Irish Gold

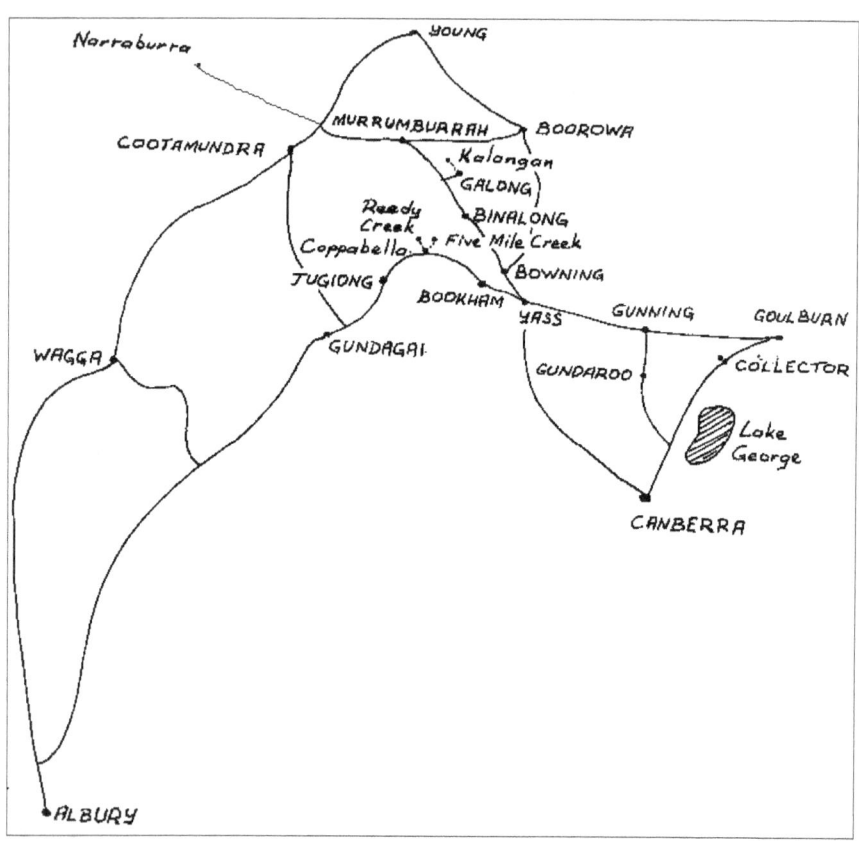

Robert Lehane

Irish Gold

Remembering John Robert Felix Lehane (1941–2001), a worthy descendant of Jeremiah and Mary Lehane and Miles and Anne Murphy.

Irish Gold
ISBN 978 1 74027 126 4
Copyright © text Robert Lehane 2002
Cover picture showing Miles Murphy's Criterion Hotel, Murrumburrah, from *Town and Country Journal*, 1 July 1876, used by permission of the National Library of Australia

First published 2002
Reprinted with minor corrections 2015

GINNINDERRA PRESS
PO Box 3461 Port Adelaide SA 5015
www.ginninderrapress.com.au

Contents

Acknowledgements		6
Preface		7
1	Leaving Ireland	9
2	A job at Yarralumla	19
3	Striking out	31
4	Gold!	45
5	Family matters	62
6	The bushranging years	73
7	Meanwhile…	88
8	Looking back, looking forward	103
9	More drama on Coppabella	116
10	Back to St Mary's	128
11	Sectarian passions rise	141
12	Black and white	154
13	Out together	166
14	Life goes on	173
15	The skies open	186
16	The biggest of all	198
17	Transitions	210
18	Farewells	222
19	Fun and games	235
20	Troubled times	250
21	A new world	266
22	Into the twentieth century	277
Postscript		288
Who's who: Lehanes, Murphys and some close relations		299
Sources		301
Picture credits		304
Index		305

Acknowledgements

James John Brown's *Yass Courier* of the late 1850s to early 1880s was my main source; I owe him, and those who have safely preserved nearly all issues of his newspaper, a great debt of gratitude. Thanks are due also to other pioneer newspaper proprietors of the region and, moving to the present, to the ever-helpful staff of the National Library of Australia's newspaper reading room, where all the papers are readily accessible on microfilm.

Having the National Library nearby was a great luxury, not just because it made frequent trips to the newspaper collection possible. Documents in the manuscripts section were the prime source of information on Jeremiah Lehane's time at Yarralumla; the pictorial section provided pictures of old Yass from the marvellous Whitehurst collection and many other illustrations; and nearly all the books consulted were read there. The Heraldry and Genealogy Society of Canberra, the Yass and District Historical Society, the Harden–Murrumburrah Historical Society and the Good Samaritan Archives, Sydney, were other valuable sources of information, as was State Records, NSW. My thanks to all.

I am grateful to Father Brian Maher, historian of the region's Catholic communities, for his interest and encouragement, and for introducing me to descendants of some of the pioneers. Thank you to my English cousin Kenneth Maclean, who made interesting discoveries, and took some excellent photos, on a visit to County Cork. And a special note of appreciation for my late brother John, who was very interested in the project, contributed family recollections and, it is good to be able to record, enjoyed reading the draft manuscript.

Preface

This is a story of two feisty Irishmen who came to Australia in the first wave of migration and did well for themselves and their families in a strange land.

Jeremiah (Jerry) Lehane was in his late twenties when he disembarked at Dawes Point, Sydney, in 1839. Miles Murphy was younger, landing two years later in his early twenties. One photo has survived of each; in both you can see the 'humorous glimmering in the eyes' that an observer in the 1880s noted as characteristic of the Irish in early Australia.

Miles headed straight to Yass, centre of a region where Irish men and women – ex-convicts and free immigrants, Catholic and Protestant – had begun congregating in the 1830s. Among them were some prominent and wealthy settlers – such as Ned Ryan of Galong, the biggest landholder in the region, and the brothers Henry and Cornelius O'Brien. According to historian Malcolm Campbell,

> the confluence of a strongly Irish population, present from the very beginning of European settlement, ready access to land and the strong leadership and substantial wealth provided by a core of influential Irish settlers, promoted a uniquely confident and assertive Irish settlement.

Miles set himself up as a carpenter, wheelwright and blacksmith in Yass, but soon turned his eyes further afield. Described in the 1860s as 'the father of Binalong and progenitor of Murrumburrah', he built hotels, stores and a flour mill and ended up owning large portions of both bush settlements. He and a son established stores on the nearby Lambing Flat goldfields almost as soon as the rush began, and the family had many encounters with the bushrangers drawn there by the wealth being extracted from the ground. Miles hosted dances that lasted till dawn and was a prominent figure at local race meetings. He possessed an 'active and enterprising disposition', the *Yass Courier* accurately observed.

Jerry took longer to seize his first entrepreneurial opportunity, but it proved a good one. After spending twelve years as an overseer on properties owned by the prominent Irish settler Terence Aubrey Murray in the Canberra and Lake George districts, he acquired an inn and grazing land at Bowning, just out of Yass. This was in 1852, within months of the discovery of gold at Ballarat and elsewhere in Victoria. Jerry's inn on the 'road' south was perfectly placed to serve the hoards of hopeful diggers heading for the rich new fields. Two years later, he moved a little further from Yass to a bigger grazing run, Coppabella, where he continued to serve the passing trade from a roadside inn. In 1861, with the gold traffic to Lambing Flat now streaming through Yass, he bought one of the biggest hotels in that bustling town.

Both Miles and Jerry married young women from Ireland soon after arriving in the colony. Miles and Anne Murphy had nine children and, as was tragically common in those days, saw four of them die. Jerry had six children, two with his first wife Mary, who died in 1861, and four with his second wife Hannah. None of the offspring displayed the entrepreneurial flair of their fathers – or perhaps opportunities were fewer after the early years of land settlement and the gold rushes.

What follows is the story of Jerry and Miles, and their families, gleaned mainly from contemporary newspaper reports. The *Yass Courier*, in particular, proved a mine of information about them and the communities they were part of. Published by a liberal-minded and obviously highly intelligent Scotsman, James John Brown, its twice-weekly four-page editions, preserved on microfilm, bring the times to life. And interesting times they were – with the gold rushes, the exploits of Ben Hall and his bushranger companions, conflicts between squatters and free selectors over land, Catholic/Protestant disputations… The latter were generally muted; as the historian Campbell notes, the 'regional ideology' emphasised harmony, toleration and cooperation. The Lehanes and Murphys, committed and active Catholics, applied that ideology in their religious lives – but, as various episodes reveal, not always to secular matters.

1
Leaving Ireland

'The finest country on the face of the earth.' That's how the *Kerry Evening Post* described New South Wales in a July 1839 article encouraging young Irish men and women to emigrate. No matter that the colony, half a world away, was established just fifty years earlier as a place of banishment for English, Scottish and Irish felons, or that convicts were still being sent there. We can be certain that the paper did not send a reporter out to check what the place was really like.

The *Post* not only promoted emigration in its columns but also provided office space for Charles Eager, an official appointed to select emigrants for New South Wales. The paper's efforts reflected the widely held Anglo-Irish view that the country was overpopulated and that a reduction in numbers through emigration might quell the agitation for reform among Catholic tenant farmers on the great Protestant-owned estates. Wrote the *Post*,

> There can be no question between enlightened men on the subject of the necessity of emigration, as a means towards providing for the superfluous population of Ireland, and the establishment of peace, comfort, and happiness in this long-neglected and long-afflicted island.

Across the county border, the *Cork Standard* was also keen to see people leave. It carried an article in July 1839 praising the work of John Besnard, an emigration agent for the colony, based in Cork City. His job was to recruit candidates for assisted emigration under schemes introduced in the 1830s to increase the supply of non-convict labour in the colony and begin correcting the severe population imbalance – about 79,000 males to 40,000 females according to the 1841 census. 'The colonists of New South Wales should feel themselves greatly indebted to Mr Besnard for his strenuous exertions in promoting the emigration of useful and virtuous persons,' wrote the *Standard*. 'The charge of selecting proper individuals as free emigrants could not be entrusted to one more capable of efficiently discharging so responsible a trust.'

With Ireland pushing and New South Wales pulling, it's not surprising that emigration – mainly from Cork and the surrounding southern counties – took off in the late 1830s. North America was, of course, an attractive alternative destination; those who chose Australia perhaps had a particularly adventurous streak. According to historian Patrick O'Farrell, the 'overwhelming weight of testimony sent back to Ireland' showed they were thankful for the decision they had made and 'full of enterprise and excitement'. No doubt, that thankfulness multiplied manyfold when they learned of the famine, caused by potato blight, that struck Ireland in 1845 and left around a million men, women and children dead and many more destitute. Some of the emigrants were able to assist relatives left behind, sending them money or sponsoring their passage to New South Wales.

Of course it was not just government propaganda that led people to emigrate – to leave their families and homeland almost certainly forever. The end of the Napoleonic Wars in 1815 had severe repercussions in Ireland. Irish farms had helped feed the British army but, when this market for agricultural produce disappeared, prices fell and landlords increasingly turned their land over to cattle and sheep grazing. Fewer hands were required; as a result, tenant farmers were forced off estates and work for farm labourers dried up. Rapid population growth, combined with the return of demobilised soldiers, exacerbated the problems.

For many families, the question became: who should set off in search of a better life abroad and who should stay behind? An historian who studied letters sent between emigrants in Australia and their relatives at home was struck by the evidence of careful negotiation within families on emigration, which 'ranked with marriage as the most important decision in most Irish lives.' Contrasting with this rational consideration of options were the emotion-charged farewells. Some descriptions survive, including this one of the departure from the Cork City dock in the late 1830s of a shipload of emigrants bound for New South Wales:

> Mothers hung upon the necks of their athletic sons; young girls clung to elder sisters; fathers – old white headed men – fell upon their knees, with

arms uplifted to heaven, imploring the protecting care of the Almighty on their departing children... It is impossible to describe the final parting. Shrieks and prayers, blessings and lamentations mingled in one great cry from those on the quay, and those on shipboard...

One young man who set out for Sydney in 1839 was Jeremiah Lehane, a farm labourer from Newmarket, northern County Cork. We'll never know whether the decision to go was his alone or a collective decision of the family – parents William and Ellen, brothers Pierce and Daniel, sisters Honora and Margaret and perhaps others unknown – and whether there was a dockside farewell. Daniel emigrated later, sponsored by Jeremiah, as did various other relatives, including sons of Pierce, Honora and Margaret. Pierce, who was about ten years older than Jeremiah, remained on the family farm at Newmarket up to his death in 1886.

The Lehanes were a Catholic family with roots in Ireland's long-vanished Celtic past. Ruins stand near Rathcormack, north-east of Cork City, of Castlelyons – originally called Castle Lehane or Castle O'Lehan. Up to late in the twelfth century, this was the seat of the Lehan sept or clan, chiefs of the surrounding locality of Hy-Lehan. The inscription recorded from a stone at the site – LEHAN O'CVLLANE HOC FECIT [built this] MCIIII [1104] – is the sole remnant of their building works; the ruins that can be visited today are from a later period.

The Norman invasion of 1170 ended Irish rule of Ireland, and saw the Lehanes soon ejected from their castle. King John granted the site to William de Barry, who erected his own castle there in 1204; his descendants were long known as the Lords Barry of Castle Lehane. The invasion ushered in more than seven centuries of increasingly resented British occupation. Gone were the fabled Irish kings who held court in the ancient castle on the sacred hill of Tara near what is now Dublin. Gone also the renowned monastic culture that arose after St Patrick's conversion of the Irish to Christianity in the fifth century.

Various decrees from London helped ensure a tense relationship between the Irish and the invaders from England. Native Irish were excluded from the first parliament of Ireland formed late in the thirteenth century. Laws that took effect in the mid-fourteenth century made it illegal for the English and Irish to intermarry, and even for Englishmen to admit

Irish musicians and storytellers to their households. Things became much worse two centuries later when Henry VIII and his Protestant successors tried to impose the practices of the new Church of England on Catholic Ireland. A series of savage Protestant–Catholic wars culminated in 1690 in the Battle of the Boyne, at which the Protestant William of Orange triumphed over the Catholic James II.

The winners introduced the infamous Penal Laws, which stripped Irish Catholics of most of their remaining rights and remained in force for more than a century; the last of them were finally repealed in 1829 following the success of the Catholic Association movement led by the charismatic Daniel O'Connell, 'the Liberator'. The Penal Laws denied the vote to Catholics and barred them from the military, the civil service, the legal profession and teaching. No Catholic schools were permitted. Religious rights were severely restricted. If a Catholic owned land, he was prohibited from leaving it to one son; it had to be divided equally between all. This meant small farms had to be divided into tracts incapable of supporting a family.

At Castlelyons, the Catholic Barrys transmogrified into the Protestant Barrymores. The castle was rebuilt and became a fashionable mansion of the 'Protestant Ascendancy' until fire destroyed it in 1771. One tale has it that the Earl of Barrymore of the time was a gambler. Before heading

The ruins of Castlelyons, known earlier as Castle Lehane.

Newmarket in Jerry's day – a painting in Newmarket Court.

to town for a session, he left instructions that, if he was not home by six a.m., the castle should be burned to keep it out of the hands of creditors, his non-return signifying that he had lost. He won handsomely, but celebrated too well and forgot his instructions. When he returned late, the castle was burning merrily.

Thirty-five miles to the west, at Newmarket, the Aldworth family from England built a handsome mansion, Newmarket Court, on land that the Protestant King James I had granted them in 1615. The branch of the Lehane family into which Jeremiah was born became tenants on

The same part of Newmarket today – many of the old buildings still stand.

Newmarket Court – then and now.

the Aldworths' 32,000-acre estate. In another connection with Australia, the mansion, built in about 1725, served as a convent of the Sisters of St Joseph for four decades after the Aldworths finally departed in the 1920s. The Melbourne-born Mother Mary MacKillop, who has been credited with one of the two miracles necessary for canonisation and is expected to be declared Australia's first saint, founded this order.

According to a topographical dictionary published in 1837, Newmarket Court was 'handsomely built of hewn limestone and situated in a demesne richly embellished with timber of luxuriant growth; an avenue of ash trees is said to have been planted in the reign of Elizabeth.' Suggesting the Aldworths were mindful of the needs of their farmers, the dictionary records that they donated the site for a spacious Roman Catholic chapel and helped fund its construction. A school and Sunday school were run in connection with the chapel. Interest from various Aldworth bequests was divided annually among the poor of Newmarket, and the town – population 1,437 – contained a fever hospital and dispensary.

Contemporary evidence indicates that the Aldworths were among the more compassionate landlords during the famine and in 1843, just before the start of that catastrophe, a local Catholic clergyman described the then head of the family, Richard Oliver Aldworth, to an inquiry as 'a kind and considerate man I must admit'. Nevertheless, the following passage from the topographical dictionary indicates that there had been major discontent among the local farmers:

> At Scarteen, a village a little to the north of the town, about 1000 of the peasantry assembled in 1822 anticipating evacuation of the military, but were repulsed by Captain Kippock and Lieutenant Green...who marched with 30 to attack the assailants, whom they dispersed with the loss of about 20 that were killed in the conflict. The gentry of the surrounding district, upon this occasion, presented to each of those officers a handsome piece of plate.

The land farmed by the Lehanes was in an area known as 'The Island', bounded by the wall of the Newmarket Court 'demesne' and a curve of the River Dalua, a tributary of the Blackwater. Its location and extent – apparently nearly 100 acres – lead one to wonder whether the family may have had a role on the estate that set them apart from most of the tenants.

The shipping documents say Jerry, as Jeremiah was known from his early days in Australia, was twenty-six years old when he boarded the 618-ton migrant sailing ship *Mary* at Plymouth in early August 1839 after crossing over by steamer from Cork. He was probably actually a bit older; counting back from the age of sixty-three recorded at his death on New Year's Day 1874 makes him twenty-eight or twenty-nine. His steerage companions on the 116-day journey round the Cape of Good Hope, across the Indian Ocean and the Great Australian Bight in the roaring forties, and up the east coast to Sydney were 104 men, seventy-six women and forty-seven children.

Jerry was fortunate in finding himself on what appears to have been a relatively well-managed and healthy ship. Heavy loss of life was not unusual on migrant voyages to New South Wales; for example, in the twelve months from early 1837 one child in every eight died out of a total of about 1,800 heading for Sydney. Whooping cough and measles were big killers, and there was always the risk of shipwreck. On this voyage of the *Mary*, though, the death toll was only one adult and three children.

Jerry and most of his fellow passengers were assisted emigrants – coming to Australia under a scheme that involved payment of £18 per head government 'bounties' to people or companies bringing out useful people. Governor Richard Bourke initiated the bounty scheme in 1835. The idea was that colonists wanting people to work for them should choose suitable candidates in England, Scotland or Ireland, bring them to the colony and receive a payment from the colonial government covering all or most of the costs of the passage. The intended result was a better match between new arrivals and the colony's needs for tradesmen, labourers and servants than the existing government-run assisted immigration scheme gave.

Not surprisingly, reality did not fully match the good intentions. An obvious problem was the inability of colonists half a world away to select emigrants. According to the historian R.B. Madgwick, the system degenerated into a commercial speculation controlled by British shipowners, the most important of whom was John Marshall. He had a dubious reputation, being accused of malpractices including helping fill his ships by making false statements about inducements offered by the colony to poor emigrants. Marshall owned the *Mary*, and received the bounties due when Jerry and his shipmates arrived in Sydney on 24 November 1839.

Regulations required that a ship's surgeon travel on each migrant vessel to try to keep deadly diseases at bay. This was in the interests of shipowners as well as the passengers, because the total bounty paid depended on the number of employable people landed. The surgeon on the *Mary*, W.E. Grove, noted in his report that the general state of health on board was good on arrival, although some people had suffered from whooping cough, diarrhoea and dysentery. To help preserve cleanliness and health, six people had been paid a salary of £3 to keep the steerage area in proper order. All passengers had been sent on deck at nine-thirty each morning while the cleaners went about their task, and when the weather permitted their bedding was aired on deck. To promote their spiritual welfare, prayers had been read every night and divine service performed morning and evening on Sundays if the weather allowed.

Sydney's *Australian* newspaper praised John Marshall when it reported the *Mary*'s arrival, saying his vessels had a record of delivering migrants in good health. In the same vein, the *Sydney Herald* said,

> great credit is due to the captain, officers and surgeon for the cleanliness of the vessel and general good discipline on board – in fact the whole of the passengers speak very highly of the officers and of their gentlemanly conduct during the whole voyage.

Sydneysiders who read this on 25 November may have been surprised to learn from the *Australian* five days later that the whole crew of the *Mary* had been brought before magistrates Charles Windeyer and H.H. Brown, charged with either refusing duty or desertion. The men complained of harsh treatment during the voyage; 'among other matters, the cook complained that the first officer forced hot coffee down his throat,' the paper reported. The first officer claimed the incident began when the cook served coffee made with salt water at the cabin table, and 'as a punishment, the doctor, second officer, and himself, insisted on his drinking it, which he refusing, they held him and poured it down his throat but it was not so hot as to scald him.' The magistrates saw no problem with this form of retribution. In fact, they considered it insufficient punishment and sentenced nine of the crew 'to be mulcted in four days' pay each'.

On arrival in Sydney, Jerry was declared an acceptable immigrant, making Marshall eligible for his £18. Those who filled in the official form noted that two Irish ministers (Rev. A. Donovan and Rev. J. Beechinor) had certified that he had been baptised in the Catholic Church, while Richard Oliver Aldworth of Newmarket Court had attested that his character was 'very good'. He could read and write, and his 'state of bodily health, strength and probable usefulness' was judged good.

Other single men on the *Mary* included bakers, carpenters, coopers, grooms, house servants, painters, shepherds and shopkeepers as well as farm and general labourers. Single women were expected to find employment as domestic servants. The *Sydney Herald* report of the *Mary*'s arrival said great numbers of the passengers were of a very respectable appearance, and they would remain on the ship, lying off Walker's Wharf, to be engaged. 'Therefore it is requested of those people who wish to obtain servants to make early application,' the paper advised.

2
A job at Yarralumla

Following his arrival in Sydney, the first reference we have to Jerry is in July 1840 as an employee of Terence Aubrey Murray on his Yarralumla sheep run where part of Canberra now stands. If he was recruited on board the *Mary*, it may not have been by Murray personally. Murray was in Sydney during November 1839, but a letter he wrote at the time indicates he had set out for Yarralumla by 22 November, two days before the ship docked. Murray was back in Sydney in the autumn of 1840, so maybe he employed Jerry then.

The Sydney Jerry landed in was still the gateway to a vast bush prison; convict transportation to New South Wales finally came to an end in mid-1840. It was also a boom town, with census figures showing population growth from just under 20,000 in 1836 to nearly 30,000 in 1841.

The emigrants' landing place, Walker's Wharf, was on the western edge of Dawes Point – near the present site of the Pier One ParkRoyal Hotel beside the Harbour Bridge. Their first impressions should have been good; James Maclehose's *Picture of Sydney* published in 1839 described the area as 'probably one of the best neighbourhoods in Sydney'. It noted that some respectable dwelling houses had been built there recently, 'mostly occupied by opulent persons'.

Sydney's streets were still dirt tracks – except for a short section of George Street that had been coated with granite – and the polluted Tank Stream discharged into mud flats at the edge of Sydney Cove. Nevertheless, Maclehose was not the only one impressed by the town. Charles Darwin was, too, when he called in on the *Beagle* in 1836. He noted gigs, phaetons and carriages with liveried servants driving about, houses of a good size and well furnished shops. He thought the town must contain much wealth; it appeared that a man of business could hardly fail to make a large fortune. The whole scene was a most magnificent

Terence Aubrey Murray.

testimony to the power of the British nation, he wrote. 'My first feeling was to congratulate myself that I was born an Englishman.'

Another side of the picture that would have greeted the new arrivals was chain gangs of convicts working on roads and public buildings. Floggings of miscreant convicts were commonplace, prisoners were held in stocks as a form of public humiliation and every now and then there was a public hanging. The governor, George Gipps, was the local representative of the government in Britain and the legislative council that advised him was an appointed body; the first hint of democracy came in 1843 when voting, limited to men of wealth, was introduced to fill most legislative council seats.

Terence Aubrey Murray, who took Jerry on as an overseer, became one of the first elected legislative councillors. He was about the same age as his new employee, and had made his mark in the colony quickly after arriving from Ireland with his father and sister in 1827. Both father and son obtained land grants near Lake George, south of Goulburn, and expanded their holdings there by purchase. Then, in 1837, Terence and a partner bought the 2,560-acre Yarralumla run from Francis Mowatt, who had acquired it four years earlier. The homestead Mowatt built, using convict labour, on the site of the present governor-general's residence, served initially as a hunting lodge. He had a pack of hounds and, with his guests, on their occasional visits from Sydney, hunted dingoes and kangaroos.

Murray bought Yarralumla in the early stages of a drought that was so severe that Lake George dried out completely, a rare event. He wasted no time in setting the property up; his friend Stewart Mowle recorded that around 25,000 sheep were running on Yarralumla in 1838, and fifty or sixty men, mostly convicts, were employed there. Murray was more than fully occupied, retaining his properties near Lake George and serving as a district magistrate from 1833 to 1840. A large part of the magisterial task involved passing judgement on errant convicts; floggings were a common punishment, although Murray was said to be among the more humane dispensers of justice.

Although Yarralumla was his home base, Murray was frequently away. Stewart Mowle usually then took charge. In 1836, when he was just thirteen, Mowle's parents decided his prospects would be brighter in New South Wales, where his uncle was prospering, than at home in England, so they sent him to Sydney. A friendship made at Sydney College, predecessor of Sydney Grammar School, led to him becoming a frequent visitor to the home of the collector of customs, Colonel Gibbes, where in mid-1838 he met Terence Murray. Murray was there on business; five years later he married Gibbes' daughter Mary.

Murray invited Mowle to ride back to Yarralumla with him; so ended

The old homestead at Yarralumla.
The sketch is from 1876, thirty years after Jerry's time there.

Mowle's schooling. Soon afterwards, Murray left the sixteen-year-old in charge for the first of many times. Although younger than everybody else on the station, he apparently was not daunted by the responsibility. 'I readily fell into my duties,' he recalled in old age. This was despite the fact that, because of the drought, 'water, feed and every necessary for stock had disappeared and nothing would grow'. Mowle's admiration for Murray knew no bounds; he was his 'best loved friend' and 'the most chivalrous, noble and refined man on earth'.

One of Murray's responses to the drought was to look for high-country pasture where he could take his sheep. He, Mowle, an overseer and two Aborigines set off in late 1838 up the bed of the Cotter River into the mountains, finding lush grazing land on the Cooleman Plain. Early the following year, Murray and his men drove their flocks and bullock drays up the same route and established a new station on the site. In subsequent years, Jerry almost certainly would have spent time up there.

Temporary relief from the drought came in late 1839. Mowle was visiting his ailing uncle at the time, and Murray wrote to him in January 1840, 'The plains are covered with grass, the river is running beautifully, we have plenty of hay and corn and the horses are all in fine condition, fit for any work.' Perhaps that was the scene that greeted Jerry when he started work at Yarralumla.

Murray's letters to Mowle when he was away from the property, and his young friend was in charge, make it clear that Jerry and the other overseers were to be treated strictly as the manager's servants. References in them to Jerry are mostly of the nature 'tell Lehane (or Jerry) to…' Mowle wrote in his reminiscences that he did not associate with the overseers. He recalled that in his early days at Yarralumla, before his marriage in 1845, he had only one companion when Murray was absent: 'a native black Tommy Murray, who I used to get to sleep on the floor in my room'.

Activities at Yarralumla included cropping as well as sheep grazing. Managing sheep was a much more labour-intensive activity than it is today. Runs were unfenced – this largely remained the case up to the 1870s – so shepherds were needed to look after the flocks. Typically, groups of three men were responsible for 1,500 to 2,000 sheep. At night they were brought into a fold; one of the men, the watchman, had the job of stopping them straying and protecting them from attack by dingoes. Soon after sunrise, the other two set off in different directions with half the sheep each, slowly moving them along as they grazed, before returning to the fold at sunset. The whole group moved to fresh pasture every few days.

Usual practice was to wash the sheep before summer shearing. On Yarralumla they were first washed with hot water and soap, then driven into the Molonglo River, where water pouring from a sluice in a dam wall finished the job. They were shorn as soon as they were dry. In his January 1840 letter to Mowle describing conditions after the rain, Murray, clearly pleased with the way things were going, wrote,

> For the last 2 months we have all, men, bullocks, horses, dogs etc, been busy haymaking, and now we are, except the bullocks and horses, equally busy sheep washing and shearing. We are in the water morning till night just as if we were amphibious.

Jerry first appeared in the Murray correspondence in July 1840. Mowle was away at the time, looking after St Omer, the property – near Braidwood, fifty miles east of Yarralumla – of his uncle, who had just died. Terence Murray was also away. His brother, Dr James Murray, who had bought a nearby station, Woden, in 1837, was at Yarralumla.

Apparently, James had sent a messenger to Mowle asking him to send farm produce from St Omer to stock the Yarralumla larder, and Mowle had despatched potatoes, four cases of pork and thirty-four hams. We learn from James' letter of thanks that Jerry received the load. 'Lehane detained your men in order to send back some seed-oats,' he wrote, 'which he now finds he cannot spare in consequence of having only a sufficiency for Yarrowlumla (the original spelling used in all the correspondence).' This suggests that Jerry had moved straight into a position of responsibility on the station.

The next reference to him is in a letter from Terence Murray to Mowle, who was again supervising operations at Yarralumla, in May 1841. Murray wrote from Goulburn on his way to Sydney to give evidence to a commission of inquiry into immigration; he was concerned about a shortage of people willing to work as shepherds and the wages they were demanding, and favoured importing coolies from India. The return from Yarralumla for the March 1841 census – a total of 108 people, comprising eighty-seven Catholics, seventeen Episcopalians, three Presbyterians and one Jew – shows Murray had greatly expanded its labour force from the 'fifty or sixty' Mowle encountered when he arrived less than three years earlier.

Murray told Mowle, among much else related to the running of the property, that 'I wish you to make it part of your daily business to see that Jerry has at least six ploughs at work.' He wanted to put sufficient grain in store to last a few years. 'You are aware of the great additional expense to which I am put this year by maintaining so large an agricultural establishment,' he wrote. He thought 'the central part of the old paddock where the heavy crop of hay was last year' should produce good wheat. 'Will you go over there and see how it looks, and take Jerry with you. If it be not too foul tell him to sow it with wheat. The horse team which I wish to see ploughing might be employed at it.'

In a letter from Sydney the following August, Murray advised Mowle on lines of command on his properties. 'You must make Lee [William Lee, an overseer based at Lake George] more attentive in reporting matters to you,' he wrote.

> It is his duty to do so and you should insist on his having no communication with Maurice [presumably another overseer] or Lehane, or only through you. It is better that you should do that than that I should interfere.

Murray wrote again from Sydney in early September. He told Mowle to insist that 'due attention' was paid to lambing and remarked that he was glad to hear 'that affairs have prospered with you in love'. This related to Mowle's courting of his future wife Mary, daughter of Dr Thomas Wilson of Braidwood Farm, not far from St Omer. 'We shall discuss this subject over a jovial bottle when I go home and I would give a great deal to be with you now. I want Lehane to ride with you to Braidwood.'

In another letter twelve days later, Murray told Mowle he was glad to see arrangements for the lambing were successful: 'I highly approve of your making Jerry as useful as possible in attending to the sheep.' Less pleasing news must have arrived shortly afterwards because Murray wrote again five days later on the same subject:

I am sorry that the lambing is not going all well – pray on no account let it be neglected but everything else give place to it. The splitters, fencers, carpenters and blacksmith should all become shepherds and watchmen while it lasts. Let all hands on the establishment be turned out for that purpose and this alone. Tell this to Lee and Jerry, and let each of them have a certain number of flocks to attend to.

He added that wages should be withheld from anyone who was negligent concerning the lambing.

Murray returned to Yarralumla in late September 1841 and spent most of his time there for the next year and a half. Mowle's recollections from old age were again rosy:

> The years 1841–42 and the major part of 1843 were passed with the usual routine farm and pastoral occupations, that was travelling to the mountains, sleeping out at times in the snow, or finding shelter in a hut through which it and rain found their way – riding round to stations to see the sheep and counting them out from the folds, giving out rations, in the water washing or looking after the men washing sheep – at the shed folding fleeces, galloping after cattle and horses – riding or driving tandem or four-in-hand with my best loved friend…

As Murray and Mowle were in the same place, there is a long gap in their correspondence and so, unfortunately, in references to Jerry. He must have taken some leave from Yarralumla because on 26 March 1842 he married Mary O'Connor at St Mary's Cathedral, Sydney. Mary, also from County Cork, was a daughter of farmer Cornelius O'Connor and his wife Margaret, formerly Roach. She was older than Jerry; according to her death certificate she was thirty-nine when they married – he was about thirty. That certificate also records that she had four children, suggesting there was an earlier marriage, as she had only two with Jerry. Why then was her name still O'Connor when they married? Information about Mary, even the ship she came out on, has proved elusive.

We know that a brother, William, and sister, Johanna, followed her to Australia with their families during the 1850s. Both families came from the north of County Cork – William's from Ballyhae near Charleville and Johanna's from Buttevant, a town not far to the south. Most likely, Mary came from the same area, which was within twenty miles of Newmarket.

After their arrival in the colony, both families first stayed with Jerry and Mary, and then settled quite close by, in the Boorowa district. Like Jerry, William O'Connor and Johanna's husband Jeremiah O'Keefe were listed in the migration records as farm labourers.

Another sister, Sarah, married a Benjamin Forrest and remained in the Buttevant region. However, their son John, born in November 1820, and younger daughter Mary Ann followed their uncle and two aunts to the far side of the world. John Forrest had a distinguished career. After achieving academic distinction in Ireland, he was ordained a priest at the Irish College, Rome, in 1847 and awarded a doctorate of divinity in theology from the Gregorian University. Newmarket was among his parish postings following his return to Ireland at the height of the potato blight famine. John set out for New South Wales, with Mary Ann, in June 1860, having been invited to become the first Rector of St John's, the Catholic residential college at the new University of Sydney. His associations with the Lehane family in the 1860s and 1870s, including presiding at the marriages of both children of Jerry and Mary, are outlined in chapters 6, 8, 10 and 17. Mary Ann married a Sydney doctor, James Gilhooley.

Possibly Jerry knew Mary before he set out for Australia, and proposed marriage after the death of her first husband. She may have emigrated under her former married name; that would explain the failure to find her in the shipping records. The discovery of links between Lehanes and O'Connors in the Newmarket area supports the theory that the pair were acquainted in Ireland. The Lehane land on the Aldworth estate became, fairly briefly, O'Connor land around the turn of the century. This was a delayed consequence of Ellen Lehane, a daughter of Jerry's

The graves at Newmarket of Jerry's brother Pierce (right) and members of the O'Connor family.

brother Pierce, marrying a Daniel O'Connor. Pierce's son William left the land to their son Jerome O'Connor. So far, however, no evidence that connects the O'Connors of the Newmarket and Buttevant regions has come to light.

Father Nicholas Joseph Coffey was the presiding minister at St Mary's when Jerry and Mary took their wedding vows. Both put their signatures to declarations that they were members of, or held Communion with, the Roman Catholic Church. Mary's address was given as Sydney, Jerry's as Limestone 'plane' (sic). St Mary's, Sydney's first Catholic chapel, had gained cathedral status on the arrival of the town's first bishop, John Bede Polding, in 1835. 'It is an excellent specimen of gothic building, being generally admired as an architectural ornament to the town,' wrote James Maclehose in his 1839 guide to Sydney. It was the most expensive sacred edifice in the colony, he added.

Returning to Yarralumla, Jerry and Mary presumably took up residence in one of the many slab huts on the property. Mary would have had little female companionship – the 1841 census recorded only eight females in the total complement of 108. It's possible she was recruited for domestic duties at the homestead, then still an all-male establishment.

Early in 1843, Terence Murray launched his campaign for the new legislative council, to which he was elected in June. He married Mary Gibbes in May 1843 and the couple moved into the Yarralumla homestead the following October. The Murray–Mowle correspondence resumed before then, with Murray writing in July that he intended to remain in Sydney until the beginning or middle of September and then go to Yarralumla for good – a strange sentiment for a newly elected legislative councillor. 'I am weary of the wandering and unsettled life,' he wrote.

The depressed economy and personal financial concerns were increasingly worrying him, and in September he asked Mowle to send 1,000 or 2,000 sheep to Sydney to allow him 'to pay all my small debts about the town'. He wanted wethers or ewes that were fat enough to bring five shillings each if boiled down for tallow. Like many other financially stressed graziers, Murray had turned to boiling sheep down in big vats – a practice pioneered by Henry O'Brien of Yass – following collapse of the wool market. He showed signs of anger with Mowle: 'You always tell me the sheep are doing well. Is it not strange that they are never fat?'

Ten days later he wrote,

> I must complain to you that all my sheep stations must be badly – very badly – managed. Royce has fat weathers, Bradley has sheep fat, but I cannot even get sheep fit to boil down. If the stock – cattle and sheep – had been attended to I would not, bad as the times are, have felt the very severe pecuniary cares at all events… I am deeply stricken at heart. I wish to retire from the world but cannot bear the thought of leaving unpaid the tradesmen or shopkeepers who trusted me, my banker who overpaid my account to serve me, or the private gentleman who made a bargain with me, trusted me to pay him when I liked… You must either send me 2000 fat sheep, either ewes or wethers fit for boiling, or 25 bales of wool at once.

The following letter contains the next mention of Jerry; Murray suggests Mowle send him to Lake George to manage shearing to obtain the urgently wanted wool. Mowle's reply evidently brought more bad news concerning the sheep, prompting Murray to write, 'Do the best you can… I want to wind up my affairs and give up the world forever.' Things got worse; ewes and wethers sent to Sydney by a man named Bourke, evidently a tenant of Murray's, were of poor quality.

> Hence Jerry and I shall serve him at once with notice to quit. These disappointments for the first time in my life reduced me to a want of money and I shall take care that my overseers shall henceforth be more attentive…

The dramatic language continued. Murray was 'suffering under my share of the general depression, with a pretty probable prospect of ruin before me…' He was not alone: '…wide-wasting ruin is overwhelming the whole country.'

On 11 October, just before setting out for Yarralumla with his bride, he wrote that he intended to remain 'up the country' for two years. 'You and I must now work hard and have no overseers,' he told Mowle. Jerry had become the object of blame for the poor state of the sheep and he, certainly, was not required any longer. 'We both and Lee could manage the whole establishment,' Murray wrote. 'Lehane I consider useless as an overseer of stock – I cannot yet get over the neglect of the wethers.'

Fortunately for Jerry, there must have been a change of heart. He reappears in the correspondence, evidently again a trusted employee, in

July 1844 – two months after the birth of the Murrays' first child, Leila. Leila was to have her own flock of sheep, and Murray asked Mowle to count out 340 ewes and 340 dry sheep for it. He instructed Mowle to tell Jerry to take charge of them.

A flurry of letters followed over the next weeks, from the Australian Club, Murray's Sydney base during legislative council sittings. First, Mowle was to tell Jerry that he (Murray) had arranged the sale of a hundred bushels of wheat. Then he told Mowle he had received a complaint that the sheep at Lake George were in a 'scandalous condition'. Murray said he had placed too much trust in Charles Massy, the man in charge.

> I may perhaps be trusting just as much to Lehane, and therefore I want you to go round all the stations at Yarrowlumla, see all the flocks, and examine the folds and make me a report of their condition in all respects… I am now determined to trust again to the management of no man.

Judging from Murray's letter two weeks later, Mowle's inspection brought bad news. 'I am sorry to hear that the sheep do not look well,' he wrote. 'Pray tell Jerry to reduce the flocks to smaller numbers each. I must have the sheep got into condition, and am content to pay for men so he has no excuse for not bringing them into condition.' Murray must have thought a further prod was needed because he wrote two days later, 'Pray tell Lehane to put the sheep in smaller flocks, so as to ensure their being in good condition.'

Murray returned south at this stage, leading to a break in the correspondence. For Jerry and Mary, the big coming event was the birth of their first child. Ellen Lehane was delivered safely at Yarralumla on 20 October 1844. Two days later, Father Michael Kavanagh, from the Catholic mission at Queanbeyan established five years earlier, baptised the child.

Murray's return to Sydney near the end of the year brought a renewal of the correspondence, but this was brief because Mowle left Yarralumla the following January. Murray had given Mowle one of his outstations – Mannus, near Tumbarumba – and at the end of 1844 one of Jerry's jobs was to arrange for it to be stocked. Jerry was to start a team of men at once with sheep for Mannus, with two pack bullocks for provisions. 'Consult Jerry upon all these points and arrange the matter with him so that there will be no disappointment,' Murray advised Mowle. Jerry evidently was not part of the expedition, because Murray's next letter a week later instructed, 'Pray see that no time is lost in getting on with the shearing and harvesting; and tell Jerry not to stop the boiling.' The good news was that the depression was over – 'wool is in great demand.' But boiling sheep down for tallow was apparently still worthwhile.

Mowle married Mary Wilson the following May. After an unsuccessful attempt to set themselves up at Mannus, they returned to the Canberra–Lake George area. Despite help from Murray, their grazing enterprise failed and Mowle started work with the Customs service in 1852. His memoirs mention Jerry once. In July 1850, he spent a night on one of Murray's Lake George properties – then 'rode to Goulburn next day with Lehane and sold my sheep skins…'

Some time between 1845 and early 1847, Jerry, Mary and Ellen had moved from Yarralumla to Murray land near Collector – probably to the main Lake George property, Winderradeen. We know they were there by early 1847, because the birth record for child number two, William Lehane, names their place of abode as Collector. William was born on 19 February. Four days later, Father Michael Brennan from Goulburn baptised him.

An April 1849 advertisement in the *Goulburn Herald* suggests Jerry still spent some of his time at Yarralumla. Murray was seeking tenants for several small farms 'near Limestone Plains', and interested parties were invited to apply to Mr J. Lehane at Yarrowlumla. The following March, Jerry gave his address as Lake George when appearing in a court case in which Murray alleged a carting contractor had stolen one of his bullocks. Jerry was described as superintendent for Mr Murray. He was still at Lake George when he signed an October 1850 advertisement warning that any cattle found trespassing on Murray's Lake George estate would be impounded.

3
Striking out

In March 1852, the Sydney entrepreneur and auctioneer Thomas Sutcliffe Mort advertised the upcoming auction of the Bowning Inn, eight miles west of Yass, together with the lease of the 15,000-acre Bowning station. Their owner, Goulburn flour miller James Sinclair, had tried to sell them by private contract in September 1850, but without success. Now they were to go under the hammer along with the rest of his insolvent estate.

The two-storey brick-built inn comprised 'four good rooms with servants' offices &c.' on the ground floor and 'likewise four good-sized rooms' upstairs. There were also numerous outbuildings, three or four cottages of two or four rooms each, and stockyards. The station's 'good pasture land' was said to be capable of carrying 4,000 sheep. Advertising the Bowning property for sale in 1850, Sinclair described it 'as a desirable place for an industrious person making a fortune.'

Perhaps the reason why it failed to sell in 1850 was that traffic on the southern 'road' beyond Yass was sparse. Things had changed dramatically when Jerry made his successful bid for the inn and station eighteen months later. Gold had been discovered at Ballarat, Bendigo and other places in Victoria in the second half of 1851, just a few months after Australia's first big gold find near Bathurst. By early 1852, people had started streaming south to try their luck – all potential customers, as Jerry no doubt figured, for a roadside inn.

Jerry paid £200 for the hotel and pastoral run. This appears a rare bargain when compared with other prices obtained at the auction. Sinclair's flour mill in Goulburn sold for £4,500, a house in the town for £660 and a 740-acre property and inn near Gunning, between Goulburn and Yass, for £700. We have evidence from the Murray correspondence that Jerry had long been interested in moving on from being an employee

*The only photo of Jerry Lehane, probably taken in the early 1870s
— from the group photo on page 209.*

– he seems to have seized a great opportunity. In July 1844, Murray asked Mowle to find out whether Charles Massy would be interested in renting the dairy at Lake George. 'Lehane has made me an offer on the subject but I think it is too low,' he wrote.

Early in 1852, before their move to Bowning, Jerry, Mary and their young children were joined at their home near Collector by Mary's brother William and his family. William, his wife Ellen and their five children – eighteen-year-old Margaret and four boys aged between twelve and seventeen – had arrived in Sydney in February. Apparently they accompanied the Lehanes on their move to Bowning. Then William and his sons joined the rush to the Victorian diggings, and had some success on the Yackandandah and Ovens fields. Afterwards the family settled at Hovell's Creek near Boorowa.

The *Goulburn Herald* referred to the exodus south in May 1852, reporting that 'a number of parties well equipped with vehicle, rations and mining tools have taken their departure from this part of the colony for the auriferous localities of Victoria, bent upon acquiring a portion of the golden wealth'. The paper's perhaps self-interested advice was that intending diggers would be better off staying at home. On the other hand, it thought those heading south with stock and flour to supply the goldfields were likely to do well, and provide a boost to the local economy when they returned.

In late June 1852, heavy rains and flooding – Gundagai was almost totally destroyed, with the loss of eighty-nine lives – brought a temporary halt to the traffic. But by September 'no fewer than fifteen carts and drays, each accompanied by parties of from three to five', were passing the *Herald* office each day on their way to the diggings. By January 1853, 'diggers, by hundreds' were moving through Goulburn every week, 'all in one confused mass'. A month later, about 150 intending gold miners were passing through the town on an average day. 'The road between Goulburn and [the] diggings is described as being literally thronged with both equestrians and pedestrians,' the paper said. Jerry must have been doing great business.

Just how long he retained the Bowning Inn is unclear, but in 1858 he became licensee of another hotel on the road south, the Star Inn, Reedy Creek. This was on the 23,000-acre Coppabella run, which straddled the main road in rolling country near Bogolong (now Bookham), about twenty miles from Yass. Jerry negotiated the purchase of Coppabella, home of the Lehane family for the next twenty-five years, in 1853 and took possession in April 1854. A Daniel Minehan took over the lease of the Bowning run in September 1854. The following month, Jerry placed an advertisement in the *Herald* offering rewards for two horses lost between Bowning and Bogolong during August – £2 for each if they had strayed or £20 following their return and conviction of the thief if they had been stolen. Perhaps the horses disappeared while he was moving his stock from Bowning to Coppabella.

Jerry paid £500 for the Coppabella lease. The seller was John Paterson of nearby Illalong, uncle of the poet Banjo Paterson. Coppabella had been occupied at least since the early 1830s, and passed through many hands before Jerry took over. Men named Connor and Bayley ran sheep there in the early days. Cornelius O'Brien – brother of Henry O'Brien, who achieved fame for promoting the boiling down of sheep – took up the lease in 1836. The O'Briens, well-to-do Irish Catholics, were prominent Yass district residents for many decades – Henry at Douro next door to the explorer Hamilton Hume's property east of the town and Cornelius at Bendenine to the west. The next lessee, a Mr Lamb, took possession in 1848, followed by Paterson in 1852.

Just where Coppabella began and ended was not entirely clear; before runs were fenced, doubts about the location of boundaries, and resulting disputes between neighbours, were inevitable. Beginning its lengthy report of a Yass District Court case in April 1860 in which Jerry claimed damages from a neighbour, Ann Byrnes, for trespass through running stock on his land, the *Yass Courier* commented,

> This is one of those squatting cases of frequent occurrence, which result in a great measure from the injudicious, thriftless distribution of the lands of the colony in olden times, by irresponsible Governors and their subordinates, occasioning great litigation, huge expense, and engendering very lamentable ill-will between neighbours.

The dispute was over a strip of fertile land between two creeks. Witnesses described it, according to the *Courier*, as the very heart of the Coppabella run and the area best adapted for lambing down a flock of sheep or camping horned stock. Rights to the land had been in dispute for decades. In 1841, O'Brien's overseer set up hurdles for sheep folds on the land; Mrs Byrnes had them knocked down and threatened to burn them if they were not removed. From then on, she claimed, O'Brien and subsequently Lamb and Paterson had kept their sheep off the land.

The jury found against Jerry in the initial case, but then his lawyer, George Allman, persuaded the judge who had heard it, Judge Callaghan, that there should be a retrial. This was held six months later. Witnesses supporting Jerry's claim to the disputed land included Cornelius O'Brien, John Paterson and the commissioner of Crown lands for the Lachlan district, Edgar Beckham, who had made a ruling on the boundary following the 1841 dispute. Jerry told the court the area in question – about one by one-and-a-half miles – was an excellent lambing station and provided very good grazing. However, he had not used it for lambing because the cattle and horses Mrs Byrnes ran there would have destroyed the lambs. He claimed that being denied the land for lambing had cost him £50. This time, the jury supported Jerry, and he was awarded £25 damages.

Witnesses at the first trial included a man named Williams (alias 'The Towney'), a shepherd on Coppabella for more than twenty years, who said he had been running sheep on the disputed land since the early 1840s. Jerry brought Williams along to give evidence at the second trial, but had to inform the judge and jury that he could not appear as he was 'drunk just now'. Jerry assured them that he (Jerry) had not supplied the drink.

Williams was one of at least eleven men working on Coppabella in the late 1850s. Their names, and Jerry's, appear in a long list in the *Courier* in April 1859 of 'Electors of the Lachlan District' requesting that the Sydney lawyer Peter Faucett allow them to nominate him as their representative in the New South Wales legislative assembly. Jerry is near the top of the list, along with notables such as Hamilton Hume. The 1859 election came a year after the right to vote was granted to all men (with a few exceptions), irrespective of wealth or social status. Voters on the Lachlan electoral roll numbered 976.

Faucett was being invited to contest the election against John Nagle Ryan, son of one of the region's earliest settlers and biggest landholders, Ned Ryan of Galong. In a sign that Jerry had acquired some standing in the region, the man who originally proposed that Faucett seek election, squatter and Justice of the Peace Nicholas Besnard, noted in a letter to the *Courier* that he had first 'ascertained the views' of Jerry and three others – including Cornelius O'Brien and John Paterson. Faucett declined to stand, so Ryan was elected unopposed.

Whether the Coppabella workers who signed the petition for Faucett to seek election were exercising independent political judgement is probably open to question; more likely they were pleasing the boss. One of them was Jerry's nephew James Lehane. A son of Jerry's brother Pierce, he emigrated from Newmarket, sponsored by Jerry, in 1856. In 1858, James was in trouble with the law, charged with assaulting Constable Richard Hassett while in the execution of his duty. The Yass Court of Petty Sessions treated him leniently. Noting that James was a new arrival in the colony, the magistrate admonished him and imposed a £2 fine. The story of James is a sad one; he died at Coppabella a year later, aged just twenty-three, of 'inflammation of the head and chest', and was buried at the nearby settlement of Jugiong.

Others on the list were shepherds Nathaniel Gorth and James Taylor. Gorth, an old man, died in suspicious circumstances on Coppabella in 1865; his story is told in chapter 9. Taylor made the news in December 1858. He returned to his hut one evening to find his wife Mary dying of strychnine poisoning. The inquest could find no reason for her suicide. The *Courier* reported that the pair had been married for about twenty years and were said to have lived free from any serious quarrels; 'they never had more angry words than, to employ Taylor's own words, 'man and wife will have occasionally'.'

Shepherd Williams made a grim discovery on Coppabella earlier in 1858 – the body of a man with two handkerchiefs tied around his neck, suspended from a small sapling. This was William Morris, a policeman from Gundagai, who had allowed a prisoner in his custody to escape. 'Dreading the consequences of his negligence, it is supposed that he rashly hung himself to a tree,' the *Courier* reported.

The escape occurred from the Star Inn, which at that time was home to Jerry, Mary and their two children. Morris and the prisoner had stopped there for the night en route to Goulburn. Evidence to the inquest suggested that the policeman had responded to the prisoner's escape by slowly and deliberately throttling himself. Wrote the *Courier* correspondent,

Although Morris proved himself too cowardly to meet a small degree of censure, he certainly showed almost unexampled determination in the means he took to put an end to his life.

At the start of 1858, major bushfires exacerbated the hardships the region was already experiencing from drought. The *Courier* reported in mid-January that alarming and devastating bushfires had completely encircled Yass, and a week later that 'the whole country for miles around has been laid waste by the recent destructive and calamitous bush-fires.' We don't know what impact drought and possibly fire had on Coppabella at that time; the *Courier* tells us, though, that around early April Jerry sold 1,200 wethers to a butcher in Beechworth, a Victorian gold town, for fourteen shillings per head.

One effect of the hard times was extensive unemployment. All along the southern road (from Sydney to Yass and beyond), reported the *Courier*, very many respectable people were travelling in search of employment in a state bordering on utter destitution. A 'respectable carrier' told the following sorry tale:

> I started from Sydney in company with two or three other teams, with my usual stock of supplies for the road. We had proceeded on the road for two or three days, when on a very frosty morning, about seven o'clock, as we were partaking of breakfast, a most respectable and genteel-looking woman, accompanied by a child, approached us, and requested a drop of tea and something for her child to eat; my eyes filled with tears to see the evident effort which she made to make the request, and I said 'Yes, my good woman, you are welcome to share whatever we have got; sit down; here's a pannikin of tea and some bread and meat.' While she sat beside us, a young man came up, carrying a 'swag'. She informed us that he was her husband, and we solicited him to join us at breakfast. He appeared thankful for the offer, and expressed his gratitude. They travelled with us, sharing what we had, for two days, when some of the horses having strayed, detained us for some time in one place, and, apparently feeling ashamed of continuing to remain dependent upon us for a longer period, they left, stating that they would push on and perhaps fall in with employment. Similar requests were made all along the road, and when we arrived at Goulburn we found that our supplies had become exhausted, and we there expended thirty shillings to enable us to have sufficient for the journey to Yass.

The southern road at the time was still little more than a bush track, and haulage of goods by bullock-drawn cart from Sydney to Albury typically took between forty and ninety days. The Reverend John Dunmore Lang travelled south from Sydney in July 1859 and described the road from Bogolong to Gundagai as 'inconceivably bad – quite discreditable indeed to a civilised country'. He wrote that it had been in better condition when he made earlier mail coach trips south in the 1840s; it had not yet been broken up 'by the passenger and goods traffic of the Golden Age'. Now,

> Think of having to get out of the vehicle, for fear of one's neck as well as in mercy to the poor horses, and to walk about two miles at a stretch in pitch darkness, where every second step takes one over the ankles in mud, and of losing sight of the lights altogether and having to cooee for the mail at last, as we had completely lost our way in the bush.

According to advertisements in the *Courier*, 'the shortest, most agreeable, and most expeditious way' of reaching Sydney from Yass was

The wool clip heads for port – a sketch from the 1860s.

via steamboat from Nelligen, near Bateman's Bay on the South Coast. No wonder the *Courier* was calling as early as 1860 for a railway to be built to Yass, which then had a population of about 1,000.

The other great mid-nineteenth-century development in communications, the electric telegraph, reached the town in August 1858. The *Courier* described it as 'one of the greatest boons ever conferred upon a community.' One advantage was that it would allow each week's paper to carry 'the Sydney intelligence up to a late hour on the previous evening!' The *Courier* reported that it had not heard yet of 'any candidate for matrimonial honours' having 'popped the question' by telegraph. 'But on Wednesday something close akin to it arrived from Goulburn, namely, an invitation to a young lady in Yass to attend a ball shortly to take place in the former town!'

As one of the region's prominent Catholics, Jerry appears among those listed in the *Courier* as donors to appeals such as that for a testimonial gift to the Reverend Patrick Magennis who left Yass in 1857 (he gave a generous £5 5s) and attending events such as the laying of the foundation stone for the Catholic church at Binalong, twenty miles from Yass, in March 1860.

A year earlier he was one of about 200 men who attended probably the biggest event Yass had yet seen, a gala St Patrick's Day public dinner. Two Irish Catholic squatters, Cornelius O'Brien of Bendenine and Ned Ryan of Galong, headed the list of organising committee members, but it also included Irish-born Protestants such as Nicholas Besnard and non-Irish immigrants, including the Scot James John Brown, proprietor of the *Yass Courier*. Brown frequently editorialised on the need for harmony and cooperation between people of different denominations, and in this spirit devoted a whole page to the dinner. He hoped to see it become 'a fixed and annual event in this town' (that didn't happen – perhaps once was enough).

The venue was a large marquee in the courthouse grounds. From its central pole fluttered a green banner bearing a golden representation of 'the harp that hung in Tara's hall'. Inside, the tables were arranged so the president (Besnard) and vice-president (O'Brien) would have an uninterrupted view of all the guests. The *Courier*'s description continues,

Behind the President's seat a large and somewhat rough, but very appropriate, painting of an old Irish harper, resting against a huge oak, the harp on his right and a large Irish wolf-dog on his left, with the motto 'Cead Mille Falthea' (a thousand welcomes) underneath. At the opposite end of the table, behind the Vice-President's chair, was a neat and chaste design of the harp, supported right and left by Australia's emblem – the Kangaroo and Emu – painted in colours upon a green ground, with the motto 'Erin-go-bragh [Ireland forever]'.

At seven o'clock, the men sat down to dinner as a 'magnificent brass band' struck up a popular air. Father Michael McAlroy of St Augustine's Church, Yass, said Grace. Then 'a most ample and excellently got up dinner was disposed of.' The dessert was 'equally well and plentifully provided,' and 'champagne and other descriptions of wine were placed on the tables with a prodigality that at one time induced the President to urge a stoppage to the supplies.'

If Mary Lehane was there, she made her entrance at about eight o'clock. According to the customs of the time, the ladies did not partake in the dinner or sit with their menfolk. They came in for the toasts and speeches, occupying a special 'draperied gallery' to the left of the top table. Their numbers exceeded 100, and they 'honoured the company with their presence', giving 'a novel and pleasing aspect to the proceedings', the *Courier* reported.

Now the toasts began. First, Besnard proposed one to Queen Victoria – 'a lady seated on the throne of the mightiest empire in the world'. This was drunk with loud cheers. Next came toasts to Prince Albert and the rest of the royal family, the governor, and the army and navy. Between speeches and cheers, the band played appropriate tunes – 'German Hymn', 'Fine Old English Gentleman' and 'British Grenadiers'. Then the focus switched to Ireland. 'I have to call for a bumper, if we ne'er drink a bumper again,' Besnard announced to cheers and laughter. 'It is Erin: Land of our Forefathers, endeared by the memory of St Patrick.'

Amid 'tremendous cheering', he offered the view that love of country and of kindred is peculiarly characteristic of the Irish. He said Irishmen in Australia had remitted immense sums to assist their friends at home, and in many cases to bring them to the country of their adoption. 'Having gathered comforts around them here, they begin to think of those dear friends they have left behind them and feel determined that they as well as themselves should share with them the comforts that they themselves possess.' The toast to Ireland was drunk 'with nine times nine – one cheer more – and tremendous cheers', after which the band played 'St Patrick's Day'.

Father Patrick Bermingham of St Augustine's responded in a long and emotional speech: 'Here, tonight, in this marquee, on a virgin soil, your hearts have felt a thrill of purest delight in toasting, with filial love, the dear old land of your sires... Being an Irishman, I cannot, on sea or land, in courtly hall or cabin home, cool down the ardour of my love for Erin – a land renowned on history's page for the virtue of her daughters and the heroism of her sons, glorious by the fame of her loving children, and of passing events – reposing lovely as Eden under cover of Nature's rarest charms, with a million claims to a people's love and the world's admiration.' ('Vehement applause.')

Bermingham then switched his focus to the injustices of British rule in Ireland, and the reporting of Irish events in the London press. 'If an evicted householder, driven from cottage hearth and unable under winter's piercing cold to shelter on the bleak roadside the perishing little one, dying perhaps in the father's arms – while the famishing mother falls to earth and sinks into an early grave – if, I say, while his warm nature is worked up to terrible excitement, he meets the heartless exterminator who has driven him to madness and fells him to earth, then 'our own correspondents' and Cockney commentators speak of Ireland as a nation of assassins.' ('Hear, hear.') Much more followed in similar vein.

Bermingham then extolled the fame of the Irish on the battlefield, in the council hall, in the hall of learning, 'at the festive halls', and 'in the walks of literature and of the occult sciences'. He quoted Edmund Burke on the anti-Catholic Penal Laws:

> a machine...as well fitted for the oppression, the impoverishment and degradation of a people, and the debasement in them of human nature itself, as ever proceeded from the perverted ingenuity of man.

'During that night of Erin's sorrow,' Bermingham went on, to further cheers, 'and while the dark hand of heavy trial was upon her, her music, thrillingly plaintive and wildly joyous, echoing her woes and the triumphs of her heroes, has lived on in the hearts of her peasantry...'

Bermingham's focus then switched to the Irish in Australia. 'We have not assembled on the banks of an Australian river, like the Hebrews by the rivers of Babylon, to offer to departed greatness the tribute of our praise and our tears. No, Hope, with radiant finger, points to the rising of a day of greater glory and renown.' He praised various Irish Australians, including Terence Aubrey Murray who had 'fearlessly and faithfully advocated and promoted…true civil liberty and religious equality.' With such men as prophets and guides, 'the unhallowed spirit of national jealousies and intestine discord shall be chased from our shores.' His closing message – 'our high and holy resolve should be to teach Young Australia to soar into the higher regions of truth, honour, and virtue' – brought 'loud and long-continued cheers'.

The next toast, to 'the land we live in', was proposed by Cornelius O'Brien and 'drunk with three times three'. Responding, lawyer George Allman, Australian-born son of an Irish Protestant, said to more loud cheers, 'I do not think it is claiming too much for Australia to say that in scarcely any other country under the sun could such a meeting as this – composed as it is of every class and opinion, both political and otherwise – have occurred, and been so free, as this has happily been, of anything like prejudice or ill-feeling of any sort.' More loud cheers followed his assertion that an Australian, unlike the people of most older, more densely populated countries, could always command success by his own industry and honesty.

> No matter what his present position in society may be, he may reasonably aspire to the highest offices in the country, if qualified for them by ability and integrity.

A toast to civil liberty and religious equality came next, proposed by Father McAlroy and 'drunk three times three and with the most rapturous applause'. He said the colony was remarkable 'all over the earth's surface' for its general good feeling, peace and harmony. 'I cherish fond and brilliant hopes of young Australia…and am confident that no power shall ever be able to immolate us on the altar of slavery.'

Then followed toasts to the ladies, the landed interests, the commercial interests, the president, the press, the vice-president, and the stewards for the dinner. One of the stewards, and a member of the evening's

Miles Murphy.

organising committee, was Miles Murphy of Binalong – storekeeper, publican, grazier, land speculator and the other central character in this story. One hopes he, Jerry and all the other guests made their way home safely at the end of proceedings. Sensibly, a secure paddock and a supply of fodder had been provided for the horses of gentlemen coming to town from the country.

It was a late night; following the arranged toasts, which finished after ten o'clock, many more speeches were made and 'toasts given and heartily responded to'. Wrote the *Courier*,

The good feeling was undimmed by any untoward event, and probably the largest, as it certainly was one of the happiest and most social dinner parties ever assembled in Yass, separated well pleased with the whole proceedings and with many hearty expressions that in 1860 there would be a renewal of the good fellowship and social harmony on St Patrick's Day.

4
Gold!

On 19 July 1860, Miles Murphy rode to Yass with half an ounce of gold from a new discovery on the lambing station of James White's pastoral run thirty-five miles north-west of Binalong. Before depositing the gold at the bank, he took it to the *Yass Courier* office to show proprietor and editor J.J. Brown, who in his next issue described the sample as rough and nuggetty.

The first *Courier* reference to the find, made by a black American cook with a group of stockmen who were rounding up horses, had appeared only a week earlier and was fairly dismissive:

> We have no authenticated report of any yield of consequence, and no gold has recently been received in Yass from that quarter...but we suppose that gold has been discovered in encouraging quantities, otherwise it would be hard to imagine what has induced certain orders for mining tools that have been received from Burrowa [now Boorowa, north of Binalong] by a store in this town.

Miles' news that about 100 people, including a number of Chinese, were already at the site and working a twenty-feet-deep lead failed to fire Brown's enthusiasm; he did not consider a 'rush' warranted. 'It would be the height of folly for persons at a distance to go there until something more encouraging has been indubitably proved,' he wrote.

The find was Lambing Flat – where Young now stands. The rich goldfields there etched themselves into Australia's history as the site of vicious anti-Chinese riots. They brought population and wealth to the region, including to Yass. And they attracted bushrangers who eluded the police for years – the legendary Frank Gardiner and Ben Hall gangs.

Miles Murphy's involvement from the start of the Lambing Flat diggings in buying gold from miners and selling it presumably for a good profit was typical of his entrepreneurial career. When the population at Lambing Flat grew – it reached more than 10,000 – he established a large general store there, and another store at the site of a large but short-lived rush nearby. From his arrival as a twenty-three-year-old assisted immigrant, occupation carpenter and joiner, in November 1841, this Irishman had his eye out for opportunities and made the most of them.

Miles was a son of Felix and Margaret Murphy of Enniscorthy, County Wexford. Only the father was still alive when he set out from Liverpool, with about 300 other emigrants, on the *Joseph Cunard*. Like Jerry's two years earlier, his voyage took 116 days. In a generally positive report, the ship's surgeon noted that two adults and nine children had died, and four babies had been born.

Miles' state of bodily health, strength and probable usefulness was rated good on the shipping record, which also noted that he could read and write. After reaching Sydney, he seems to have headed straight to the Yass district. He quickly found a soulmate, Anne Ellis, an emigrant from County Antrim, and their first child – John Aloysius – was born in March 1843 at Kangiara, a small settlement between Yass and Boorowa.

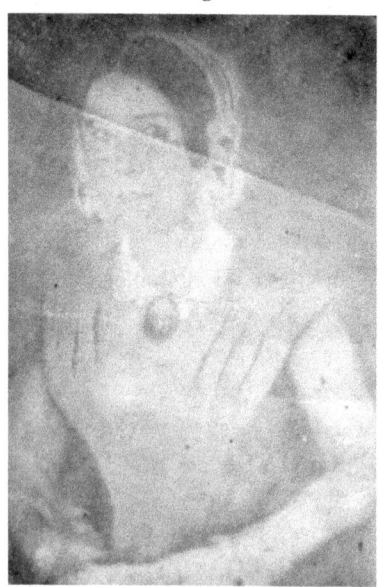

Anne Murphy.

Miles was probably engaged in building work there at the time. Showing that the entrepreneurial spirit was alive from the start, he acquired grazing land in the Weddin Mountains, near Grenfell (the town didn't exist then), from William Charles Wentworth the same year. He soon transferred this run, Arramagong, to Patrick O'Meally, who is remembered as father of the bushranger John O'Meally. Arramagong was a centre of action in the Ben Hall saga (chapter 6).

A second child, Felix, was on the way when Miles and

*Part of Yass in 1858 – from an oil painting by J.E. Grube.
St Augustine's Church (centre left) is without a tower – as it was when Miles and Anne were
married there four days after the church was consecrated in February 1844.*

Anne married at St Augustine's, Yass, on 18 February 1844. This was just four days after Archbishop Polding, head of the Catholic Church in the colony, consecrated the newly completed stone edifice. The town's pioneering Catholic priest, Charles Lovat, performed the ceremony. He had taken charge of the 24,000 square miles Yass mission shortly after Father Michael Brennan, based in Goulburn, inaugurated it in 1838 (Brennan baptised William Lehane in 1847). Achievements credited to Lovat include raising £14,000 in four years for the erection of churches and school buildings in Yass and surrounding settlements. His work was commemorated in 1868 with the installation of a bell in the tower built as part of extensions to St Augustine's completed in 1860 (Jerry contributed £20 and Miles £16 of the £1,272 11s 6d collected for that work). The bell was 'as loud as a bullock bell' and could be heard nine miles away on a calm day, the *Courier* observed.

Felix Murphy was born in Yass in June 1844. An advertisement placed by Miles in the *Sydney Morning Herald* six months later shows that, for the moment, the family had settled in the town. 'Miles Murphy, Carpenter, Wheelwright, and Blacksmith, begs respectfully to acquaint the inhabitants of Yass, and country settlers generally, that he has engaged a first rate

St Augustine's with the extensions completed in 1860.
The artist was Dr Morgan O'Connor, whose signature can be seen on the path.

blacksmith, who is capable of performing all work in the most masterly manner,' it said.

> M.M. further assures the public, that any work in the above three branches entrusted to his care shall be executed with the greatest strength and neatness, and at the lowest possible charges ever yet introduced into Yass.

Anne gave birth to two more boys in Yass – Robert in November 1845 and Joseph in June 1847. Five more children – four boys and Sarah, who in 1872 married Jerry Lehane's son William – were subsequently born at Binalong, the Murphys' home until the mid-1860s.

In April 1847, presumably at Miles' instigation, the police at Binalong recommended that the small settlement's first hotel be built and that Miles would be a suitable person to run it. Later that year, he opened the Swan Inn and, nearby, a general store. In 1849, Miles contracted to carry the mail by horseback between Binalong and Yass once a week for £28 a year – the first mail run west of Yass.

Miles' other interests included horse-racing, and in April 1849 he entered a horse called Binalong in a hack race – prize £10 – at a meeting in Yass. A year later, he hosted a gathering at the Swan to plan the first Binalong races. This decided that six races should be run over two days

– the Binalong Plate carrying a £20 prize, a hack race, a hack hurdle race, the District Purse worth £15, the Stockman's Sweepstakes and the Beaten Stakes for horses beaten in the earlier races. Ned Ryan of Galong was to officiate as judge. Five stewards were appointed, including Cornelius O'Brien and Crown Lands Commissioner Beckham.

Miles entered two horses – Short Tail, which came last in the hack race, and Alice Grey, which won the District Purse. The *Goulburn Herald* correspondent described the race-day scene:

> *And there was mounting in hot haste, the steed,*
> *The must'ring stockmen – and the nobby one*
> *Came pouring onward with impetuous speed*
> *And swiftly forming in the ranks of fun.*

Such was the scene that every avenue leading to Binalong presented on the morning of our First Race Meeting – and when the bell tolled forth its first summons to 'make ready' – the course presented a most animated and lively appearance: on every side, beneath the greenwood-tree, pranced horsemen on their mettled steeds – or stood in clustered groups around their favorites, as, their clothing withdrawn, they displayed their glossy coats, and perfect symmetry to their admiring eyes: from forth the booths came the sounds of music and merriment, waking the echoes of the surrounding woods, while the crowds about them imparted an air of bustle and life to the picture that strongly contrasted with the repose of the more aristocratical marquees in the distance; while as if by magic all the paraphernalia of the turf was there – the roped 'run in' – the 'stewards' stand,' with all its accompaniments, executed in a manner indeed surprising in such an incipient 'location' and giving undeniable evidence of the untameable love of racing in our British nature.

The writer, after noting the Irish origin of a large proportion of those present, said the people of Binalong deserved the highest credit for 'the spirited way in which the races were got up, and the peaceable manner in which they were conducted':

> ...to be admired above all, was the thorough spirit of harmony that seemed to pervade every individual, permitting the meeting to pass off without a single disturbance, which, looking at the Tipperarian statistics of the district, was truly marvellous; but so it was; not a shillelah described a flourish in

The Swan Inn, Binalong – now the Black Swan restaurant.

the atmosphere, and any one might have said 'pase' without the slightest molestation – for though the 'Rosy God' shed his spirit plentifully all around, he did not make any heart more than glad.

While Miles opened his hotel and store in 1847, the approved plan for Binalong was not drawn up and made available for inspection – at the surveyor-general's office in Sydney or the police office, 'Bennelong' (evidently the originally intended name of the settlement) – until January 1850. The following July, Miles bought five of fourteen allotments sold at the first auction of town sites; other buyers included Edgar Beckham and Nicholas Besnard. By the mid-1850s, two inns had been opened in competition with the Swan.

The life of a bush publican must seldom have been dull; incidents that reached court provide some insights. For example, in 1853 a man named Howe or Howard was found guilty of stealing sixty-nine ounces of gold in a chamois bag from a box in a horse-drawn cart parked opposite the Swan. In the lock-up, he allegedly told another prisoner, arrested for robbing Miles, that the owner of the gold would never get it 'as he had planted it amongst some rocks behind Murphy's house.'

Aired at the same court hearings was an incident at the Swan that led to Thomas Gleeson being charged with wounding with intent to cause bodily harm. He and the victim, William King, had been employed by Miles to build a well. 'About dinner time they had a quarrel and blows ensued,' the *Goulburn Herald* reported.

> ...on going towards the tap room of Murphy's house [King] felt something wet inside his trousers, and on feeling found that he had been wounded in the lower part of the abdomen... It came out in the course of the evidence,

that the prisoner, at the time of the altercation, was using the knife for the purpose of cutting his victuals, and that he and the prosecutor had been on good terms up to the time of the assault: the inference drawn was that the cutting was unintentional.

In July 1854, the *Herald* published an article about Binalong that was full of praise for 'that spirited and enterprising colonist Mr Miles Murphy':

> That 'mine host' of the 'Swan' merits the patronage and support accorded him, few persons acquainted with his frank and upright, yet respectful demeanour, and truly obliging disposition, will be found to gainsay, while he derives no small share of popularity within his homely sphere, from frequently acting as 'pacificator' between parties, whose cases of petty dispute would otherwise only waste the time and patience of the local bench.

The article predicted that Binalong, although 'as yet nothing more than the nucleus of a town', would take a prominent position among the towns of the southern interior.

> With an area of three square miles, abundantly supplied with water, and having on all sides land of the richest nature for agricultural purposes, it has also the advantage of lying on that line of route from the Metropolis to the Murray, to which teams and travellers are now giving a decided preference, and in the direct track from the Southern to the Western gold-fields.

Binalong could 'boast of possessing two requirements of a rather superior class' – the Swan Inn and Miles' general store. The inn afforded 'every necessary or required comfort and accommodation to the resident or wayfarer'. The store, 'whether as regards a show of goods or moderation in price', was 'fully competent to vie with most of those establishments which lie in far closer proximity to the great mart of the colony'.

Three months later, the same reporter had more nice things to say about Miles, this time praising him for spending some £200 of his own money on a bridge, to replace a decaying ford, over Binalong (now Balgalal) Creek on the road through the village. He wrote,

> Mr Murphy declared his intention of building a substantial and durable

bridge, at his sole expense…and right manfully and spiritedly has he carried out that liberal and patriotic undertaking. Placing himself at the head of half a dozen men acquainted with the general run of bush work, to whom he allowed a most liberal rate of wage, and having two hired bullock teams in readiness for drawing in, the banks of the creek were soon excavated, so as to admit of a foundation tier of logs, nearly three feet through, being laid at right angles with its bed; across these, secured by grooving, was laid another tier of equal dimensions, and so on until what may be termed the piers had attained an altitude of 20 feet above the bed of the creek, being fully 2 feet clear of the highest flood mark; those piers, formed each of 35 logs, and allowing a water-way of 23 feet in width between them, are united (or spanned) by logs 40 feet long and from 18 to 20 inches mean diameter, over which is laid a flooring of squared logs, or slabs, from 8 to 9 inches in thickness, closely fitted and coated with a thick layer of stone; stout handrails, somewhat curved, contribute not a little towards giving the whole an air of skilful construction and stability.

The bridge took less than six weeks to build. On its completion, continued the *Herald*, 'its kindly disposed founder was resolved the occasion should not pass without bearing with it those tokens of joyous festivity which usually characterise such events'. An 'excellent dinner' had therefore been prepared, 'and a tent capable of holding one hundred persons, or more, having been pitched close to the bridge, tables loaded with viands equally substantial and palatable, with a liberal supply of the needful in a liquid state, greeted the assembled guests, who, fully aware that 'Caed milleh faltheh' [a thousand welcomes] was the password of the day, cheerfully responded to its meaning, by devoting the passing hours to conviviality and social enjoyment.' Loyal and patriotic toasts were proposed and drunk 'with a becoming degree of enthusiasm', and the company testified 'by occasional bursts of hearty acknowledgment, the high sense it entertained of the great public service rendered by the hospitable 'founder of the feast'.'

A naming ceremony followed the dinner. After a procession of 'the principal persons present' over the bridge, Edgar Beckham's 'amiable and highly-respected' sister named the structure Beckham's Bridge. Then £140 was collected from those assembled to establish a fund to maintain the Binalong races as an annual event.

Miles' next major move, early in 1856, was acquiring the leases of the Murrumburrah pastoral run, about twenty miles west of Binalong on the track to Wagga Wagga, and the nearby Kalangan run. The Murrumburrah property contained a small, unofficial village on the banks of Murrimboola Creek; settlers had built houses and an inn there from the late 1840s. On taking up the lease, Miles issued them with notices to quit. They objected and got up a petition asking the surveyor-general to name their chosen location a town site. They claimed it enjoyed a better water supply than Cunningar, four miles to the east, which had been earmarked as the site for a town. One of their arguments was that the Murrumburrah village was on important transport routes that were likely one day to include a Sydney to Wagga Wagga rail link (they were right; the railway came through in 1877).

Crown Lands Commissioner Beckham became involved, opposing the petition. He was critical of Miles' predecessor on the Murrumburrah run, John Harris, for permitting settlement on a site of which he disapproved. He reported that the presence of the villagers, some alleged to be sly-grog sellers, was scarcely tolerated by neighbouring squatters, and thought Miles' decision to remove them was in the public interest.

That did not settle the matter. After protracted correspondence, Murrumburrah became the preferred site, although the go-ahead was also given to development of Cunningar. Evidently a major factor favouring Murrumburrah was increasing activity at the nearby Demondrille goldfield. This had been discovered in 1854, and thirty to forty miners were at work there in 1856. Miles, despite having opposed the development of Murrumburrah, was the biggest early buyer of land in the town and nearby. His holdings there eventually totalled 125 allotments. He opened the second hotel built after the official go-ahead, the Criterion, in 1860. An inn owned by John English, who was also Murrumburrah's postmaster from September 1860, had begun trading a little earlier.

According to a description published when Miles advertised for a tenant publican in 1862, the Criterion contained eight bedrooms, three parlours, a taproom and a bar. The bar was 'fitted up with spirit fountain of six taps and pipes, complete, together with six ten-gallon oval kegs, neatly painted'. The hotel had a large kitchen, cook's room and laundry,

The Criterion in 1876. The old building was demolished in the 1930s and the two-storey hotel that replaced it suffered the same fate after World War II.

and a stable containing eight stalls and loose boxes. The premises were built of brick, and constituted 'one of the most commodious and best arranged houses for business in the Southern District'. Other features included 'a small enclosed paddock for travelling stock; three-quarter acre of green barley, ready for use, and a splendid well of water in the yard'.

Perhaps wanting to concentrate on his new Murrumburrah interests, Miles put the Swan Inn up for sale in March 1858. It comprised, according to an advertisement in the *Yass Courier*,

> A substantially-built House, shingled, with verandah running the entire length of the building, in good repair, containing two parlours, tap-room, seven bedrooms, a bar, private store, and a stone-built sitting and bed room, for the use of the family.
> A detached Slab-built Kitchen, with oven and cook's room.
> A detached Slab-built Laundry.
> A Brick-built Water-Closet.
> A Slab-built Fowl-House.
> The Stabling consists of a commodious six-stalled stable, harness-room, and coach-house, with a loft for hay, and eight separately enclosed box stalls.
> A large enclosed Yard, a paled Yard for travelling sheep, and a commodious Milking Yard.
> A strong-built Shed, for drays, carriages, &c.

The advertisement claimed the inn was doing a trade of about £2,400 a year, the present proprietor had 'amassed a large fortune therein' and a more safe or desirable investment for persons wishing to realise a rapid fortune had seldom been offered to the public. It seems no sale occurred; rather, the property was tenanted for some years. Miles was back in charge in 1863.

A few months earlier, a *Yass Courier* correspondent had cast a more critical eye over Binalong – and by implication Miles – than the earlier *Goulburn Herald* writer, suggesting a bit more business competition would be beneficial:

> The township...only wants a few enterprising persons to make it go ahead rapidly. The publicans and storekeepers have all the sway in their respective businesses and as a natural result the accommodation at the inns is very indifferent and expensive, and the goods at the stores very dear...

A *Sydney Morning Herald* reporter took a similar line nearly two years later, in August 1859. He described the town as comprising a store, a courthouse, three or four public houses and a sprinkling of huts. 'Most of the township has become the property of a publican and storekeeper [clearly Miles]; and here, buried in the mountains, it progresses very slowly.'

The *Herald* reporter also visited 'Murrimboolla' (Murrumburrah), which he wrote comprised 'one public-house complete, two others building, a tent, a hut, and a blacksmith's shed'. He noted that the unnamed lessee of the pastoral run on which the town was being built (Miles again) had bought all the land recently offered for sale by the government there. The reporter noted that the purchaser was said to be still unsated:

> After a few more such purchases he may climb to the top of one of his own hills, and there, enthroned upon a granite boulder, look round upon the wilderness he has perpetuated, and exclaim with Robinson Crusoe: I am monarch of all I survey, My right there is none to dispute.

It's hard to imagine that Miles was much fazed by such criticism.

Like Jerry, Miles frequently took part in fund-raising efforts for Catholic causes. In 1857 he gave two guineas to the testimonial collection for the Rev. Magenis and £25 to a building fund for St John's College, University of Sydney. The following year, he was a member of a committee formed to raise subscriptions for the Donegal Relief Fund, which aimed to assist the 'persecuted and famishing Celts' of that Irish county.

He also took an interest in politics and, in October 1858, was a leading light at a public dinner held at Binalong – in a marquee beside the Swan – to honour William Macleay and John Paterson, the members of parliament for the region. As at the 1859 St Patrick's Day dinner in Yass, Nicholas Besnard took the chair. Other notables present included Edgar Beckham, Cornelius O'Brien and Andrew Bogle Paterson, brother of John and father of Banjo. The event began with a procession. A 'cavalcade' of Binalong's inhabitants, headed by 'Mr Ashton's fine brass band', first proceeded down the road to Illalong, the Paterson property. There, 'the concourse was joined by several carriages containing the honourable guests and a number of gentlemen resident in the vicinity'. The party then returned to Binalong, the band playing favourite airs as they went. 'The whole affair was one such as seldom is witnessed in Binalong, and occasioned a great deal of excitement,' the *Courier* reported.

In December 1860, Miles headed a Binalong committee backing the election of John Nagle Ryan to parliament for the seat of Lachlan. Unlike in the 1859 election, Ryan had an opponent, the Sydney lawyer James Martin. His supporters placed an advertisement in the *Courier* advising 'free selectors' that 'John Ryan is dead against you but hasn't the honesty to say so'. The Robertson land legislation allowing new settlers to 'select' land within squatters' runs was before parliament then; it took effect at the start of 1862. Many of the squatters, who held their land under lease from the Crown, naturally saw it as a threat.

Ryan won the election convincingly – 248 votes to 180. The margin was 153 to eight at Boorowa but a closer forty-two to twenty-eight at Binalong, perhaps because John Paterson threw his support behind Martin. Those who thought that by voting for Martin they were backing the liberal candidate against a conservative may have been disappointed by later events, as Martin went on to serve three times as premier backed by the colony's conservative forces. Martin Place, Sydney, is named after him.

The main excitement in the district, though, was gold. In early 1860, Kiandra, in the Snowy Mountains, was the focus of attention. The *Courier* reported in February that it had received information of 'satisfactory and tempting a character' about the goldfields there. The news in early March was that large parties of diggers were passing through Yass on their way to Kiandra and local storekeepers had dispatched bullock teams with supplies for the diggings. Later that month, things were looking less hopeful. Yass people returning from Kiandra reported little success, and cold weather would soon make the place close to uninhabitable.

Perhaps the *Courier*'s early optimism about Kiandra – it went so far in early March as to appoint an agent to take subscriptions there – partly explains its initial caution about Lambing Flat. Its view soon changed. At the end of July 1860, a miner brought a 'very excellent' sample of gold to the *Courier* office. Three weeks later, the paper reported that nearly 300 people were working the diggings, with some good finds being made. Shortly afterwards, Crown Lands Commissioner Beckham sent a highly positive report to the secretary for lands, saying diggers were describing the goldfield as very extensive and rich, and were behaving in a most orderly manner.

In early October, a *Courier* correspondent forecast that the country in and around Lambing Flat would produce more gold than any other goldfield in New South Wales. In the same issue, another correspondent wrote that he had been on Miles Murphy's property Kalangan one day recently, and had seen upwards of a hundred people pass through on their way to Lambing Flat. 'The night was wet, and some fifty persons camped in a shed on the farm,' he wrote. Nobody was leaving the diggings, except those who only rode up to have a look without taking their tools.

The following February, the *Courier* reported that the best way from Yass to the diggings was via Binalong (where 'first rate accommodation' was available 'for man and beast') and then a track leading through Kalangan. Perhaps aiming to help cater for the needs of the travelling diggers, Miles advertised in the same issue for 'one or two milkmen or tenants for a good dairy' on the property. Lambing Flat's first newspaper, the *Miner*, appeared the same month, and Miles immediately placed an advertisement offering to agist horses – presumably he had in mind those ridden to the diggings by prospective miners – on his 'large grass paddock' at Murrumburrah; 'saddles and bridles taken charge of by the man at the gate'. Shortly afterwards, advertisements began appearing for a new coach service from the Criterion Hotel to the diggings.

In the meantime, things had turned nasty at Lambing Flat. On 13 November 1860, a large party of diggers marched on the Chinese miners 'accompanied by a brass band playing enlivening airs'. When the Chinese fled, their tents were burnt. According to the *Courier*, one storekeeper was 'much chagrined' as seven tons of rice he had ordered to meet their demands was on its way but would now not be needed.

The Chinese returned, however, and agitation against them increased until another mob of diggers, again accompanied by a band, drove them from their camp on 31 January 1861. Again, tents were burnt. With the aim of quelling the continuing disorder, in late February the colonial government despatched a military force from Sydney. This comprised two ensigns, six sergeants, two drummers, one sapper and 125 rank and file soldiers under the command of a Captain Atkinson.

After marching about thirty miles a day, they reached Yass in early March and immediately disgraced themselves in Hamilton Hume's orchard. He had given permission for the contingent to gather some fruit, but they were asked 'not to pluck the grapes nor touch the fruit on two particular trees'. This request was ignored, and considerable damage was done to Hume's garden and fences before Captain Atkinson restored order. 'Yesterday morning an apology was send to Mr Hume, which we have no doubt he will accept, in consideration of the novelty of a body of infantry and artillery having been encamped close to his peaceful residence,' the *Courier* reported.

Just before the military arrived at Lambing Flat, the premier of New South Wales, Charles Cowper, paid the settlement a visit. He told a meeting of 1,500 miners that he had come to hear their grievances. He trusted they would not compel the government to act against them, 'but law and order were more sacred than any other question'. He asked the diggers whether they would let the Chinese return, without interference, to the one area where they were permitted to mine. This provoked 'great uproar and cries of 'No, no' - Yes, yes,' and it would be difficult to say which side predominated,' wrote the *Courier* correspondent. 'The confusion was so great that I could not catch the concluding sentences of the hon. gentleman's speech.'

Before the meeting, Cowper had been entertained at a dinner presided over by the local member, John Ryan, and attended by notables including Miles Murphy, who had recently established his store in the rapidly developing town. A week later, a grand public banquet for the premier was held at a Lambing Flat hotel. This had a sequel three months later when the hotel's owner, Charles Quail, took the members of the organising committee, who included Miles, to the Yass District Court. He claimed they had failed to pay him £80 12s 6d for the wine supplied for the banquet.

Quail told the court his waiters had kept careful account of the liquor served to the eighty or so diners. One of the waiters said the prices charged were those generally prevailing at Lambing Flat. Quail's lawyer, George Allman, said the party was a very happy one, and 'a very considerable quantity' of wine must have been drunk. Counsel for the banquet organisers, John Devereux, put forward a variety of defences – that the Publicans' Act made it illegal to sue for liquor purchases of less than two gallons at a time; that the defendants were neither lodgers nor travellers; and that the liquor was promised at wholesale prices. He told Judge Callaghan that his instructions were to do all he could to oppose the claim, 'on technical or any other grounds'. The judge found in favour of Quail.

Premier Cowper visited Murrumburrah briefly on his way back to Sydney, and told the locals he expected it to become 'a leading township not many years hence'. Back at the diggings, according to the *Courier* in mid-April, the premier who had been 'applauded to the very echo' the previous month had now been 'transmogrified into a demon of mischief'. The 'ancient feeling' against the Chinese was as strong as ever, and 'it requires but one occasion to fan the latent sparks of rebellion into a flame.'

Peace reigned through May, however, with mining operations now centred on a place called Tipperary Gully. 'In a few weeks quite a township has arisen on this place... It is wonderful how rapidly storekeepers, publicans, butchers and bakers follow in the track of the diggers,' the *Courier* observed. A census that month put the population of the Lambing Flat goldfields at 10,097 Europeans and 489 Chinese. By comparison, Yass had 1,145 people, up from 660 in 1856.

Miles was among those who set up stores at Tipperary Gully. In June 1861, he was one of four representatives of the area appointed to a committee to begin organising a Lambing Flat hospital. The following month, 'a woman who bears a very unenviable notoriety on these goldfields' appeared in the local police court charged with tendering a forged cheque at his store. The *Miner* carried a brief report of proceedings:

> ...prisoner said that she received the cheque from her sister...believing it to he genuine, and as no evidence was forthcoming to disprove her statements, the case was dismissed. As prisoner was leaving the courtroom, she turned round to Mr Fitzsimons [the magistrate] and said, 'I shall be always ready when you want me, sir!' With a shrug of utter contempt, the worthy magistrate replied, 'Go, by all means; I shall never want to see you again.'

Captain Atkinson and his troops did not spend long at the diggings, departing in late May 1861. With them, noted the *Courier* correspondent, went 'all the pomp and circumstance of glorious war.' He added, 'Although we miss them as devil-may-care fellows, ready for a spree, we have not as yet experienced any inconvenience from their departure. Indeed, I do not think the Chinese will be again troublesome here...' The correspondent spoke too soon. Early in the morning on Sunday June 30, again accompanied by a band, 1,000 to 2,000 diggers armed with guns, sticks and pick handles, and bearing flags inscribed 'Roll up; no Chinese', moved on the Chinese camps. As well as destroying tents, stores and equipment, they humiliated the Chinese by cutting off their pigtails and inflicted some serious injuries. 'Many...had severe cuts about the head and body, one had a bullet wound in his leg, and some four or five are represented to be in a very precarious state,' the *Courier* reported.

Two weeks later, a mob of more than 1,000 attacked the police camp where three men arrested as leaders of the assaults on the Chinese were being held. Shots were fired, and one digger killed, in the defence of the camp. In response, the government proclaimed martial law at Lambing Flat, with all processions banned. Another force was despatched from Sydney, this time including two howitzers, 'a full complement' of artillerymen, about sixty 'men-of-war's men' and 'a strong body of the mounted patrol'. On arrival in Yass on 27 July, they 'received salutes of five shots... The seamen were armed each with a musket, revolver and cutlass... It appeared to be the general opinion that the rioters would never oppose, though small, such a well armed and disciplined body of men.' They were greeted with jeers and laughter when they reached Lambing Flat on 30 July, but 'there was no breach of the peace whatever'.

As peace returned, so did the Chinese; the *Courier* reported in early September that 800 were working at the Back Creek diggings, with fresh arrivals daily, and they were doing well. The military force was quickly scaled down. The sailors and marines left just a week after they arrived and more units departed in September. Following gold discoveries at Forbes, NSW, and Otago, New Zealand, many diggers and some storekeepers also left. 'Opinions as to the probability of a continuance of the reign of peace are very diverse,' the *Courier* told its readers in late September. As insurance, the mounted and dismounted police were being increased in number, and a howitzer – with five artillerymen – was to remain in place.

5

Family matters

One man caught up in the June and July 1861 riots was John Henry Vicq, publican of the Empire Hotel, Lambing Flat, which had opened for business the previous April. After a day of assaulting the Chinese and destroying their property, the diggers gathered opposite the Empire to hear inflammatory speeches from their leaders. Then, following the attack on the police camp two weeks later, a 'madman' called Dolby set fire to the hotel.

Fortunately, the flames were extinguished 'before any serious mischief was done'. Dolby, who had lit other fires, including one that burnt down the Lambing Flat courthouse, 'was taken in charge of by Mr Vicq, who keeps a man to look after him,' the *Courier* reported.

The reason for John Vicq's appearance in this story is that on 3 January 1861 he married Honora Lehane at the Reedy Creek (Coppabella) residence of Jerry and Mary Lehane. John had been a lieutenant in HM 57th Regiment, and was the only son of the late Colonel Vicq. But who was Honora?

According to the marriage notice in the *Courier*, she was the eldest daughter of J. Lehane Esq. of Reedy Creek (that can only be Jerry). Her death certificate – she died, aged eighty-two, at Miller's Point, Sydney, in March 1914 – also names Jeremiah Lehane as her father. It says she was born in County Cork and does not name a mother.

To confuse matters, though, the immigration record shows Honora Lehane, aged twenty-two, occupation girl servant, arriving with James Lehane – both sponsored by Jerry – in 1856, and names her parents as Daniel and Martha Lehane of Clonfert, near Newmarket. It notes that she had an uncle near Yass; that must be Jerry. However, her father, Daniel, is said to be dead and her mother still living – so the father cannot have been

Jerry's brother Daniel, who came to the colony in 1862. On her marriage certificate, 'unknown' has been inscribed in the spaces provided for the mother's and father's names. (And, although the shipping record says she could read and write, the certificate carries her 'X' mark rather than a signature.) When Ellen Lehane, born at Yarralumla in 1844, married John Perry Lyons in February 1867 the *Courier* notice described her as the only daughter of J. Lehane.

Whatever the answer to this mystery, the marriage was duly performed by Father McAlroy of St Augustine's. Then, presumably, the couple set off for Lambing Flat where John – who, according to the *Yass Courier*, was 'so well and favourably known on the southern gold-fields' – ran the Diggers' Arms. Almost immediately he began building the Empire, a grander hotel, which was apparently funded and owned by Jerry. When this opened in early April 1861, the *Miner* was impressed:

> It contains a fine and commodious bar, parlours without number, bedrooms ditto, and a splendid ball-room. The stables and outbuildings are also on a very extensive scale. The victualling department is first-rate, the wines, spirits, &c., have been selected from the principal houses in the metropolis. The forage is all that can be desired. In fact at the Empire Hotel will be found every necessary for 'man and beast.' Let us not forget the bar-man, he is an American clipper.

Vicq placed large advertisements for the Empire in the *Miner* under a coat of arms inscribed 'Advance Australia'. The hotel's ballroom, which was open for dancing every evening, seems to have been a prime attraction. A grand ball 'on a scale of unusual splendour' was held soon after the opening. Another, to coincide with a race meeting, was advertised shortly afterwards. In May, a burglar appeared in John's and Honora's bedroom early one morning; he beat a hasty retreat when John woke up. This was fortunate because, as the *Miner* reported, there was a lot worth stealing in the room:

> Two valuable watches, the property of Mr and Mrs Vicq, lay upon the dressing table, and which were untouched; besides which Mr Vicq had under his pillow the sum of £500. £200 of this were his own property; the remainder of the money belonged to parties who were staying at the hotel.

John and Honora left the Empire, and Lambing Flat, in December 1861 and settled at Bogolong. John ran a hotel there for a few years and in 1864 was appointed the town's first postmaster, a position he held until his retirement in 1889, when a son, William, briefly succeeded him. He ran a general store in conjunction with the post office for many years and became involved in various mining ventures (chapters 14 and 18). The Vicqs had seven children, four of whom – William, Mary, Amelia and Arthur – were still living when Honora died in Sydney in 1914. John died at Bookham, as Bogolong was then known, in 1895.

Mary Lehane, who had been ill for a long time, lived just long enough to see Honora's wedding. She died at home on 28 January 1861 at the age of fifty-eight. The death certificate names the cause of death as inflammation of the lungs, and says she had been suffering from it for eighteen months. Dr Morgan O'Connor of Yass – from Westmeath country, central Ireland, so probably no relation – attended her the day she died. Mary was buried at Jugiong on 30 January.

We have no direct information about Mary's life in Ireland or – beyond the bare facts of her marriage, the births of her children and her death – in Australia. The fact that a brother, sister and nephew followed her to the colony suggests she sent positive reports of life in the bush to relatives in County Cork. Presumably Jerry did too; it's a pity their letters have not survived. When William O'Connor and his family landed in 1852 they were the first relatives to arrive – four years before the first family members sponsored by Jerry (Honora and James Lehane and another nephew, David Walsh). Mary's sister Johanna arrived with her husband Jeremiah O'Keefe and their nine children, ranging in age from six to thirty-one, in June 1858. They spent some time at Coppabella before settling near Boorowa.

Mary was still alive when the Very Rev. Dr John Forrest reached the colony in the second half of 1860, but probably did not see her nephew, who was installed as rector of St John's College in September that year. The family ties remained strong, though, with Forrest officiating at the weddings of both Mary's children (Ellen was sixteen and William thirteen when their mother died).

Jerry's first appearance in the *Courier* after Mary's death was in July 1861, following the bailing-up of a mail coach near Jugiong. Word of the assault, by three men, was received at the Five Mile Creek Inn bordering Coppabella, which was evidently owned by Jerry. On hearing what had happened, he sent the groom employed there to notify the Jugiong police. A police party traced the criminals as far as Miles Murphy's Kalangan station but then lost the trail in a thunderstorm.

The *Courier* accused the police of being slow to act, and provided space for a denial by the trooper in charge. In a foretaste of things to come in the days of Gardiner and Hall, the paper wrote of hearing almost daily of armed desperadoes stopping wayfarers and bailing up households:

> [This] reminds us of the olden times of 'bushranging', when runaways from stockades roamed through the interior, and by their daring acts – acts that in many cases they were driven to by sheer desperation – struck terror into whatever neighbourhood they might visit.

In the same month, Jerry won a court case against Charles Byrnes, a relative of Ann Byrnes of the trespass affair related in chapter 3. Byrnes had accused him of illegally impounding sheep that were grazing on the land under dispute in the earlier case. Jerry gave half the £20 damages awarded by the magistrates to the roofing fund for the Catholic church then under construction at Binalong, and the other half to the village's school. At about the same time, he sold 4,000 sheep to Miles to build up the flock at Kalangan – 3,000 ewes at eleven shillings each and 1,000 wethers at twelve shillings each.

Jerry's next deal was the big one. In late September, he bought the Globe Hotel in Rossi Street, Yass, and nearby property including the Braidwood Store, from Charles Quail (whose dispute with Miles and others was related in chapter 4). Quail had opened the hotel, one of the busiest in Yass, in 1847. He was now expanding his interests at Lambing Flat, and the deal with Jerry included buying the Empire Hotel there, run by John Vicq, from him. Quail renamed this the Royal to avoid confusion with another Lambing Flat hotel called the Empire. Jerry paid £6,500 for the property in Yass, and in return received £1,500 for his Empire.

Originally, according to an advertisement in the *Courier* in early September, Quail had intended to let the Globe. Perhaps Jerry made an offer for purchase that was too good to refuse. Quail's advertisement

The Globe, Rossi Street, Yass – restored as a bed and breakfast establishment.

described the Globe as 'that Old Establishment' and 'one of the Best Mailing Establishments in the Southern Districts'. The hotel (now restored as the Globe Bed & Breakfast) had 'stabling for 30 horses, a good garden and a well of water'.

After sealing the deal, Jerry employed Alexander and Mary Patison to run the hotel; Alexander became licensee in December. A month later, on Sunday 26 January 1862, the Globe joined in celebrations for the colony's seventy-third anniversary. In a gesture apparently mixing loyalty to the empire with a healthy dose of nationalism, the Patisons flew a flag comprising 'the Southern Cross with the jack at one corner' from the roof. Probably this was the flag first flown in the 1820s as the NSW ensign, which featured a blue cross on a white background with the Union Jack in the top left-hand corner. Five stars representing the Southern Cross were embedded in the cross. Supporters of federation flew this flag widely during the 1890s.

In tune with the spirit of optimism in Yass at the time, Jerry initiated a major refurbishment of the Globe. According to the *Courier*, 'vast alterations' were undertaken inside. Nearly all the partition walls and ceilings were pulled down, altered and improved: 'indeed, those who were acquainted with the old establishment will scarcely recognise the different apartments...' Patison placed an ad in the paper saying the Globe would 'be found replete with every convenience, combining the advantages of an hotel with the privacy of a private residence', and offered 'good, secure stabling, coach-houses, with first-rate forage.'

The reference to changes at the Globe was part of a long article about building works in Yass, which included the town's first plate-glass shopfront – nine feet high and framed in polished cedar. 'We may congratulate ourselves that Yass is going ahead and is becoming, as its geographical position and splendid agricultural and pastoral country entitles it to be, one of the leading and most flourishing towns of the colony,' the *Courier* commented. It predicted Yass would become the most important town in the southern district. A few weeks later, Henry O'Brien told a meeting called to agitate for a better road to the Lambing Flat and Forbes goldfields that Yass would be entitled, 'some years hence', to be ranked as a city.

A letter to the *Courier* by Henry Godfrey, a local storekeeper who had set up branch stores at the goldfields, gives a feel for the impact they were having. At a cost of more than £400 a month, his company employed thirty to forty teams to carry goods between Yass and the diggings: 'This money is afterwards expended in the town of Yass, amongst the lawyers, storekeepers, butchers, publicans, shoemakers, millers, and tailors.' The *Courier* reported a constant traffic of diggers and their families through Yass – in coaches and vans, on horseback, and on foot. The goods traffic was just as heavy: 'It would be hard to form anything like an accurate estimate of the number of drays laden with goods for the Flat, that are travelling thitherward; but on some days in the week a continuous line of these and waggons, carrying all kinds of merchandise and materials for building, move through Cooma-street' (Yass's main road, now Comur Street).

Clearly, these were good times to own a hotel in Yass. The Globe, as well as offering rest and refreshment to locals and those passing through, was in demand for other purposes. A Masonic ball was held there in February 1862. In May, a large room was fitted out as a court because renovations were in progress at the courthouse. A dais at one end was partitioned off and carpeted for the judge, a dock and witness box were built, and accommodation was provided for the police and press. Rooms were also prepared for the judge, jury, clerk of the peace and the prisoners awaiting trial. The *Courier* commented after the hearings that the arrangements made were 'exceedingly satisfactory. The police, under the charge of Senior Sergeant Brennan, kept the space within the bar free from unnecessary intrusion, and consequently afforded ease and comfort to those whose duty compelled them to attend.'

Business was brisk, but running the Globe presented challenges. On the same page as its story about how well the court sittings had gone, the *Courier* reported a garrotting at the hotel. Between five and six on a Monday evening, Samuel Dinnir, who had 'just completed one of his usual quarterly imprisonments', noticed that a fellow patron in one of the Globe's parlours, William Grew, a shoemaker, had some money on him. Dinnir 'caught hold of him by the neck-handkerchief and twisting it round endeavoured to choke him', at the same time extracting 'a sovereign and some silver' from his pocket. 'The cries of the man attracted the attention of Mrs Patison, who, on running into the room, noticed that Grew had grown almost black in the face from the strangulating process under which he had gone,' wrote the reporter. 'Dinnir made himself scarce.'

Two weeks later, somebody stole the kerosene burner from the lamp in front of the Globe, opening Patison to risk of prosecution because hotels were required to keep a lamp burning though the night. 'Of course, such little expensive inconveniences never entered the heads of the mischievous fools who perpetrated the 'lark',' said the *Courier*. Patison offered a £5 reward 'on conviction of the thief or thieves.'

The Globe was one of the town's main entertainment venues. For example, in September 1862, Mr D. Murray and his troupe performed the 'well-known farce 'The Happy Man'…with considerable spirit', together with 'songs, legerdemain, &c'. Mr Murray improvised some local verses to the tune of 'Billy Barlow', which, while pointed in their application, were free from vulgarity – 'a rare quality on such occasions'. An 'astounding feat', 'the boy who sleeps in the air', was performed with complete success, the *Courier* reported. In December, as a Christmas holiday amusement, the Globe presented a 'Grand Exhibition of Dissolving Views & Chromatropes'. As well as views of England, Scotland and the Continent, this included 'numerous laughable comic views, including the amusing series of the Tiger and the Tub'. 'Oh! Mamma, do take us to see the Dissolving Views. Where, my dear? At the Globe Hotel, on Boxing Night and the following evening', the advertisement concluded.

A special exhibit made its debut at the hotel in November 1862. Two months earlier, the *Courier* reported that a remarkable lamb had been dropped at Coppabella:

> It had two heads, four fore legs, and was otherwise perfect as two distinct lambs until the portion between the ribs and loins were reached. The hind quarter was that of a single animal with the exception of there being two tails. Of course the lamb did not long survive its birth.

It seems Jerry thought this freak of nature was worth preserving. He enlisted the aid of a Mr Pearce, 'who thoroughly understands the art of preserving and stuffing specimens' and who, according to the *Courier*, 'has great taste in the difficult task of setting the subject in a natural attitude'.

'The other day we were shown the result of his labour,' the report continued.

> He has accomplished his task very artistically, and we must give him credit accordingly. The animal is enclosed in a glass case, and as it is undoubtedly a great curiosity, many persons will be glad to learn that Mr Patison, of the Globe Hotel, will be happy to afford anyone who is so desirous an opportunity of inspecting it.

While business was booming in Yass and the region, so was the workload of the courts, with Jerry and Miles among those making frequent appearances. The *Courier* was distressed, editorialising in May 1862,

> There is not a more melancholy object for contemplation than a litigious community... Society is in an unhealthy state when the law is being continually appealed to, for it indicates that there is a desire, either on the one side or the other, not to abide by those natural obligations which form the base-course of all social relationships.

After appearing in two cases in 1859 – one a claim for libel against him that was settled out of court – and the 1860 and 1861 trespass cases described earlier, Jerry was back before Judge Callaghan in November 1862 successfully suing an Arthur Zouch for unpaid rent. Miles' court appearances were even more frequent. In February 1860, he sued successfully for £38 6s, the value of two promissory notes. In November 1861, he lost a case in which he alleged a neighbour had stolen cattle from Kalangan, but won another for recovery of a £23 19s 2d debt. The following February, in one of his then roles as a subcontractor carrying the mail between Yass, Binalong, Murrumburrah and Lambing Flat, he was ordered to pay £19 13s 6d in a dispute over contracts. Then, in August 1862, an action he launched against a son of Charles Quail was settled out of court.

Although not a participant, Miles was mentioned in Judge Callaghan's court in May 1861 when an old man was being tried for stealing a watch that Murrumburrah innkeeper John English kept in the drawer of a safe behind his bar. Watches were valuable items, but English did not report the loss immediately. Why? 'I thought it had been taken as a lark, and as a caution, by Mr Murphy of Binalong, as he had often told me it would be taken some day if I left it where I did.'

In the summer of 1862–63, Miles was caught up in a dispute, conducted through letters to the *Courier*, over responsibility for the loss of cans of nails delivered to Binalong for roofing work on the town's Catholic church. According to the paper's report of the incident, the contractor, Mr Hawton, placed the nails on the veranda of Murphy's store having been assured they would be safe there. 'A few days afterwards, however, when he went for the nails, it was found that the bulky and weighty parcel had disappeared, no-one on the premises knowing whither or by whom it was carried off.'

The first letter-writer, using the pseudonym 'Fair Play', addressed the question: who should pay?

> I think all will agree that the poor contractor, having placed his nails in possession of a respectable Catholic in the town, should not lose the price (£10) when they disappeared. Either the Rev. Dean Hanly, who signed the agreement with Hawton, or Mr Murphy, who received the property, should pay for the nails. The common opinion is that the bucket of nails were accidentally mixed up with Mr Murphy's goods and sent off in mistake to his store at Lambing Flat, and, if so, of course he has the benefit. It is incredible that Hawton's heavy kegs of nails could have been stolen from the store, while he (Mr Murphy) missed nothing. Mr Murphy gives no explanation.

Fair Play suggested Judge Callaghan be enlisted to arbitrate the matter on his next visit to Yass.

Dean James Hanly was first to reply. 'There can be no personal claim on me, as Hawton was to find all materials,' he wrote, 'but I concede that he should not suffer loss if he placed his goods in charge of a 'respectable Catholic in town'. Mr Hawton must receive the price of his nails, and as agent for the Catholics of Binalong I am quite willing to let Judge Callaghan, or any other competent arbitrator, decide whether the wealthy storekeeper or the rev. dean is to give Hawton a cheque for £10.'

In the next *Courier*, Miles responded to Fair Play at length and with spirit. He wrote,

> If 'Fair Play', whoever the individual may be, thinks he has the shadow of a claim against me with respect to the cans of nails he refers to, why does he not, in a manly way, represent the subject to me, and not write an anonymous and scurrilous letter, doubting my honesty and commercial integrity. This from the writer who dares not sign his name affects me but little, knowing well that my statement with respect to the cans of nails will show the gross, unmanly, and false attack made upon me...

Miles accused Fair Play of insinuating that he had stolen the cans of nails and forwarded them to his store at Lambing Flat for sale. He went on,

> The simple facts of the case are these: About nine months since three broken cans of nails were left under the verandah of my store at Binalong by some carriers; they were never delivered to me, nor to any one in my employ; neither was it known to whom they belonged until Mr Hawton, some days afterwards, called and asked about them; he received all the information that could be given to him, and was told that no one had taken any charge of them, not knowing to whom they belonged. Mr Hawton made inquiries in the town respecting them, and found one of the cans, that he could positively swear to, empty, in the possession of a person residing in the town; and applied to a magistrate for a search-warrant – with what success I cannot say. 'Fair Play's' statement that 'it is incredible that Hawton's heavy kegs of nails could have been stolen from the store, while he (Mr Murphy) missed nothing,' is scarcely worth noticing – considering that my stores are under the charge of responsible persons, and the nails spoken of placed under a verandah, in the charge of no one, with no owner, and at the mercy of any dishonest person who could not resist so great a temptation. That they could be sent to my store at Lambing Flat is impossible; for any person

having any knowledge of storekeeping must be aware that goods received at a store are invoiced, marked, and numbered; and the cans referred to could not possibly have my mark on them; and considering Mr Hawton identified one of the cans at Binalong a few days after he applied at my store, is a sufficient answer to this statement.'

He added,

I now leave the public to judge between 'Fair Play's' statement and mine, and whether it is reasonable that I should be expected to pay Mr Hawton's 'wages for his toil and sweat,' because he neglected looking after his own business.

Miles also asked what could the Binalong Catholic church, Dean Hanly or Judge Callaghan possibly have to do with the matter? Fair Play pounced on this in his reply. 'The answer is very plain,' he wrote.

It is a dishonour to the Catholic community that a poor mechanic, engaged in building their church, should be robbed of his materials which he had placed in possession of one of their *great* men. Judge Callaghan is a clever man – an honest man. Is Mr Murphy afraid of him? Will Mr Murphy name a day to let all the parties concerned meet the judge, and abide by his decision?

Miles shot back,

I do not pretend to be the *great* man 'Fair Play' would make it appear I am; but I most distinctly state that neither I nor anyone in my employ ever had or took possession of the cans of nails 'Fair Play' is so interested in. There is one part of 'Fair Play's' letter I most cordially agree with, viz., the character he gives Judge Callaghan (who, by-the-bye, ought to think himself highly honoured, coming, as it does, from an individual who is ashamed of his own name), when he says that he (the judge) 'is a clever man – an honest man.' Would that I could apply the same words to 'Fair Play'!

That seems to have been the end of the matter.

6

The bushranging years

At Coppabella, around New Year 1863, the Lehanes entertained a distinguished visitor, Dr John Forrest. The 'learned divine', the *Courier* tells us, had earlier paid a visit to the Lambing Flat goldfields. Jerry's discussions with the rector of St John's College, University of Sydney, probably included thoughts of sending son William to the college; William entered St John's in 1864. Also discussed may have been Jerry's intention to remarry. His marriage to Hannah Maria O'Hehir on 4 February 1863, like that to Forrest's aunt Mary O'Connor twenty-one years earlier, was celebrated at St Mary's Cathedral, Sydney.

Hannah, daughter of Michael and Mary Bourke of County Clare, Ireland, was the twenty-eight-year-old widow of John O'Hehir, also from Clare, whom she married in Melbourne in 1853. The couple's only child, Mary, was three years old when John died in May 1859. John had been publican of the Emerald Isle Hotel, George Street, Sydney, since 1853, and Hannah ran the hotel after his death. Jerry may have met her there; alternatively, as there were O'Hehirs in the Yass district, the meeting may have occurred closer to home. Hannah was about twenty years younger than Jerry.

Another family development around this time was the arrival in the colony in November 1862 of Jerry's brother Daniel, whose eldest son Jeremiah had come out nearly five years earlier. Jerry sponsored the emigration of both father and son. Young Jeremiah was working on Coppabella in 1862; he is listed, with fourteen other people from the station, as a donor to an appeal for Lancashire cotton industry workers who lost their jobs when the American Civil War cut cotton supplies. He gave £1; Jerry senior gave five guineas.

Daniel found work as a shepherd on Samuel Barber's Bogalara run,

St Mary's Cathedral, Sydney, in 1865.
Additions had made it a much grander building when Jerry married Hannah there in 1863 than when it was the venue for his marriage to Mary O'Connor twenty-one years earlier.

next to Coppabella. He subsequently sponsored the emigration of his wife Ellen and eight other children, who arrived in January 1865. Sadly, Daniel died of heart disease in October the same year, aged fifty-five. The death certificate names Jeremiah Lehane (which one?) as undertaker at the Jugiong burial. One of the children – Catherine, who was eighteen in 1865 – subsequently found work at the Bookham Inn not far from Coppabella (chapter 12) and three others – William, Ellen and Nora – married into the Mayoh family, who had a property in the Young district. The widow Ellen lived to a great old age, dying at Young in September 1912.

For a period from mid-1862, Jerry was fairly prominent as a public citizen. In July, both he and Miles were coopted to the Lancashire Distress Appeal Committee, which Henry O'Brien chaired. Then in October he was elected to the committee of the Yass Pastoral, Agricultural, and Horticultural Society, also presided over by O'Brien, which organised the town's first agricultural show. Despite a renewal of drought in the district, this was held successfully in early March 1863. Jerry was one of the speakers at the after-show dinner, responding to O'Brien's toast to the society. The *Courier*'s brief report of his speech suggests he believed those prepared to make the effort could expect to succeed in Australia:

> He believed that the pastoral and agricultural interests were identical, and that any man who devoted his attention to either could become independent in this country. He was confident that if the farmers devoted their attention to the proper cultivation of the land, they would succeed in getting excellent crops.

In April 1863, Jerry and Miles were among those collecting signatures for a petition calling for Yass to become a site for circuit court hearings. Reasons advanced included its proximity to a 'large and permanent' goldfield, its 'large and commodious' courthouse and its 'extensive and well ventilated' gaol. In the same month, Jerry was elected to a committee to raise funds for a monument in Ireland to O'Connell, 'the Liberator'. The *Courier* noted that many 'Englishmen and Protestants' had attended a meeting in Yass to support the monument appeal, 'as proof that the merits of Daniel O'Connell as a friend and champion of the sacred cause of civil and religious liberty are recognised by men of all countries and creeds.' It regretted that few Irish Catholics were present.

For those living out of town, perhaps the danger of being accosted on the road by bushrangers was sufficient reason for not appearing. One episode early in the resurgence of bushranging that Miles was apparently lucky to avoid was an armed hold-up, in September 1861, on the road between Binalong and Murrumburrah. 'It is believed that these highwaymen were in expectation of falling in with Mr Miles Murphy on his way to the land sale at Burrowa, calculating that he would have a considerable sum of money on his person,' the *Courier* reported. 'Mr Murphy fortunately escaped the encounter.'

In March 1862, three bushrangers bailed up a Yass resident, Thomas Jackson, as he rode home from Lambing Flat and robbed him of £18 3s. According to the *Courier*'s report, Jackson was riding a horse he had borrowed from Miles' property Kalangan:

> One of the men...asked Jackson what sort of a horse he was riding; Jackson told him that it was not of much account, but the bushranger was incredulous, and said he would change horses with him... He was then

ordered to take the saddle off, the highwayman saying he would put his own on in its place, but on finding the animal had a sore back, he said he would not ride a scabby horse.

The paper commented, 'We suppose that some time before the millennium the roads will be cleared of a *few* of these highway gentry.'

A month earlier, a coach travelling between the Forbes goldfields and Lambing Flat had been bailed up at Patrick O'Meally's inn on Arramagong run. Patrick was the father of John O'Meally, soon to become notorious as a member of the Ben Hall gang. According to a Lambing Flat newspaper report reprinted in the *Courier*, an armed bushranger ordered the six passengers off the coach and made them join eleven captives taken when the inn was held up. 'We can scarcely comprehend how the seventeen persons at Meally's (the spelling was variable – sometimes also O'Maley or O'Malley) could stand quiet and allow themselves to be kept prisoners and robbed by one armed man,' the paper commented. 'Why, there were enough present to eat him.'

O'Meally, lessee of Arramagong, obtained his licence for the inn in April 1860. Miles and a Boorowa district squatter, George Eason, who was the husband of a sister of O'Meally's wife, provided the necessary £50 sureties. Three Justices of the Peace signed the licence, which was to remain in force for four years. According to historian D.J. Shiel, the inn quickly 'gained notoriety far and wide' as a haunt of bushrangers:

> The O'Meallys were usually among the first targets for any police interrogation... It became a meeting place for the 'flash' men of the Weddin, receiver of stolen goods and sympathetic harbourer of wanted law-breakers.

Miles' connection with Arramagong dated back to his first years in the colony (chapter 4), but one can only speculate on why he supported O'Meally's application for a publican's licence there (he provided sureties for many district publicans, including Jerry at Reedy Creek and hotel-keepers in competition with him at Binalong and Murrumburrah). According to Shiel, O'Meally was 'forced' to transfer the run back to Miles in late 1861; this suggests Miles may have maintained a financial interest in it. Apparently Miles immediately passed the lease on to a Patrick Throsby, but by 1864 had regained it. Shiel describes these transactions as a sign that civilisation was moving swiftly to take on the wild men of the Weddin; 'businessmen had come to the Weddin now that land had become such a valuable commodity.' As well as displacing Throsby, Miles dispossessed William Turland, who ran another inn on Arramagong. Shiel records that he profited nicely from Turland's eviction through selling the former inn to the police, who had established barracks nearby.

The *Courier* noted the stationing of police there in March 1863, seeing it as a sign that the government was vigorously carrying out plans for suppressing bushranging in the region. 'If a few more of these resorts of bushrangers were served in a similar manner the roads about Lambing Flat and Forbes would again assume a state of order,' it commented.

One of the most dramatic episodes in the region's bushranging saga occurred nine months earlier, in June 1862. This was the bailing up and robbery by Frank Gardiner's gang near Eugowra, east of Forbes, of a police-escorted coach taking gold and banknotes worth more than £10,000 to Sydney. John O'Meally and Ben Hall were among those arrested as suspects, but they were not sent to trial. Hall discovered on his release that Sir Frederick Pottinger's troopers had burned down his house; some have suggested that this set his future course as an outlaw.

Whatever the provocation, the crimes came think and fast – the Hall gang's toll between February 1863 and April 1865 included ten mail coach robberies, bailing-up twenty-one stores and homesteads, stealing twenty-three racehorses, and the capture (twice) of the village of Canowindra. Two policemen were killed in encounters with them. Hall himself is credited with committing sixty-four robberies under arms. Gardiner, having masterminded the Eugowra affray and various other hold-ups and raids, left for Queensland during 1863, leaving the leadership vacuum that Hall filled. (Gardiner was arrested there in 1864, tried and sentenced to thirty-two years' gaol, but released in 1874 on condition that he leave the colony.)

Returning to the Eugowra affair, Pottinger's men soon captured two other suspects and seized 240 ounces of gold and a roll of banknotes from them. The next day, bushrangers attacked the troopers taking the prisoners to Forbes, and the two escaped in the melee. Pottinger kept hold of the gold and cash, but one of the attackers was heard to 'swear, by all that was impious, that Sir Frederick should never take the recovered gold to Forbes', the *Courier* reported. To keep the gold safe, 'in the dead of the night, when it was dark, cold and raining, [Pottinger's party] quietly sallied forth' and proceeded to Narraburra, a pastoral run west of Lambing Flat. Here the gold 'was safely planted', and 'the party prepared to resist any attack which might be made upon them, and of which they were in constant dread'. Pottinger sent a messenger to Lambing Flat with news of what had happened. Nine troopers were dispatched to Narraburra, and they and Sir Frederick's men succeeded in conveying the gold to Forbes 'without molestation'.

The reason for mentioning this episode is that Narraburra features later in the story. Jerry bought it in 1865, his son William managed it for about eight years, and William's son John Augustine was born there in 1873. The Lehanes themselves do not appear to have been troubled by the Gardiner or Hall gangs, although, following a sighting of Gardiner, O'Meally and others near Yass in June 1863, police scoured the Reedy Creek area, presumably including Coppabella.

The Murphys, though, as storekeepers at Lambing Flat and landholders nearby on one of the main routes to the diggings, had many encounters. During 1863, the government gold escort from Lambing Flat to Yass used the track through Kalangan rather than the main road through Murrumburrah. A *Courier* correspondent questioned this arrangement, saying several slip panels that enclosed private property had to be opened each time the coach passed, and a similar number of 'bad creeks' had to be crossed. 'It is not necessary that I should point out how these difficulties are so many helps to bushrangers.'

In June 1863, a Murphy employee, William Howard, was stopped near Lambing Flat and robbed of £5. 'The ruffian…quietly hinted to Mr H. that money being a scarce commodity with travellers now, the bushrangers would be compelled to visit the township for a supply,' the *Courier* reported. 'It appears they were looking out for Mr John Murphy' (Miles' eldest son, then running the Lambing Flat store). The second Murphy son, Felix, also working at the store, was the next victim about ten days later – stuck up within sight of the Lambing Flat police camp:

> He was on horseback at the time, and two men, after the usual fashion of the craft, told him to stop, and persuaded a compliance with their order

Bushranger victim William Howard (left) and the apparent intended target John Murphy.

by each pointing a revolver at him. Fortunately he had little or no money on his person, but he was placed to great inconvenience and loss in being compelled to give up his new saddle for an old one which one of the men had.

In August, the driver of a team carrying a load of hay from Binalong to Lambing Flat for the Murphys received a visit from Johnny Gilbert and four bushranger companions after setting up camp for the night. 'They remained all night, feeding their horses with the cut hay; and in the early dawn took their leave quite leisurely,' the *Courier* reported. One of the horses was 'a superior animal' belonging to William Howard; it had been stolen from John Murphy a week earlier.

Shortly before this episode, the *Courier* gave a cryptic account of a strange episode involving the twenty-three-year-old Gilbert and other members of the Gardiner–Hall gang. A Catholic priest visiting country parishioners 'was somewhat surprised to have the outlaws pointed out to him at a short distance from where they were staying':

The rev. gentlemen at once approached the bushrangers and entered into conversation with them. He took advantage of the opportunity to point out to them the inevitable fate of their lawless career, the enormity of their offences against God and man, and strongly urged them to discontinue their reckless life. The outlaws listened attentively to the admonitions of the rev. gentleman, thanked him warmly for his kindness in addressing them, and stated that they were prepared to give themselves up if the Government would guarantee that no worse fate would be awarded to them than imprisonment. They dreaded being hung, although the life they were now compelled to lead was a most unhappy one. We understand the rev. gentleman promised to lay the matter before the Government, and that he has already done so.

Probably any hopes the bushrangers might have had of lenient treatment disappeared the following month when John O'Meally shot dead Murrumburrah shopkeeper John Barnes. He had opened his store in 1860, the year Miles' Criterion Hotel began trading. Barnes encountered O'Meally, Gilbert and some companions while riding to Cootamundra to visit his son. Apparently, O'Meally chased and shot Barnes after he refused to hand over his saddle. 'O'Maley has plainly indicated the ferocity of his disposition by his valuation of the life of another,' commented the *Courier*. 'Until this man, above all others of the scoundrels who infest the bush, is taken, no one's life is worth a straw.'

More shots were fired when O'Meally and Hall held up two stores at Lambing Flat in mid-September 1863. A few days later, O'Meally and others bailed up a shoemaker named Yuill and seized the four pairs of boots he was carrying on his saddle. A *Courier* corresondent reported,

> Mr Yuill has known O'Maley for a number of years, therefore he pleaded hard for one particular pair of highly finished napoleons to be returned; whereupon O'Maley jumped off his horse, pulled off his boots, tried on the good-looking napoleons, and found them such a capital fit that he said with an oath he could not think of returning them; but, for the sake of old times, he would not search him; consequently Mr Yuill was allowed to ride on. This is, I believe, the first instance on record of any traveller leaving Johnny O'Maley's presence with sound pockets.

Gilbert apparently was involved in this incident, using a ploy he had tried before. Shortly before Yuill was accosted, he met, striding along the road, what appeared to be a 'tall, ungainly looking woman'. According to the correspondent, this was almost certainly Gilbert:

if so it is not the first time Gilbert has adopted female apparel, for I'm credibly informed that when he stuck up Hammond's station at Junee, one of the servant girls there was making some remarks upon his long and well oiled hair and he laughingly observed 'I'm obliged to wear it long for I've sometimes to dress in women's clothes, and I intend to escape out of the country in petticoats.' It is well known that he attended the last Young races, mounted on horseback, disguised in a lady's riding habit, hat and feather. His smooth good-looking face much assists him in this respect.

In late September, a police party burnt down the former O'Meally inn on Arramagong, which was still occupied by John's father and other members of the family. The *Courier* compared this to the earlier firing of Ben Hall's house, describing it as retaliation that 'smacks of the medieval ages, and is unworthy of the enlightened nineteenth century'. The bushranger's end came less than two months later during a raid, in company with Hall and Gilbert, on a station near Forbes. Squatter David Campbell staged a clever ambush and shot O'Meally with a fowling piece. His death 'ridded the neighbourhood and the country of one of the most remorseless and bloodthirsty ruffians the colony ever produced,' said the *Courier*; its sympathy for old man O'Meally did not extend to the son.

The death of O'Meally brought no let-up from attacks by Hall, Gilbert and their companions. The bushrangers bailed up the Boorowa to Binalong mail in early December and, four days later, the Binalong to Yass mail. They were after money; according to the *Courier*, while examining the mail following the second encounter, they 'expressed themselves eminently disgusted with the conduct of those who send cheques by the post instead of ready money'. Noting that Gilbert had reportedly said he would leave the country if he had the means to do so, the *Courier* put forward a radical proposal:

> As the police have failed…to be masters of these two men, it might become a serious matter for consideration whether it would not be the most advisable course for the Government to pocket for once its morality and sense of public justice, and pay a good round sum to Messrs Gilbert and Hall to quit the country.

This was 'almost worth trying', despite the risk of 'others of the same class imitating [the bushrangers'] example.'

The government did not take up this suggestion, and the attacks continued unabated. In two days of frenzied activity in mid-December, about fifty people were bailed up and robbed on the Binalong to Bowning road. In late January 1864, bushrangers accosted ten people on their way to races at Young, and then continued their assaults – on the Kalangan to Murrumburrah road – as race-goers returned home. In March, they again preyed on returning race-goers, this time from a meeting at Binalong at which both Miles and Jerry officiated as stewards (this is the first evidence encountered of an interest by Jerry in horse-racing). Among those 'cleaned out' of their money, the *Courier* reported, were the gold commissioner and a representative of the Oriental Bank.

In April 1864, Felix Murphy recognised at the local pound a racehorse, Troubadour, that Ben Hall had stolen from a property near Young. It had been impounded with other horses found running wild in the bush, and presented 'the usual wretched appearance of all horses that have been ridden and relinquished by bushrangers'. Troubadour was entered in the Ladies' Purse at the Burrangong (Young) races a month later – 'we hope not much the worse for his short acquaintance with Ben Hall,' the local reporter commented. A forlorn hope: instead of finishing the race, Troubadour bolted. On the night after the race, Hall, Gilbert and a third man again stole Troubadour. After 'rousing up the groom' at the racecourse stables, they 'quietly rode' it and another horse away. Hall apparently later returned Troubadour to the stables.

A few days earlier, the trio had held up about twenty people at a nearby inn and been caught in the act by two policemen. Shots were fired, but the bushrangers escaped unscathed. One police shot knocked Hall's hat off, but 'being connected by a string with his coat, he quickly replaced it'. The bushrangers stayed in the district, and two days later encountered a Mr F. Russell on horseback near Kalangan, heading towards Boorowa:

> Hall and his two companions rode up to him, and, without the usual ostentation of presenting a revolver, enquired whether he had a cheque or two about him. Mr Russell told him that he had come just a day too late, as he had on the previous evening transferred all the money he had on him to the bank.

After telling Russell about the encounter at the inn, which he treated

Bushranger Johnny Gilbert.

'as a capital lark', Hall asked where he could get some oats. 'On being told that Mr Murphy had plenty, he said he would not go there,' the *Courier* reported. Nevertheless, on leaving Russell, the bushrangers headed towards Kalangan.

Action in late May and June included an attack by Hall and two companions on the Lambing Flat to Yass coach near Binalong and more stick-ups on the Binalong to Bowning road. The region was also experiencing floods, with the Murrumbidgee River, Galong Creek and the Boorowa River rising higher than on any occasion since the great flood of 1852. Suffering the attacks of bushrangers and destruction by flood, the *Courier* editorialised, 'at the present time we must appear in the eyes of the civilised world as a truly unfortunate people'. Referring to the 'ungoverned state of society', the article went on,

> We have culpably neglected to implant in the hearts of the people, as a body, a just appreciation of moral goodness, and a sense of the duty they owe to their God and their fellow creatures.

In July 1864, the Troubadour episode had a sequel when a jockey, John Doyle, called at the Murphy store in Young. A tailor recognised the breeches Doyle was wearing as a pair he had made for Troubadour's owner, Frederick Chisolm, and Chisolm confirmed that they were his. Apparently, Hall had stolen the breeches as well as the horse. 'The police got scent of the circumstances' and arrested Doyle, as receiver of Hall's booty, at a nearby inn.

Three months later, Hall, Gilbert and another gang member, John Dunn, robbed Chisolm of £3 as he was riding to Goulburn to give evidence against Doyle. During this encounter, Hall told Chisolm of plans, soon put into effect, to bail up the Yass mail. Around this time, according to the *Courier*, bushrangers were perpetrating about two mail robberies a week on the main southern road within sixty or seventy miles of Yass. These had a deadly culmination near Jugiong in mid-November, when a bullet fired by Gilbert killed Sergeant Edmund Parry of Gundagai, one of two policemen escorting a mail coach as it headed for Yass. Apparently undaunted, Hall and Gilbert bailed up the Yass to Binalong mail, carried by packhorse, a week later.

These were desperate times for the bushrangers, with their attacks generally yielding little cash and their prospects of being captured or shot growing by the day. According to a stick-up victim called Hayes, Hall spoke of living, night and day, in jeopardy of his life. He told Hayes he was hatching a plan to bail up the Anglican bishop of Goulburn and the attorney-general, both of whom were planning trips in the region. He intended to hold them hostage until the government granted him and Gilbert their liberty. Hall was quite amused, the *Courier* reported, 'at the idea of making the Attorney-General of the colony his humble and obedient servant'.

This plan was not put into effect, but the gang's bushranging continued remorselessly. In late December, Hall, Gilbert and Dunn bailed up a Yass auctioneer, David Davis, as he returned home after a sale in Murrumburrah. He had the proceeds with him in an envelope – nearly £110 in cheques but little more than £1 in cash. 'Hall tore open the envelope,' the *Courier* reported, 'looked at the contents, exclaiming, '— the cheques'.' Gilbert asked Hall whose cheques they were; he said he did not know – there were so many of them. 'Take them, we'll ride in and smash them,' Gilbert reportedly replied. The bushrangers rode off with the cheques, and an advertisement – headed 'Highway Robbery' – appeared in the *Courier* on 31 December setting out the details. It listed sixteen cheques, including one written by John Murphy for £17, and cautioned the public against negotiating them.

Three policemen and a black tracker spotted Hall, Gilbert and Dunn soon after this encounter, and set off in hot pursuit. The bushrangers put spurs to their horses and headed for Kalangan, 'every now and then looking back under their arms to see what progress the police were making', the *Courier* reported. The police lost sight of them a few times, but 'the tracker…quickly recovered the scent'. On reaching Kalangan, they were only a few minutes behind their quarry, but the bushrangers had taken three fresh horses from the Murphys' stables and by this stage two of the police horses were 'baked' and the other not much better. No one at Kalangan knew which way the bushrangers had headed, but the black tracker again found the trail, which the troopers followed until a 'terrific hail, thunder and lightning storm' obliterated all signs. 'Thus ended a very close, but unfortunately fruitless, pursuit.'

One of the horses taken from Kalangan was John Murphy's 'second-class racer' Lumpy Leg, 'well known on the neighbouring turf'. Its unspectacular form included third place in the £25 Publicans' Purse at the 1860 Binalong Races and another third in the £7 Farmers' Purse – for horses that had never won a prize exceeding £5 – at the 1863 Murrumburrah Races.

Raids and stick-ups by the Hall gang continued unabated, and in late January 1865 a second policeman met his death at their hands. A shot fired by John Dunn killed Constable Samuel Nelson during a raid at Collector, near Lake George. Two weeks later, the colonial government changed the rewards offered for information leading to the bushrangers' capture to try to increase the chances of success. Instead of offering £2,000 for information leading to the apprehension of both Hall and Gilbert, £500 would be paid for information leading to the capture of either of them and another £500 for the actual arrest. An important point, as a *Courier* correspondent observed, was that individual policemen were now eligible; rewards would not go into general police funds as had occurred in the past. 'So now my gallant blues you have no excuse, therefore go ahead,' the correspondent exhorted.

In the case of Dunn, the sums were slightly lower – £375. But the reward notice contained another potent incentive for people to lead police to this bushranger, who had been declared guilty of wilful murder by the inquest into the death of Constable Nelson:

> ...all persons are hereby cautioned that by harbouring, assisting, or maintaining the abovenamed offender, they will make themselves accessories to the crime of murder, and be liable to prosecution accordingly.

A month later, another set of reward notices appeared in the newspapers. This time, the threat of prosecution as accessories to murder applied also to those providing any assistance to Hall and Gilbert. At the same time, a bill was introduced into parliament providing harsh sentences – five to fifteen years gaol with hard labour and forfeiture of all property to the Crown – for those convicted of harbouring bushrangers. This was enacted on 8 April. One *Courier* correspondent feared the law went too far:

> [It] places the honest settlers of these parts in an awful position, as by it they are bound to give immediate notice to the police after receiving a visit from the bushrangers, in the performance of which they [are] very likely *to be shot on the road*; but if the dread of the robber's bullet prevents them giving the said notice, they render themselves liable to fifteen years' penal servitude with forfeiture from themselves and families of *all* the property they possess...

Clearly, however, those with most cause to feel desperate were Hall and his companions. They were active in the Murrumburrah area in mid-March; shots fired in one encounter with police left Gilbert and a policeman with arm wounds. The bushrangers were said to 'look wretched', the *Courier* reported, 'owing to their long exposure to weather and hard living. Gilbert says they often have to go four and twenty hours fasting, as they are so hunted by the police. They complain that no one carries any money about them, and that even at the stations it is rarely to be found.'

In early April 1865, a particularly ruthless bushranger operating to the south of the Hall gang's territory, 'Mad' Dan Morgan, was tracked down and shot dead. The same fate befell Ben Hall on 5 May after his whereabouts, near Forbes, had been betrayed by a former associate; the new law was having its intended effect. Gilbert's turn came just over a week later, on 13 May. This time the informer, who the following month received his £500 reward, was Dunn's grandfather, John Kelly. Police shot Gilbert dead as he tried to escape after an early morning raid on Kelly's house near Binalong, where the bushrangers had spent the night. Dunn managed to get away.

Miles performed the undertaker's duties when Gilbert was buried in the police paddock outside Binalong on 16 May. One historian suggests this may have been 'his ex officio duty as local storekeeper – or simply because of his expertise as a carpenter'. The *Courier* reported,

> We learn that an excellent cast of [Gilbert's] face was taken by an inhabitant of Binalong. It is said that a number of persons secured a lock of the deceased bushranger's hair, for what reason we cannot imagine. Tastes differ; and whether these mementoes were secured out of respect and admiration of Gilbert's conduct while in life, or because of his notoriety, the parties are best able to state.

7

Meanwhile...

Bushranger John Dunn escaped on foot from the 13 May shoot-out and the same day stuck up Richard Julian's Bogolong station, neighbouring Coppabella. Dunn's clothes were covered in blood when he staged the raid, suggesting he had been wounded. He made off with a horse, saddle and bridle. Julian was apparently an old friend of Jerry's; in 1861 he was a witness at the marriage of Honora Lehane and John Vicq, and shortly afterwards at the burial of Mary Lehane.

At the end of May, the *Courier* suspected Dunn was still near Bogolong, being 'sheltered and harboured by persons resident not far from that locality'. Nearly three weeks later, it reported 'rumours' that he remained in the neighbourhood of Bogolong and Jugiong, 'and the police stationed at the latter place are constantly in search of him, night as well as day, but presently without success'.

Dunn remained at large until late December 1865, when he was wounded and captured during an exchange of fire with police near Coonamble hundreds of miles to the north; apparently, he and a companion were heading back to his 'old haunts' in the Lachlan district. As with Hall and Gilbert, an informer had told police where to find the bushranger. Dunn escaped from Dubbo lock-up two weeks after his capture, but was taken again the next day 'almost dead with thirst and exhaustion'. In late February, he was sentenced to death for murder, and a month later hanged in front of a crowd of seventy at Darlinghurst Gaol, Sydney. According to the *Courier*, he had been most attentive to the exhortations of the Catholic clergymen who had constantly attended him, was apparently deeply penitent for his past offences, and had 'looked forward to their expiation with much resignation'.

Dunn's capture, finally bringing the perils and excitements of the

Gardiner–Hall era to an end, came at a time of severe drought. Both the Anglican and Catholic churches declared Friday 12 January 1866 a 'Day of Humiliation and Prayer', and businesses closed as the people prayed for rain. As the *Courier* put it two days before, 'we are all invited to… seek at the throne of the Giver of all good things that mercy and that consideration we are scarcely worthy to ask – only that we are the subjects of His will.' The paper said an 'anonymous writer' had endeavoured to argue that the visitations of flood and drought were governed by the laws of nature – in other words, that they were ruled by a system whose laws were yet undiscovered by man. It was convinced this couldn't be so:

> Were such a doctrine accepted there would at once be an end to the belief in Divine interposition in extreme events, such as those we refer to, and the privilege and efficacy of prayer would be rendered nugatory by the reflection that whatever occurs is beyond the power of the Almighty.

By now, the heady optimism about prospects for Yass and the region fired by the Lambing Flat gold rush had long since dissipated. The depredations of the bushrangers contributed to this, as did drought in the early and mid-1860s, punctuated by severe flooding in the winter of 1864 (Hamilton Hume's garden at Cooma Cottage was briefly under three and a half feet of water).

Probably more important was the reduction in activity at Lambing Flat. In August 1863, the *Courier* reported that fewer than 4,000 people – down from a peak of more than 10,000 – were now scattered over the goldfields, and 'the reduced population and the moderate success being met with by the miners causes a stagnation in business generally'. By November, local storekeepers were agitating for a new influx of Chinese diggers to boost trade. This was despite the fact that, as the *Courier* pointed out, 'it is only a little over two years since the unfortunate Mongolians had their property destroyed and their lives placed in jeopardy for attempting to gain a footing at Lambing Flat'. In July 1864, a correspondent wrote that traders were discovering 'they had built too expensive stores and public houses, and had stocked themselves far beyond any probable demand. They had failed to watch the incomes of the people, and suddenly awoke to a consciousness of the fact that the population was decreasing as rapidly as snow under the influence of the sun.'

The Murphys maintained their Lambing Flat store, one of the largest on the goldfields, located in what became the main street of Young, until early 1865. Then they opened a new store in Murrumburrah. John Murphy was in charge of Murphy and Son, Lambing Flat, for most of its life as a general wholesale and retail store and wine and spirit merchant. He was also active in the community. For example, in November 1861 the eighteen-year-old made 'a brief but appropriate speech' at a meeting called to push for the construction of a Catholic church in the town. During 1862, he was treasurer of the provisional hospital committee and a member of the Burrangong Progress Committee and the local committee raising money for the Lancashire Distress Fund (chapter 6).

The local *Burrangong Argus* bade John a fond farewell:

> No man who ever was connected by commerce with the Flat could be more sincerely sorrowed after than is Mr Murphy; and every one who has ever known him most earnestly wishes for his prosperity in the future – be his location at Murrumburrah, whither he has gone, or at any spot to which Providence may call him. Mr Murphy has made for himself a name here as an excellent specimen of what can be produced in Australia, and there is but little chance that he will ever lose it.

The *Argus* added that John was 'remarkably and deservedly popular with all classes of the community', and as a result 'his commercial transactions can hardly fail to thrive.'

In Yass, while the goldfields initially provided a major boost to business they also brought the temporary loss of one essential service. 'The only severe loss our town has sustained by the opening up of the Lambing Flat diggings is the migration of our hairdresser to that favoured region,' the *Courier* reported in March 1861. In its whimsical way, it added that only 'a perruquier of undoubted taste and proficiency' would be acceptable as a replacement. Two and a half years later, in September 1863, it noted that Yass now had two barbers:

> Two barbers in a small town – and thriving too – must prove to the most sceptical that we are going ahead. The youngest devil in our office says people can now travel from pole to pole without experiencing the slightest change of atmosphere.

While noting that storekeepers and publicans were reporting a 'stagnation in business', and that Yass would feel the exodus of diggers from Lambing Flat more than any other town, the *Courier*, at this stage, retained its optimism. It was encouraged by the recent opening of a new shoe store, tailor's establishment, tannery, brewery and restaurant, as well as the second barber's shop. By the end of the year, things looked less promising, with the paper reporting, 'Never within the recollection of the oldest inhabitant of Yass has there been such a dull Christmas and New Year's time.' The rot continued; one result was a decision by the *Courier* in July 1864 to revert from twice-weekly to once-a-week publication because of a shortage of advertising support.

Despite noticing 'no favourable alteration…in business prospects in this or the surrounding districts', the *Courier* reversed this decision the following November – because weekly publication meant much news 'becomes stale before its publication' and competition for space was so tight that 'it is utterly impossible to find room for much that is interesting.' It appealed to readers to subscribe rather than borrow other people's papers, and to pay their accounts promptly. It evidently had strong reader support, claiming it lost only one subscriber during its time as a weekly. One reader noted that he had 'always felt satisfaction in the manly, independent, and truly impartial manner in which our local paper has been conducted'. Another wrote,

> I should like to know what a man could lay out a few pounds on yearly that would yield the comforts enjoyed from the perusal of a well conducted newspaper. I watch the arrival of the newspaper as a school boy does the approach of a holiday; and how much more so must a man who is in a remote part of the bush rejoice to receive the news which a paper contains.

Presumably, the slowdown in business affected trade at the Globe Hotel. We don't know whether that's why Jerry's first tenants there, the Patisons, moved on in mid-1863. However, when he advertised in the *Courier* for a replacement the emphasis, as one would expect, was firmly on the positive:

THE GLOBE HOTEL, YASS

A MOST favourable opportunity is now open to any respectable person who is desirous of realising a speedy independence, by renting the abovenamed first-class substantially brick-built licensed HOTEL and PREMISES.

To enter into minute detail, by way of advertisement, of all the advantages and conveniences which the above far-famed Hostelry possesses, would be both lengthy and expensive: suffice it to say that the house is doing a first-rate trade, and which can be greatly improved, and that the premises are, for extent, capability, and convenience, without exception, second to none in the Southern district.

Sarah Benjamin, formerly owner of a Yass store, the Red House, selling 'drapery, grocery, crockeryware and fancy goods', became the new licensee in September 1863. Presumably thinking that a change of image might boost business, she renamed the hotel the Prince of Wales. Advertising her 'large and commodious hotel', she promised to 'pay every attention to the convenience of her customers, the house being well stocked and re-furnished. One visit will prove the fact.'

The name change was no doubt prompted by the bout of royal fervour marking the marriage on 11 June 1863 of Queen Victoria's heir, Edward, Prince of Wales, to Princess Alexandra of Denmark. Yass closed down for the day, and put on a show in the evening advertised as a grand display of fireworks and general illumination. 'At Nine p.m. the 'Big Gun' at the Court-house will announce to the public that a Red Light will appear at different places in Cooma-street, immediately after which a magnificent display of Rockets and other Fireworks will take place on the Hill near the Bridge, which will continue for some time', locals learned from the previous day's paper.

> At the signal of a Blue Fire from the Globe Hotel, several Fire Balloons will be sent from the front of the Court-house, in search of the stars. At Ten o'clock p.m. a Red Light from North Yass will announce the continuation of the Fireworks. GOD SAVE THE QUEEN!

Afterwards, the *Courier* expressed its pleasure with the way things had gone, reporting that the main street was thronged with family groups viewing the sights. 'The town of Yass never before exhibited so happy and pleasing an aspect,' it said. In its leader the day before, the paper observed that the holiday, celebrated throughout New South Wales, promised to be

> the most general and most heartily concurred in which has ever been witnessed in this colony... It will mark no triumph of arms, it will commemorate no deeds of carnage, it will not celebrate with pomp the extinction of an enemy, but be a dedication to a coming era of peace and wisdom, which, so far as human foresight can decide, is destined to characterise a race that are to be our kings hereafter.

Besides changing the Globe's name, Sarah Benjamin entered into the loyal spirit by setting up a Theatre Royal in the hotel's large saloon. The Yass Amateur Dramatic Club presented the opening show, advertised with the slogan 'Vivat Regina!', on 26 April 1864. Admission cost four shillings for front seats and 2s 6d for back seats. The troupe, managed by tailor Joshua Shipway, performed three items – a 'light comedy' *The Blue-Jackets or Her Majesty's Service*, a 'screaming farce' *The Railroad Station*, and a 'never-to-be-forgotten nigger-farce' *The Post-Office*. The *Courier* described the venue as 'a neat little theatre' and regretted that 'the hour at which we were compelled to go to press in order to be in time for the mails precluded us the pleasure of attending the opening entertainment.'

Soon after, in June 1864, some difficulties Mrs Benjamin was having in running the hotel found their way to court. First, she brought an ex-employee, Harry the Cook, before the local bench on an assault charge. 'I told him the kitchen was in a very dirty state, and ordered him to clean it...' she said in evidence. 'He jumped up from his chair, and struck me in the mouth and on the shoulder; I have been obliged to get a doctor to attend to my shoulder.' Harry denied the charge and in turn accused Mrs Benjamin of assault. He said he had gone to the courthouse seeking a summons against her for failure to pay him. When he returned to the kitchen she came in 'in a terrible passion, and wanted to know what I had gone over to the court for; she called me a — old vagabond, and struck me on the ear...; in trying to get to the fireplace I pushed, and very likely struck, defendant; if I struck her, it was in my own defence.' The magistrates found in Mrs Benjamin's favour, fining Harry £2, or one month's gaol.

A week later, Mary Hibberd, whose husband the *Courier* informed its readers 'is a purveyor of tripe and cowheel', appeared before the magistrates charged with steeling ale. She had been caught in the act by Mrs Benjamin's son, who told the court, 'I watched prisoner, and saw her walk through the hall, and go behind the bar, and take a bottle of ale from off the shelf and put it under her dress, and then go out.' Mary was sentenced to three days in the Yass lock-up.

Sarah Benjamin left the hotel within weeks of these events. The new publican, Owen Hilly, was granted the licence for the premises on 12 July 1864. Previously owner of another Yass hotel, the Squatter's Arms, he was to remain Jerry's tenant there for the next five years. The Prince of Wales sign came down immediately; the hotel was again the Globe.

Jerry also ran into trouble during Mrs Benjamin's tenure of the hotel. Its previous owner, Charles Quail, took him to the Yass District Court in October 1863 claiming £2,000 damages for breach of agreement. This related to the 1861 deal under which Jerry was to buy the Globe and Quail's other property in Rossi Street, Yass, for £6,500 while Quail was to pay £1,500 for the Lambing Flat inn managed for Jerry by John Vicq. Presumably because of the amount of money at stake, both Jerry and Quail employed two lawyers to represent them. The *Courier* did not report the arguments put to Judge Callaghan, just noting that the case was referred to arbitration:

> The arbitrator...closed his labours after two sittings, the award being, by consent, £200, the defendant [Jerry] to pay all costs, which include those in the District and Supreme Courts, and those having reference to arbitration.

Clearly, Jerry had lost, although the result could perhaps have been worse for him. It seems from the following report, which appeared in the same column of the *Courier* as the outcome of the arbitration, that his mood as he rode home from Yass was not good:

> VIOLENT ASSAULT ON THE LAMBING FLAT COACHMAN
> The coach from Lambing Flat not arriving yesterday afternoon about the usual time surmises were entertained of it having been stuck on the road, which is in many parts very boggy, but these were dispelled by the arrival of a messenger from Bowning, who stated that George Miller, the coachman, who is a very steady, inoffensive young man, had been violently assaulted by Mr Jeremiah Lehane, of Coppabella. From the account which has reached us

it appears to be the custom to turn out the horses at Bowning for a portion of the day, which bring in the coach to Yass. Mr Lehane was on his return home after the conclusion of the arbitration case yesterday, and had hung up his horse at the inn door when Miller came in to Bowning with his team from Binalong. He asked permission of Mr Lehane to take his horse to fetch in his own four, which were as usual feeding about. It would seem that consent was given, but Miller was somewhat longer away than he promised to be. Whether this irritated Mr Lehane, or there was any other cause, an altercation ensued, during which Mr Lehane struck Miller on the back of the head with a stick, felling him to the ground and rendering him insensible. The blow was considered to be of so severe a nature that a messenger was despatched to Yass for medical assistance, as well as for some person to bring in the coach. This is an outline of the statement which has reached town, and we can only vouch for its truth so far as that.

As there was no follow-up report or letter in the *Courier*, we can probably assume that Jerry did not dispute the story and that the 'inoffensive' Miller did not take the matter to the police. A desire to get home quickly to Hannah may have influenced his behaviour. A week earlier, Judge Callaghan had exempted Jerry from jury duty at his criminal sittings 'on account of the dangerous illness of his wife'. Miles also won an exemption, on the grounds that his role as postmaster at Binalong required him to stay there because the person who usually acted in his absence was away. For Jerry, a more cheering recent development was a very successful lambing season; he informed the *Courier* that the lambing percentage on Coppabella was ninety-nine per cent.

Miles had been in court earlier in 1863, taking action to eject the then tenant of his Swan Inn, Jacob Marks; a February sitting of the Binalong Court of Petty Sessions ordered Marks to deliver up possession in fourteen days. Miles was also in dispute with Marks over the agistment of horses. A few days before the court hearing, he placed an advertisement in the *Courier* warning Marks, who was also a mail contractor, to pay agistment costs for three horses in his paddock at Murrumburrah or see them sold. Marks was having a bad summer; in late 1862, two bushrangers had bailed up his Binalong to Yass mail coach, threatened to 'blow his brains out' and robbed him of £9.

Having sent Marks on his way, Miles resumed his publican's role at the Swan. Sixteen months later, in June 1864, he placed an advertisement seeking a tenant or buyer for the 'old-established and much-frequented' inn, saying it was his 'desire to retire from public business'. He must have been referring to a wish to relinquish the day-to-day running of a hotel rather than to quit business affairs, because the following year he established a store and a flour mill at Murrumburrah and his Binalong store apparently continued to flourish. A pre-Christmas 1863 advertisement claimed it offered 'the BEST, CHEAPEST, and LARGEST STOCK of GOODS of any store in the Southern District', including rum at eighteen shillings a gallon, brandy at twenty-one shillings a gallon, and wines, port and sherry at from twelve to eighteen shillings a gallon.

Presumably, no buyer or satisfactory potential tenant for the Swan came along, because the Murphys were still in residence in mid-May 1865, when Miles buried the bushranger Gilbert. Ten days later, about nine in the evening,

> ...a young man of very respectable appearance walked in...and was first noticed when in the middle parlour. From thence he walked into what is known as the best parlour, where he was seen by the housemaid who, observing that he had taken one of the candles off the table, and was looking about, imagined that he was desirous of washing himself after having come off the road after a long journey. Directly he saw her he put out the light, took the candles out of both parlours, passed by her in the verandah, and went towards the end of the house. She reported the affair to Mrs Murphy who immediately went into the middle parlour and found all in darkness. Lights were immediately got, a search was made, and a pair of blankets and a feather pillow were found missing...

The robber escaped, but was apprehended next day with the blankets and pillow, some books belonging to the Murphys, and three silver watches and some clothing obtained elsewhere. Both Miles and Anne gave evidence at the trial in Yass the following September – Anne saying she had not given the prisoner, John Scott, permission to enter the premises and Miles identifying the books as his sons'. Scott was sentenced to eighteen months' hard labour.

During these years, despite the activities of Ben Hall and his companions, the Murphys expanded rather than curtailed their horse-racing activities; their involvement now extended beyond Binalong and Murrumburrah. Miles served as a steward at the 1863 Burrangong (Lambing Flat) races, and horses owned by his son John took second place in races with £30 and £20 prizes. A horse owned by Miles won the £15 Consolation Stakes. At the April 1864 Yass races, two of Miles' horses ran second, with one of them declared winner after a protest. Miles entered three horses in a £5 Cart Horse Race but, for reasons not given in the *Courier*'s report, 'the race lapsed'.

Immediately after the Yass races, Miles and thirteen other enthusiasts, including Owen Hilly of the Globe, put their names to a proposal to form a jockey club – 'for the purpose,' the *Courier* reported, 'of keeping up the fine old English sport, and securing and fencing in a race course.' Miles, Hilly and three others made £3 3s donations to the cause. The paper expressed the hope that no attempt would be made to make the club too exclusive. 'The black ball has often proved the apple of discord in small communities, and we see no good reason why any person should be debarred from being a member of the Yass Jockey Club, unless it be upon the grounds that he has been guilty of some discreditable practice in racing matters.' Despite the *Courier*'s prediction that the club would attract a considerable number of founding members, the proposal lapsed.

The Murphys continued to be involved in various other community activities. Miles and John were members of a local committee formed in April 1863 to support the proposed national monument to O'Connell in Ireland. Miles was to collect money for the cause in Binalong, and John at Lambing Flat. When Archbishop Polding visited Lambing Flat in November 1863, John read the address of welcome from the local Catholics. This expressed their 'appreciation of the love and kindness shown by your grace in travelling so far to visit us, and by your advice in the vicissitudes of life, and we most sincerely and humbly thank you and fervently pray that our Heavenly Father may protect you from all peril and sickness, and prolong your life amongst your children whom you have so long protected by your wisdom and care, and edified by your talents and piety.' The archbishop 'replied in a touching and pathetic manner', the *Burrangong Times* reported.

> He trusted his visit to Burrangong would be productive of much good, and

*St Mary's Church, Murrumburrah.
A window behind the altar commemorates John Murphy.*

thanked the deputation for their kindness and attention to him, and after requesting them to kneel, bestowed on them a solemn benediction.

The following month, Miles and three others launched a fundraising effort for construction of a Catholic church at Murrumburrah. Two of the three were John English and John Dillon, owners of the two hotels that competed for the town's trade with Miles' Criterion; each innkeeper put in £20. The fourth contributor was James Murray, the town's first blacksmith, who put in an even more generous £50. A meeting of local Catholics ten months later, presided over by the Boorowa-based priest in charge of the Murrumburrah flock, Father O'Neill, moved matters along by formally appointing a fundraising committee that included Miles and John Murphy, the other two innkeepers and Murray. 'A subscription list was at once opened, when the very handsome sum of £84 4s was subscribed in the room,' the *Courier* reported. The church, St Mary's, had a long gestation. Although tenders for the masonry and wood work were called in September 1866, with plans and specifications available for inspection at the Murphys' Murrumburrah store, it was not completed until 1871.

Fire destroys St Mary's Cathedral.

In mid-July 1865, both Miles and Jerry came to Yass for a meeting at the courthouse called to begin local fundraising for the rebuilding of St Mary's Cathedral, Sydney. The cathedral, whose foundation stone was laid by Governor Macquarie in 1821, had been destroyed in a spectacular blaze on the evening of 29 June. According to the *Courier*, sixty to seventy people attended the Yass meeting, including some of the town's prominent Protestants. One of them, lawyer George Allman, spoke as mover of the resolution to open a subscription list. He rejected the argument of some Protestants that it was wrong to contribute to the rebuilding because this would 'assist in what they term the errors of the Roman Catholic Church'. He thought that 'the fact of our all worshipping the same merciful Creator, and relying for redemption on the same glorious Redeemer, ought rather to produce a hope of our mutual salvation, than narrowly limit that salvation to those only who entirely agree with us in doctrine.' Flour miller John Higman argued a similar case:

> As a Protestant, following according to his conscience what he believed to be the right path to heaven, and which he hoped to reach, he was not so bigoted as not to believe that he would meet Catholics there.

Miles and Jerry were elected to the fundraising committee and given responsibility for collections in their districts. About £700 was handed in at the meeting, with the *Courier* report indicating that Jerry made the biggest contribution – his own £50 plus £20 3s 6d collected at Coppabella. Perhaps the Old Testament story of the prophet Jeremiah's lamentations over the ruins of the temple at Jerusalem following its destruction by Babylon's King Nebuchadnezzar in 586 BC influenced his response.

Elections at the end of 1864 saw Miles and Jerry again fly their political colours. In the Lachlan electorate, Miles headed the list of supporters of James Martin, the outgoing conservative premier. Martin was opposed by a man named Lynch, whose platform included support for free trade and railway building. Martin won by 673 votes to 218. Voting in Miles' territory was even more convincing – eighty-two to six at Binalong and 106 to five at Murrumburrah. Across the colony, though, support for the conservatives collapsed, allowing the more liberal Charles Cowper to again form government.

Jerry's name was high on the list of Martin supporters, and he evidently was also interested in the outcome in the adjacent Yass Plains electorate. There, he again backed the conservative Peter Faucett, solicitor-general in Martin's government, whose long list of supporters included notables such as Hamilton Hume and Henry O'Brien, Yass's three doctors, and Dean Hanly of St Augustine's Church. Faucett had a harsh critic in the *Yass Courier*. In January 1864, the paper complained of his inactivity in the legislative assembly and described him as the *mis*-representative of the Yass Plains constituency. A month later, under the heading 'That's the way the money goes', it claimed he worked five hours a week and added, 'Ah, Peter, Peter, if you take the pay you ought to face your work and perform it like a man.'

The *Courier* backed Faucett's opponent, Mr Harbottle, a Sydney businessman 'universally esteemed and respected by all who know him'. It thought Faucett's 'utter neglect of his duties' should rule out his re-election, and suggested that all electors holding liberal opinions vote for Harbottle; 'his views are moderate, yet progressive'. After Faucett won by 305 votes to 112, the *Courier* described the election as 'an honorable contest honorably conducted' and hoped that 'whatever side was taken by our fellow townsmen in the late contest, the friendly relations which previously existed amongst them will continue.'

We know that Jerry, although evidently not supporting its politics, was

The building built beside the Globe Hotel for the Yass Courier.

a reader of the *Courier*. John Vicq wrote to the paper in January 1865 as postmaster at Bookham replying to a complaint about irregular letter and newspaper deliveries, and claimed that a copy of the *Courier* 'picked up on the road' by the complainant 'belonged to Mr Lehane'. From late 1865, Jerry was also the *Courier*'s landlord, with the paper occupying a new building beside the Globe Hotel. He laid the foundation stone on 21 August 1865. 'The new building will be two storeys high, fifty feet long, and will be connected with and form part of the premises next the Globe,' the *Courier* reported. 'The front shop is to be opened as a bookseller's &c.' After the ceremony,

> about twenty friends met at supper at the Globe Hotel to celebrate the event. Mr Lehane, the proprietor, occupied the chair. The evening was passed very pleasantly, and the arrangements were highly creditable to the host and hostess of the Globe.

It must have been the season for laying foundation stones; eight days later, Anne Murphy performed the duty for her husband's new flour mill at Murrumburrah, next to the Criterion Hotel. Miles had been preparing to enter the milling business for some time. He visited Sydney in July 1864 to make arrangements to acquire the necessary sixteen-horsepower steam engine and other machinery, and brick-making for the building started at Murrumburrah the following April. The *Courier* correspondent waxed eloquent:

I have something to record that will, it is hoped, in no small degree increase not only the importance of the town but the welfare of the surrounding district.

He quoted rival hotel owner and master of ceremonies for the occasion, John Dillon, as saying that no town between Boorowa and Wagga Wagga, except Gundagai, had a flour mill – 'too wide a district to be unrepresented'. The correspondent went on,

> Mrs Miles Murphy then proceeded in the usual form to the business of the day, which having been duly performed, and after a few remarks from Mr Miles Murphy, stating how anxious he was to promote the comfort and well-being of his neighbours here and elsewhere, this part of the proceeding terminated by each person present drinking success to the mill and long life and prosperity to Mr Miles Murphy and family. Shortly afterwards most of the company met to partake of an excellent repast provided gratuitously by mine host Dillon, of the Commercial, and after many toasts being drank, the party separated, fully convinced of the hearty hospitality of Mr and Mrs Dillon. Thus terminated a red letter day in the history of Murrumburrah, and with a hearty 'God speed the plough,' I say farewell.

8
Looking back, looking forward

The ups and downs, and rapid change, of the early 1860s saw writers in the *Courier* both look back nostalgically and extol the march of progress. For example, a report in 1863 about the construction of a new store in Yass with 'a handsome modern plate-glass front' prompted a letter from 'Old Yass' praising 'old verandah cottage stores' and decrying the trend to undignified touting for custom. This brought a spirited response from 'One of the new generation':

> The march of intellect and the march of improvement generally go hand in hand. The intellect devises, and the hand executes material improvements. Liberal institutions take the place of antiquated modes of Government. Railroads and telegraphs take the place of antiquated modes of communication. Rivers are bridged, and the old inconvenient and dangerous punts are set aside. And why should not the mode of conducting business be improved also? Why should not light and elegant buildings be substituted for the dark and dingy dens that have served their time?

In March 1864, the *Courier* published the first of a series of 'Early recollections of Yass' by a 'Late Digger' who had 'wandered many a mile, and toiled through many a weary day, in search of the yellow deity', and had now 'returned once more to 'our village' to…muse on the turmoil and vicissitudes of life…' This was James Wood, a Scottish immigrant who arrived in Yass in 1838 and set up a tailoring business. Many of his contributions described good times and admirable people from the past, but his January 1865 piece looked ahead with optimism. Having spent nearly thirty years based in Yass, he reflected,

> How changed is Yass; how altered the district from the time when the 'old hands' were sparsely scattered o'er the waste, when one's nearest neighbour

lived twenty miles off. The contrast in the year of our Lord 1865 is certainly highly gratifying to every reflecting mind, and speaks well for the future of Australia. Having lately visited a considerable portion of the surrounding districts, nothing struck me so much as the great number of beautiful farms, the neat and cleanly homesteads, and the respectable and comfortable occupants... Everywhere the eye is delighted with well-cultivated fields, clean neat houses, tidy housewives, stalwart sons and daughters, and nice chubby children, ready at all times to let down the rails and show you the way... Most of the farm homesteads are beautifully and picturesquely situated... Some of the landscapes, viewed from the houses, are worthy to be copied by any artist. How I regret my inability to paint these scenes: the neat slab cottage, the well laid out brick house, the carefully arranged flower-garden, the barn raised from the ground to keep it from vermin and damp, the nicely cleared and well cultivated paddocks, the surrounding hills casting their shadows on the plains below, the neatly built church, erected by pious hands and dedicated to the glory of Him who liveth for ever.

The *Courier*'s editor, with his feet perhaps more firmly on the ground, promoted the view that future prosperity required a more diverse economic base – the region was too dependent on gold, the vast runs of the squatters, who employed few people, and the free-selector farmers, whose prosperity was at the mercy of produce markets. He was glad to see that two tanneries had been established in Yass, and suggested soap and candle manufacture as two more possible industries for the town.

The *Courier* was critical of the small amount of revenue the government obtained from the squatters. Jerry's annual payment for the Coppabella lease was £120 in 1865, and Miles paid £30 for Murrumburrah and £40 for Kalangan. Runs were being transferred 'at almost fabulous profit', the paper claimed in May 1865. As an example, it noted that £3,000 had recently been paid for a run in the Lachlan district; from the context, it is clear that this referred to Jerry's purchase of Narraburra earlier in the month. The article noted that the seller had given no guarantee that there was a single beast on the run, although a herd of unmustered cattle formed part of the deal. It went on,

> The purchaser has, however, stated that if he cannot find fifty head of cattle he is well content with his lot, as the bare run itself is worth every penny of the money he paid for it.

Jerry was in his mid-fifties when he bought Narraburra. Seven months earlier, he had become a father again when Hannah gave birth to baby Jeremiah at Coppabella. Showing how unbelievable some of the information on birth (and death and marriage) certificates can be, Jerry was said to be forty-eight and Hannah thirty-two when Jeremiah was born. When their next child, Josephine, arrived in July 1868 the stated ages were fifty and thirty-six. A year later, when son John Thomas, who lived only five months, was born, time had apparently run backwards – Jerry's age was given as forty-nine and Hannah's as thirty-four. For Jerry, at least, the count was more accurate when their last child, Gertrude, was born in November 1870. He was said to be sixty, but Hannah only thirty-three.

Son William was eighteen when the Narraburra purchase was made, and he soon took charge of the 28,000-acre property as superintendent for his father. Presumably, Jerry bought it to secure William's future. His will, drawn up in 1872, provided for Coppabella to pass to young Jeremiah.

Earlier, another life – professional, academic, priestly? – may have been envisaged for William. We have no information on his early schooling but perhaps, as was common among squatter families, Jerry and Mary employed a tutor. This could explain why the eight-year-old was at home when in mid-1855 a carrier, Joseph Cooper, lost two of his bullocks near Coppabella. Cooper complained in a letter to the *Goulburn Herald* about the way Jerry treated him. After searching for the bullocks for eight days, he had received a message that Jerry had seen them about twelve miles from his house.

William Lehane.

I started very early the next morning for the residence of Mr Lehane, and to my great surprise I saw my bullocks confined in a small paddock. After waiting a considerable time Mr Lehane made his appearance, and demanded £3 before I could get possession of them. Not having the money with me, he sent his son a distance of five miles to receive the money.

For William's secondary education, Jerry chose St Mary's College, Lyndhurst, at Glebe Point, Sydney. Archbishop Polding established this boarding school in 1852 to provide a traditional English education – centred on Latin, Greek and mathematics – for the sons of Catholics who had done well in the colony and for outstanding pupils from poorer backgrounds; Catholics were urged to contribute to scholarships for those boys. Many ex-students rose to prominence, especially as lawyers and politicians. Lyndhurst was also a seminary for Benedictine priestly vocations.

One of William's classmates was Joseph Murphy, the fourth son of Miles and Anne, who, like William, was born in 1847. Joseph and William won the two prizes awarded for their age group in 1860, their first year at the school. Both did well again the following year – William first, Joseph third. Results started to slip in 1862; William came fourth and Joseph thirteenth out of the sixteen candidates examined. In his final year, 1863, William was fifth in a class of ten. Joseph was absent for the exams, probably with the disease that culminated in the sixteen-year-old's death in April 1864.

Felix Murphy, born in 1844, was also at Lyndhurst during William's time there. He won prizes for his academic work and for catechism in 1860. He also did some public speaking outside the school that year, addressing the Australian Catholic Young Men's Society in October on 'The past and present fidelity of the people of Ireland to the true faith'. In a performance that, according to the *Freeman's Journal*, frequently elicited loud plaudits, Felix argued that Ireland stood pre-eminent for its virtue and national fidelity:

> Every means have been tried for ages to deprive her of the old faith; banishment, confiscation, and death have been employed in vain. Like her fidelity for the faith is the love of her people for Fatherland, in whatever part of the world they happen to be; neither time nor place creating any change in their love for their persecuted land.

The eldest Murphy boy, John (born 1843), was also a Lyndhurst student. He topped his class in 1857, his second year there. Greek and arithmetic seem to have been among his best subjects.

William, too, was good at Greek, coming first with a score of ninety-five per cent in his final year. The school used external examiners to assess students' progress, and it was William's cousin Dr Forrest, rector of St John's College at the University of Sydney, who tested the fifth form boys on Books I and II of Xenephon's *Anabasis*. He found their performance, presumably William's in particular, 'highly creditable'. William also did well in catechism (ninety-six per cent), but failed to shine in most other areas. His Latin marks were: Virgil's *Aeneid* forty-one per cent, Sallust (*Jugurthine War*) forty-two per cent, and Latin composition twenty-one out of forty. He scored fifty-six per cent in geometry and thirty-two per cent in algebra, but a more impressive eighty-four per cent in arithmetic. He just passed French, with forty-three out of eighty.

In 1864, at the age of seventeen, William entered St John's as a pre-matriculation student. This institution's purpose was 'to prepare Catholic Students for the University Lectures, and to supply courses of study in Metaphysics, Ethics, and Modern History, as well as Religion'. An annual fee of £50 covered board, accommodation in a single room, and the academic program.

Dr Forrest, described in the *Freeman's Journal* on his arrival in Sydney in 1860 as a 'gentleman of rare learning and a thorough Irishman', had a constant struggle to attract students. The 1861 enrolment of three had fallen to two when the college moved from temporary accommodation near the university to its grand building on the campus towards the end of 1863. Things began to look up in William's time; the new structure housed ten students in 1865. However, by 1873, numbers had fallen again to one. The problem was by no means confined to St John's; the university's only other college at the time, the Anglican St Paul's, also had very few students in its early days. So did the university as a whole; twenty-eight matriculated students were enrolled in 1860, forty-four in 1865 and forty-seven in 1869.

The failure of St John's to flourish appears to have weighed heavily on Forrest. In a speech welcoming Archbishop Vaughan, newly arrived from England, on his first official visit to the college in May 1874 he said,

'We deeply regret that, owing to causes which it would be out of place here to discuss, this college has not hitherto realised the aspiration of its founders.' Obviously unimpressed, Vaughan is said to have accused Forrest of succumbing to drink and offered to pay him £400 a year to resign. The bishop took on the rector's role himself, and had little more success in attracting students. Despite his ejection from St John's, Forrest remained in high public regard. On his death in 1883, the *Sydney Morning Herald* wrote of his 'liberal and enlightened views' and 'sympathies…as broad as his heart was kind'. According to the *Daily Telegraph*,

> His learning, his great hospitality, his broad mind and big heart, combined with a humorous, good-natured manner, made him popular, not only with his own people, but with those who were, in a religious sense, opposed to him.

Soon after construction began in 1861, the college building attracted admiring commentary from Sydney's *Empire* newspaper. Although the walls were massive and the workmanship very elaborate, the project was proceeding rapidly, it reported.

> This result is facilitated by means of powerful cranes, which traverse the building by means of a railway carried on a strong framework, about thirty feet high, from end to end of the works. With the aid of this machinery the heaviest blocks of stone are lifted into their places with almost as much ease as if they were no larger than bricks; and the wall, buttress, arch, and clustered column are growing up as if by enchantment. The saving of heavy manual labour, by the excellent mechanical contrivances here brought into operation, is enormous.

Work on the twenty-acre grounds also impressed the paper. Large areas were being planted with ornamental trees and shrubs, which were already flourishing:

> …so that by the time the college halls are ready to receive the students 'academic groves' will be there for shade, shelter, and ornament.

In April 1865, after the first full year's activity in the new structure, the college held a prize-giving ceremony in its 'magnificent gothic chapel'. William was among the students present, along with nine fellows and various 'friends' of St John's. At this stage, Forrest was evidently pleased with the way things were going, reporting that the progress of the students and prospects for the college were satisfactory, discipline was good, and studies 'both general and special in the University and College' were most satisfactory. He thanked six men whose donations of books had given the college a 'splendid library'; the biggest donor, James Hart MLA, had presented 3,964 volumes.

Chairman of the proceedings, the Venerable Archdeacon McEncroe, urged the students to remember the blessings they were enjoying, which had been denied to their forefathers. 'In no part of the British Empire were Catholics better circumstanced,' the *Freeman's Journal* reported him saying.

> They had a college affiliated to the University where they could take all their degrees, while their countrymen at home had built a University at very great cost, and were unable to obtain a royal charter to confer degrees. In Canada the Catholics possessed a University, but which was principally indebted for its existence to the liberality of one ecclesiastic, the Bishop of Quebec, whilst in this colony they owed their position to the munificence of the Legislature. He hoped to see St John's College prosper, and each year have an accession to its inmates.

The prizes awarded included a silver medal with the image of Pope Pius IX, donated by Archbishop Polding, for the best divinity student. This went to Matthew Maher, who proceeded to take a Master of Arts degree. Maher was also the top history student. William was among the other prizewinners, coming third in history and in 'Greek, Latin and mathematics for non-matriculated students'. It seems that his efforts in 1864 earned him matriculation; a list of former residents of St John's gives his university 'fresher' year as 1865. Why William did not go on to take a degree will probably remain a mystery – family legend suggests he had a wild time at college. Maybe Jerry summoned his son home because he needed somebody to look after Narraburra, or because he thought the responsibility of running Narraburra would settle William down. Or did William make the decision himself, deciding to take the option of following in his father's footsteps on the land?

Whatever prompted the decision to quit St John's, William came home to Coppabella in early September 1865 – just in time to be a player in a major drama for the family. The good news, reported in the *Courier* at the end of the month, was a very successful lambing – 100% plus three or four extras. This was 'despite the bad season, which has certainly had no parallel for many years past'. During October, the paper reported a tremendous dust cloud over Yass that 'completely concealed every object within a very considerable distance'. Accounts from the Fish (upper Lachlan) River spoke of cattle dying in great numbers and people being able to pull ten- to twelve-pound fish out of the river with hay rakes because the water level was so low. In November, a bushfire raged for several days between Bowning and Bogolong, 'sweeping before it every vestige of herbage remaining from the long-continued drought'.

Sub Inspector O'Neill of the Gundagai police must have crossed a parched landscape when he rode the forty miles to Coppabella on Monday 16 October 1865 to arrest Jerry for cattle stealing. A grazier neighbour, John P. Sheahan, another of the region's prominent Irish Catholics, made the complaint, accusing Jerry of stealing a red and white bullock. Sheahan had other business interests, including an inn at Jugiong and local mail coach runs. He was one of the earliest settlers and in 1853 was awarded a watch and chain, and a silver tankard, by the government for gallant conduct during the previous year's devastating floods. The *Goulburn Herald* reported,

> Mr Sheahan, so long known and deservedly respected in that neighbourhood [Jugiong], at the imminent risk of his life, and at the sacrifice of his property, gallantly went to the rescue of thirty-three persons, whose lives were perilled by the awful visitation, and succeeded in saving them from the fate which they had no power to avert.

Jerry spent two nights in the Gundagai lock-up before being brought before the local police magistrate. Proceedings began with evidence from Sub Inspector O'Neill, who said the hide of the allegedly stolen bullock had been found at Coppabella. He quoted Jerry as telling him at the time of the arrest, 'I can take my oath I did not kill the bullock, but I won't be answerable for what others on the station have done.' He had advised Jerry not to say any more, but Jerry had offered the information that he killed all the meat required for his residence at Coppabella.

The accuser, Sheahan, appeared next. He said his son Philip and the man in charge of his cattle, Peter Hart, had brought him the hide, and given him 'certain information', on 11 October. He agreed with Jerry's counsel, Mr Ryall, that he had sold Jerry four bullocks and a cow the previous July. He could not swear that the red and white bullock was not among them; he had not been present when the cattle were delivered, and did not remember Hart giving him a description of the animals.

Hart was the next witness. He said he and Philip Sheahan had gone to Coppabella on suspicion that a cow belonging to John Sheahan had been killed. He said a man named Peter had shown him two hides in a shed, and one, with Sheahan's brand, was that of the bullock in question.

> I knew it by the peculiar spots on each side, and the white patches about the flanks… I have seen the beast that owned it very often, the last time about September, when it was put into the yard and jumped the fence.

He claimed to remember distinctly the colours of the five animals sold to Jerry, and swore 'most positively' that none had the hide's red and white colouring. Philip Sheahan, who was with Hart when the cattle were delivered, also told the magistrate that none of them matched the hide found in the Coppabella shed.

The first witness for the defence was John Conroy, a bullock driver employed by Jerry. He said the hide did come from one of the bullocks sold by Sheahan: 'I noticed it particularly, making the remark that the beast was not fat enough to kill, and would make a capital worker.' He said about one beast a week was killed at Coppabella. Next to give evidence was 'Black Jack', an Aboriginal stockman. He also said the hide came from one of the bullocks delivered by Hart. He said he had killed it on Jerry's instructions; Jerry's nephew Jeremiah was with him.

The final witness was Edward Bourke, a nephew of Hannah Lehane; he was employed at Coppabella 'looking after stock and lost sheep'. He said the Peter who had shown Hart and Philip Sheahan the hide, Peter Waring, was an 'acting hut-keeper' whose jobs included cooking for station workers. He had ushered the visitors into the Coppabella shed and 'bolted' that evening. According to Bourke, young Jeremiah remarked of Waring's actions, 'The old scamp – I didn't think he would do that.'

Winding up proceedings, the magistrate committed Jerry to stand trial at the quarter sessions in Gundagai five days later. After the required bail – £200 and two sureties of £100 – was 'at once offered', he was discharged from custody.

There was no quick conclusion to matters as foreshadowed. Instead, the quarter sessions hearing was postponed to the next sitting in Gundagai in February 1866. This followed advice from the Crown prosecutor that Waring, as a material witness, needed to be located. Sub Inspector O'Neill told the court Waring could give evidence that the bullock Jerry was charged with stealing was killed with his knowledge and sanction. The case was later postponed to the April 1866 circuit court sitting in Wagga Wagga.

In the meantime, the police were active. First, in late October 1865, Waring, evidently an elderly man, was apprehended near Douro, Henry O'Brien's property near Yass, and despatched to Gundagai under escort. Then, a few days later, young Jeremiah was arrested at Junee charged with being implicated in the case. He had left Jerry's employ shortly after the visit of Hart and young Sheahan to Coppabella. Next, charges were laid against Black Jack and Edward Bourke and both were taken into custody.

Young Jeremiah appeared in the Gundagai Magistrate's Court in early November. The only witness was Black Jack, who had said at Jerry's first court appearance that Jeremiah was present when the bullock whose hide was at the centre of the case was killed. Under Jeremiah's cross-examination, Black Jack agreed that the hide had in fact not come from the bullock killed then. 'The examination of Black Jack extended over three hours, during which he varied considerably in his evidence to that given on a previous occasion,' the *Courier* reported. Jeremiah was discharged.

The paper reprinted an indignant item from the *Gundagai Herald* questioning whether Aborigines – 'benighted beings, such as this' – should be allowed to give evidence on oath as there was 'no guarantee that the truth will be adhered to in any shape'. Jerry evidently had a very different opinion of Black Jack, a long-time trusted employee. The Aboriginal stockman makes a larger appearance in the story in chapter 12.

The *Courier* was highly critical of the way young Jeremiah had been treated. It said that between being 'taken from his honest employment at Junee' and appearing in the Gundagai Court he had 'in his vile prison house been unnecessarily detained and degraded for eleven days'. The article went on,

> The law holds that a man is innocent till proved guilty, and whose fault is it that so great a wrong has been done upon what so far as the evidence goes seems to have been an innocent man. Loss of situation, loss of reputation, contact with the loathsome of society for eleven days may be nothing to the dull eye of officialism, but it is everything to those whose case it may be to-morrow, and whilst endeavouring to right the wrong inflicted upon this young man, our community will be only protecting itself. The authorities to whom our liberties are confided will surely deem this a fitting subject for enquiry.

Finally, on 23 April 1866, Jerry appeared before Mr Justice Faucett and a jury at the circuit court in Wagga Wagga. As a political candidate, Peter Faucett had enjoyed Jerry's support at elections in 1859 and 1864. He was elevated to the judiciary in October 1865. Jerry faced two charges: that he had stolen a bullock the property of John P. Sheahan, and that he had received the bullock knowing it to be stolen. The solicitor-general, Robert Isaacs, conducted the prosecution. Jerry's defence team was headed by the noted Catholic barrister William Bede Dalley, later acting premier of New South Wales. He was supported by George Allman and another solicitor named Walsh.

Sub Inspector O'Neill, the first witness, said Jerry 'manifested very great indignation' when charged, the *Wagga Wagga Express* reported. John Sheahan, called next, admitted he knew very little about his stock. He had known Jerry thirteen or fourteen years, and had been on good terms with him. Hart then acknowledged under cross-examination that he had not told Jerry the colour, brands or marks of the cattle he delivered. He said Sheahan had about 600 cattle at Jugiong; he might be able to recognise as few as twenty or as many as 300 of them. Appearing for the prosecution, young Jeremiah said he could not be sure whether the hide taken by Hart and Philip Sheahan belonged to one of the bullocks sold to Jerry, although he did not think it did. He told the court that Jerry had dismissed him.

Peter Waring's appearance lifted the level of drama in the court. He said Jerry had shot the bullock with the disputed hide in the presence of himself, Jerry's son William, Black Jack and Bourke. He left Coppabella after Hart and Sheahan took the hide, and claimed Jerry had said he would send the police after him. 'I told him he had better look out that I did not send them after him for shaking cattle,' Waring told the judge and jury. 'He replied that if he caught me by myself he would 'make me so that I could not tell anyone'; after he killed the beast I left his service; he threatened to take my life and I was frightened.'

Under cross-examination, Waring agreed he had taken off from Coppabella two days earlier than he first said, but had returned having been permitted to by William. On the night he first departed, he had visited the Five Mile Creek Inn, run by George Bodkin. 'When I was at Bodkin's public house, I will swear the landlord did not discover me trying to commit an unnatural offence and flog me for it,' Waring said. 'I did tell Bodkin a man wanted to maul me; Bodkin put the man out.' Bodkin disputed this account. The *Express* said his description of what he found Waring doing was unfit for publication. Bodkin went on, 'I shoved Waring out through the gate and told him if he came back I would horsewhip him; I put him outside because the men in the house had heard something of what had occurred and would have killed him if he came in.'

William was called for the defence. He said the hide at the centre of the case was one that had been hanging on a fence when he returned to Coppabella from St John's College on 7 September. Later, he had seen his father, watched by Black Jack, Waring and Bourke, shoot a bullock with Jerry's JL brand; hence the animal Jerry shot was not the source of the hide. William said Waring had asked Jerry's permission to leave with a settlement of his wages. Jerry had refused.

Summing up for the defence, barrister Dalley expressed amazement that a friend and neighbour of Jerry's had instituted the proceedings. 'It would have been extraordinary if no claims of friendship but those alone of neighbourhood had existed,' he added.

Sheahan had heard from that unnatural old scoundrel [Waring] that a beast had been shot. A hide that once had belonged to a beast of his had been found, not at Lehane's residence, but on a fence miles away from his house. Putting all friendship out of sight, his first step ought to have been to have ascertained if it had not belonged to a beast that had been sold; to have asked Lehane if there had not been some mistake, or if he or his servants knew anything about the matter. No – the first thing he did was to take out a warrant.

Dalley commented on the evidence of each of the other prosecution witnesses. Hart's inability to say how many cattle Sheahan had on his land bordering Coppabella, and other aspects of his evidence, showed he was either a fool or a liar. Young Jeremiah Lehane, although 'no friend of the prisoner's', would not swear that the hide did not belong to one of the beasts delivered. Dalley was particularly scathing about Waring:

> He first said he bolted on the Tuesday, and, on cross-examination, he said he bolted on the Sunday. On that day, he told young Lehane that he would inform against his father for cattle-duffing if he was not paid his wages. But he was treated as an absconder, and his wages had never been paid… If Lehane had been guilty, would he not have paid Waring his paltry wages, and have then offered five, ten or a thousand pounds to have stopped his mouth?

Dalley also referred to the innkeeper Bodkin's evidence against Waring:

> Bodkin charges this man with one of the most awful of crimes; he can have no interest in perjuring himself, and yet he charges him with a crime which dare not be named amongst Christian men, and put him from his house that he might not be murdered by the men that were there. Such a man's evidence could not be worthy of the slightest credit.

Jerry's behaviour was further proof of his innocence, Dalley observed. Sub Inspector O'Neill's evidence showed Jerry had 'expressed great indignation at the charge, and certainly did not bear himself like a guilty man'. And if he were guilty would he have left the evidence, in the form of the hide, lying around?

The *Express* did not report Solicitor-General Isaacs' reply, beyond saying it was a very long and able speech that most elaborately reviewed the evidence and Dalley's comments on it. After Judge Faucett 'summed up very favourably for the prisoner', the jury immediately – without leaving the box – returned a verdict of not guilty. Two day's later the solicitor-general informed the judge he would not proceed with the cases against Black Jack and Edward Bourke, and both were discharged.

9

More drama on Coppabella

On the day the *Yass Courier* reported Jerry's arrest for cattle stealing – 18 October 1865 – it also brought its readers news of the apparent murder of one of his workers on Coppabella. The victim, Nathaniel Gorth, was aged in his early seventies. His body was found in a waterhole in Reedy Creek, near an outstation where he and two others were employed minding sheep.

Jerry notified the Jugiong police of the incident on Saturday 14 October. Two days later – the day Sub Inspector O'Neill called at Coppabella to arrest Jerry for cattle stealing – Gundagai police magistrate A.C. Rose proceeded to Bodkin's Five Mile Creek Inn to conduct an inquest into Gorth's death. Perhaps O'Neill and Rose rode out together. Whether they did or not, the timing explains why Jerry was not among those who gave evidence at the inquest.

The first witness, Constable Chapman from Jugiong, said information he had received led him to suspect that a young man named John Hoare, who had been living in the same shepherd's hut as Gorth, had murdered the old man. Next to appear was Thomas Johnstone, the third occupant of the hut. He said he and Hoare were working as shepherds, with Gorth the night watchman. As he left the hut on the day Gorth disappeared, the watchman had shown him a bruised eye, allegedly the result of a blow from Hoare. He said Gorth had begged him not to go away because Hoare was sure to kill him that day. 'I told him not to be afraid,' Johnstone recalled.

According to Johnstone, before setting off with his flock for the day he had told Gorth to 'go and tell Mr Lehane that I had lost some sheep'. When he returned to the hut that evening, he found Gorth missing. He asked Hoare whether Gorth had been to Jerry to report the lost sheep. 'He said deceased had told him I had said nothing about the lost sheep,' Johnstone told the magistrate, adding that Hoare suggested Gorth had collected his pay from the homestead and gone. 'I suspected something was wrong, but to save myself from harm I said nothing.' Johnstone went on,

> The prisoner was more jovial and freer that night than he was other nights. The deceased did not return that night or the next day. The prisoner remarked that his ghost would be haunting us. He said on Tuesday night, 'I had the — down, and would have killed him only the knife wasn't sharp enough.' I have repeatedly heard the prisoner say to the deceased, 'you —, I'll kill you.' On Thursday morning the prisoner called me to the creek and pointed to a hat lying on the ground, and said, 'There's the —'s hat; he has gone and drowned himself to get me into trouble because Lehane has a down on me.

The next witness, a local sawyer named Michael Corby, said he had reported Gorth's disappearance to Jerry and a day later found the old man's cabbage-tree hat on the bank of the waterhole and retrieved the body with a grappling hook. The water was about three feet six inches deep. He noted that one of Gorth's eyes was blackened. The final witness was a medical practitioner, Dr William Lyons, who had examined the body. He said he had detected 'no external marks of violence which of themselves would account for death', and the appearance of the body was compatible with death by drowning.

The wheels of justice turned slowly for John Hoare after the magistrate committed him to the circuit court, Goulburn, charged with wilful murder. First he was to face the judge and jury on 9 April 1866, but the case was postponed to a later sitting. After a year in custody, he was finally brought to trial in October 1866.

Like Jerry in the cattle-stealing case, Hoare was defended by William Dalley. The witnesses who appeared at the inquest were called again and gave much the same evidence, although Johnstone's testimony, if the newspaper report is an accurate reflection, was less dramatic than before. For example, when Hoare had talked about planning 'to cut the old fellow's throat' he had taken this to be 'flash talk'. Addressing the jury, Dalley contended that the prosecution had not proved that a murder had been committed, let alone that Hoare was guilty of one. The jury, after only a 'short absence', found him not guilty.

In its first account of the incident, the *Courier* said it appeared Gorth had been frequently threatened by Hoare 'for some time past', and the evidence at the inquest and trial suggests this is likely to have been the case. Whether he was murdered or committed suicide, the story of Nathaniel Gorth is a sad reminder that life could be extremely harsh, as well as lonely, for the shepherds – often old men – on Australia's vast sheep runs.

By 1865, though, the shepherding days were drawing to a close. The *Courier* reported in May 1866 that a new type of wire fencing had been introduced in Queensland. This could be erected at little more than a third the cost of 'the ordinary three-railed fence'. A year later, the paper's subscribers read that 'a regular revolution in the conduct of pastoral properties' was under way as fences went up.

> The cost of working stations properly fenced and subdivided is found by experience to be considerably below that of those worked under the old [shepherding] system.

Jerry may not have been among the first to adopt the new technology; another sorry tale, from 1868, of antics in a shepherds' hut is told in chapter 11. However, fencing must have been well advanced on Coppabella by the start of lambing in June 1870. 'We understand,' noted the *Courier*, 'that this season, for the first time on an extensive scale, Mr Lehane has adopted the plan of leaving the sheep unshepherded, and finds it highly advantageous – both ewes and lambs thriving better than if folded nightly.'

While the dramas were unfolding on Coppabella in late 1865, a swindler was busy in the neighbourhood. His victims included George Bodkin of the Five Mile Creek Inn and John Vicq, temporary publican of one of the two hotels at Bogolong (his appointment as postmaster, at £12 a year, in August 1864 was on condition that he give up his publican's licence, but apparently a lengthy transition period was allowed). Vicq was experiencing difficult times. Shortly before the swindler's visit, he had lent a caller to the hotel a valuable horse; when it was returned, it had a number of stab wounds, apparently inflicted with a knife. 'In explanation, the man said the horse ran him against the branches of a tree, fell, and inflicted the injuries,' the *Courier* reported. 'But on closer examination the story appeared to have been concocted, as the wounds were evidently clean incisions.'

The swindler purported to be John W. Windeyer, who ran Wantabadgery station near Wagga Wagga with his brother Walter. He made a morning visit to the Bogolong inn, where, Vicq told the magistrate's hearing after his eventual arrest in Yass in late December 1865, he ordered breakfast and had a few glasses of brandy. Vicq let him leave without paying as he said he was going to overtake his brother and would pay by cheque on his return. The swindler did return, and presented Vicq with a cheque for £2 signed 'John and Walter O. Windeyer'. Bodkin told the court a somewhat similar story. This time the swindler stayed the night, left with the innkeeper's agreement without paying, returned as promised but again asked if he could defer payment, and then, as he said he would, sent a cheque in the mail from Jugiong.

The swindler, who had deceived a long list of traders in a similar manner, turned out to be Frederick Pryor, a man of 'somewhat common appearance' but 'perfectly self-possessed', with whiskers and beard 'cut after the American fashion'. Explaining the choice of the Windeyer name for use in his deceptions, the *Courier* reported that 'it would seem he has for some time been employed in the culinary department at Wantabadgery station.'

The new year, 1866, started dramatically in Yass when a fifty-year-old relative of the distinguished Catholic prelate Archdeacon McEncroe gave himself up to the police, claiming he had lit the fire that destroyed St Mary's Cathedral. Edward McEncroe said his spectacular act of arson, which he believed would be punished by hanging, was a response to the failure of both the archdeacon and a relative in a prominent Sydney firm to help him find employment. Proof soon emerged that McEncroe was at Jamberoo, south of Sydney, on the night of the blaze. A letter in the *Freeman's Journal* claimed the Yass police and magistrates were 'very credulous' to have believed his story:

> Any sane man could have seen at a glance that the fellow was crazy, or that being too lazy to work for his bread, he preferred a cool cell and good ration at the public's expense.

January 1866 also saw the death of Henry O'Brien, at the age of seventy-eight. The *Courier*'s obituary praised his involvement 'in every movement that had for its object the advancement of Yass', and described his introduction of boiling down stock for tallow during the 'great pastoral depression' of the early 1840s as his greatest public act. Remembering other early settlers who had died recently as well as O'Brien, the paper noted,

> Old familiar faces that we have been in the habit of greeting for years past – men who have been, as it were, the patriarchs of the community – have passed away from us for ever, but whose memories will be cherished with fond affection.

The tone of the *Courier* through much of 1866 was gloomy, because of the continuing drought and economic hard times. Even when reporting progress, articles sometimes had a resigned air. For example, an item on 27 January marking the seventy-eighth anniversary of the founding of the colony observed,

> Seventy-eight years ago Captain Phillip made his camp on the border of the tank stream; the live stock of the settlement consisted of one bull, one bull calf, four cows, one stallion, three mares, three yearling colts, a few sheep, goats and pigs. The population consisted of 707 convicts (of whom 150 were women), and about 200 soldiers, sappers, and miners. The transport fleet comprised six vessels, and three store ships. The reader can easily draw a comparison between the state of things at that time and the present.

In March, editor James John Brown wrote of 'the direful seasons experienced in the colony during the past three years'. An article in May spoke of 'a pinching poverty hitherto unexperienced in this colony' among farmers, with many families short of food and one forced to live off the flesh of possums. Another article advanced the case for improving the region's stock. Although grass was very scarce and forage dear, a smaller number of better-bred animals could be maintained and bring good prices. The writer thought it 'impossible to speak in too strong terms of disparagement' about the cattle and horses around Yass, and added, 'The miserable donkey-like horses we see ridden into Yass every day are a libel on the species'.

By August, the *Courier* was wondering how Yass continued to support ten hotels, including many first-class establishments (presumably Jerry's Globe was in that category).

> How some of them pay their owners is a mystery, for the number of travellers, and also of 'bar' customers, could with ease have their wants provided for by one, or at most a couple, of these establishments.

Things were so bad, the paper added, that people with the means to do so were leaving the colony. And vast numbers of those without means were on the move:

> The number of young able-bodied men who have recently passed through the town in search of work has exceeded anything of the kind known for more than twenty years past. In conversation with some of these unfortunate fellows we have learnt that in many instances they have come from the border of the colony, and in some cases from the furthermost parts of Victoria, and in their travels have been unable to obtain any kind of work whatever. Some of the men are mechanics, such as carpenters, smiths, plasterers, bootmakers, &c., but the bulk are of the labouring class generally. We have good reason for believing that some of these poor fellows have undergone the disagreeables of a compulsory fast for four or five days together. They say there are so many of their class travelling in the bush that it is a difficult matter to obtain any assistance at the stations, the owners alleging that the cost of relieving strangers in search of employment is considerably greater than the whole expense of their establishments.

We don't know whether many unemployed men were seeking work at Coppabella, but the property certainly had one unwelcome visitor in August – the bushranger Robert Bourke, who rode in after sticking up the Gundagai mail. Jerry's overseer was tending a flock of ewes on a lambing station when Bourke turned up there. Bourke seized the overseer's horse, leaving the worn-out one he had been riding.

Described as about twenty-five years old – with fair hair, a thin face, no whiskers and 'bearing every appearance of being a quiet, inoffensive traveller' – Bourke had a short but busy bushranging career in the district after leaving his job as a station cook. His solo exploits included further mail coach hold-ups and numerous other armed robberies. In early September, he staged a stick-up at Bodkin's Five Mile Creek Inn, and stole a 'valuable' horse belonging to one of the five customers there. He rode this horse when he again bailed up the Gundagai mail the next morning.

A *Courier* article suggested that 'had a little more courage been shown' at places where he had stuck up groups of people, Bourke would already have been captured or killed. The raid on Bodkin's was a case in point. He stole a pair of boots from one of the customers, and while trying to put one of them on 'his foot became so fastened that he could neither withdraw it nor put on the boot'.

> He got a knife, with which he coolly cut the leather from near the toe to the instep, stooping down all the while to do so. It is said that some one made a sign to the others present to rush him, but as they had no firearms [!] they considered it unwise to do so. We learn that there was a fowling-piece and plenty of ammunition in the house, and which was known to one of the party, but any little valour he or any of the persons there might have had evaporated in the presence of the single-handed bushranger.

Later that month, or in early October, Bourke left the district for Victoria, where he was captured after a hold-up on a property at Diamond Creek, not far from Melbourne. A shot from his gun killed a man named Hurst in this encounter, and although the evidence indicated Hurst had initiated the shoot-out Bourke was convicted of murder. Despite a recommendation of mercy from the jury, he was duly hanged.

At the height of Robert Bourke's bushranging career, in September 1866, his description was published in the *Gazette* distributed to police posts around the colony. Constable Edward Brady of Carcoar, between Bathurst and Cowra, thought he had made the prize arrest when he apprehended a man named Bourke in early October and charged him with highway robbery under arms and horse stealing. 'His description exactly corresponded with that of Robert Bourke,' Brady told the Carcoar Magistrates' Court. The young man arrested turned out, instead, to be Hannah Lehane's nephew Edward Bourke.

His identity having been sorted out and the highway robbery charge dropped, Edward, who no longer worked for Jerry on Coppabella, remained under arrest for horse stealing. Constable Brady claimed at the Carcoar hearing that Edward gave two conflicting answers when asked where he had obtained a mare with a PL brand. When the case moved to the Yass Court of Petty Sessions, a man named Patrick Langan claimed the horse was his and the magistrate remanded Edward in custody to face judge and jury the following February.

The charge had changed by the time the trial began; Edward was now accused of stealing a horse belonging to a John Jones. With the key exhibit, the horse, tied up outside the courthouse, both Jones and Langan were called as witnesses. Langan appeared first, saying he had bred the horse, it was five years old, and he had lost it two years ago. 'I am certain the mare outside the court is mine,' he said. Jones claimed he had owned the horse for seven years. It was branded PL because a Patrick Lennan had given it to him after branding. Judge Purefoy remarked that the case, with two people swearing the allegedly stolen property was theirs, was one of the most remarkable he had ever heard. The jury acquitted Edward Bourke.

For the Murphy family, end-of-year celebrations a week before Christmas at St Augustine's School, Yass, marked the transition from 1865 to 1866. In front of parents, Dean Hanly of St Augustine's Church and J.J. Brown of the *Courier*, the teacher, Edmund Flannery, quizzed the students and set reading assignments. Brown was most impressed with the way the boys performed. In geography, for example, 'the smartness with which questions were answered, not alone relating to position on the map, but to general characteristics, products, connection with sacred or profane history &c. was most pleasing…' Reading, of both prose and verse, displayed strict attention to punctuation 'and an entire absence of that 'sing-song' drawl sometimes heard in public schools on such occasions'. In mental arithmetic, 'the rapidity with which calculations were made and answered was truly wonderful'. Brown noted with approval that many non-Catholic children attended the school, and received 'a sound secular or commercial education without their religious views being in the slightest way interfered with.'

Two of Miles' and Anne's boys, presumably boarders at the school, were among the pupils awarded prizes. Fourteen-year-old Thomas took the reading prize in the 'head' class and eleven-year-old Miles junior was top of fourth class. At the end of the ceremony, the pupils presented their teacher with 'a handsome tea and coffee service' and Thomas read the following address:

Dear Sir – We, the boarding and day pupils of St Augustine's School, before our separation for the Christmas holidays, have great pleasure in addressing you, and in conveying to you our grateful acknowledgments for the care with which you have directed our studies during the past year. We also beg to present to you the accompanying testimonial, as a slight mark of our affection and regard. – We are, Dear Sir, yours very truly…

In his reply, Flannery praised the boys, saying, 'any success which may have crowned our united labours during the past year has been owing more to your ability than to my instruction'. He added that, while he had worked in schools with as many as a thousand students, 'I can safely aver that in no school have I ever met children more capable of acquiring instruction or more desirous for its acquisition.' No doubt everybody departed for the Christmas–New Year break with a warm glow, although Flannery reminded his pupils that school was to resume on 8 January. There were no long summer vacations in the 1860s.

Back home at Binalong, Dora Garry, widow of James Garry who ran Miles' Swan Inn for a few years up to his death in 1862, was a sorry focus of attention in late 1865 and early 1866. First she appeared before the local magistrates claiming a Binalong shoemaker named Mulgrew had come up and struck her while she was standing at the bar of the Swan. In answer to a question from Mulgrew, she said, 'I did not say you were a mean scruff; you asked me what I was saying about your wife's character: I told you to go and look.' The assault was proved and the defendant ordered to pay £1.

Mulgrew responded by launching an action for slander with a claim for £100 damages. Appearing before Judge Purefoy in Yass, he said Mrs Garry had accused him of stealing her fowls. He claimed that in an altercation on the veranda of the Swan she had 'told me in public that I had been living by thieving and — for the last ten years'. In earlier encounters she had 'slapped her buttocks and said kiss that you fowl-stealing wretch' and called out, 'there goes the fowl-stealing telegraph'. Mulgrew was awarded £2, so he ended up £1 ahead.

More sober activity around this time at the Swan included a meeting in early February 1866 to form a local committee to back James Martin's re-election as Member for the Lachlan. As well as Miles, the committee

Murrumburrah in 1880, showing the flour mill beside the Criterion.

included the familiar names Cornelius O'Brien, Nicholas Besnard, John Paterson, John Sheahan and John Vicq, but there was no sign of Jerry. Martin was returned unopposed, and the conservative Robert Isaacs, who had succeeded Peter Faucett as both the local member and solicitor-general when he became a judge, won easily in the Yass Plains electorate despite the *Courier*'s opposition. The paper seems to have made a poor choice in backing his apparently more liberal opponent, Robert Scott Ross, who in June 1866 was found guilty of various frauds on Yass businessmen in the lead-up to the election and sentenced to eighteen months' hard labour.

For Miles, the major event of 1866 was the opening of his flour mill at Murrumburrah, beside the Criterion Hotel, on 9 August. The day began unpropitiously. Rain was coming down in torrents, the *Courier* tells us, and Miles had been called before a visiting police magistrate from Young to answer a charge of selling liquor without a licence. He was found guilty and ordered to pay £30 5s 6d, a result 'which drew a long face from the person concerned, and a lull of astonishment from the audience at the court'. The reporter had no doubt that Miles was innocent – 'there was not a syllable [in the evidence presented] to prove the defendant's guilt' – or that the conviction would be overturned on appeal. His prediction proved accurate when the case was heard again in Yass in October.

Miles arranged a dinner on the premises, beginning at eight p.m., to launch the mill. 'When the bell sounded, about 150 persons were immediately at its call to partake of the good things supplied with so much liberality by the host,' the *Courier* reported. Jerry was among those at the top table with Miles. James Welman, a long-time squatter near Murrumburrah and neighbour of Miles, chaired the evening's proceedings.

Toasts began 'after ample justice had been done in the eating line, which was proved by the pleasant countenances that shone from the large assemblage.' The toast to Miles, proposed by Welman, followed those to the Queen and the Prince and Princess of Wales. Describing Miles as 'the father of Binalong and progenitor of Murrumburrah', Welman said he could well remember 'when there was not a slab in Binalong'. He said Miles was 'the first to inhabit that district'. He could also well remember 'when the former lessee of Murrumburrah, Mr Harris, had but a small hut on the same spot of ground on which the mill now stands, where he was in the habit of boiling down his scabby sheep'.

Welman praised Miles' Criterion Hotel, saying it 'could not be excelled out of Sydney' in the excellent accommodation it afforded all travellers. Then he turned to the flour mill, saying 'the district had been hitherto imposed upon by the obnoxious charge of 1s 6d per bushel for grinding, which Mr Murphy found himself capable of doing at 1s', and 'heretofore, the wheat-grower could only get from forty-two to forty-three lbs. of flour for his bushel of wheat, whereas Mr Murphy could afford to give forty-five lbs. of flour out of sixty lbs. of wheat.' Welman 'was frequently interrupted with shouts of applause' during his speech.

In reply, Miles conceded that he did not know much about flour milling but promised 'to give the business his attention' and offer even better prices and service where this could be justified. 'He returned grateful thanks for the unanimous feeling expressed at the drinking of his health,' the *Courier* added.

After further toasts – to, among others, the ladies, the agricultural and pastoral interests, and 'the mechanics' – the tables were removed so a ball could proceed. 'At about ten o'clock dancing commenced, and was continued unceasingly till sunrise on the following morning.' The reporter continued,

> This certainly was the largest and most successful night's enjoyment that has ever been known in the district, and I am sure that all who were present will join me in wishing Mr Murphy every prosperity in his new enterprise.

The opening seems to have been well timed. In early October 1866, the *Courier* was still writing of deepening economic gloom, with a 'disruption in mercantile affairs' unparallelled since 1842–43. But within weeks things were looking better as waggons heavily laden with wool passed through Yass on their way to Sydney and prospects appeared increasingly bright for an abundant wheat harvest. Business was also looking up in town, with 'a complete revival' in prospect for the New Year. 'We have a lot to be thankful for,' the editor wrote towards the end of November. Not only was there 'every appearance of a splendid harvest', but the new Weddin Mountain (Grenfell) goldfields promised to be as rich as Lambing Flat in its best days.

In late November, Murphy and Son (Miles and John) placed an advertisement in the *Courier* addressed 'To Squatters, Farmers, and Others' seeking custom. This offered 'liberal advances on the present clip of wool' if consigned to the firm's Sydney agents, or on ensuing wheat crops if delivered to the Murrumburrah mill. A *Courier* item in February 1867 suggested the mill was doing a great job: 'we hear that the machinery is most excellent, and the finest silk-dressed flour can be turned out there.' Also, 'we are told that the customer there has another advantage, namely, that he gets from 4 lbs. to 5 lbs. more flour to the bushel…' This may not have been the whole story, because another item three weeks later said the Murphy firm had changed millers, and 'the present one is giving very general satisfaction'. That satisfaction was short-lived; dramatic events later in 1867, including an episode in which the new miller, John Wilson, allegedly ordered Miles out of the mill, are related in the next chapter.

10

Back to St Mary's

In early February 1867, Jerry, his twenty-two-year-old daughter Ellen and perhaps other members of the Lehane family set off for Sydney where Ellen was to marry a twenty-three-year-old lawyer, John Perry Lyons. They may have caught the train for the last part of the journey as the southern railway, gradually snaking south, reached Picton, about forty-five miles south of Sydney, in 1863. Had the ceremony taken place a month later, they could have left the Cobb and Co. coach at Mittagong, not far past the mid-point of the journey, as a rail terminus opened there on 4 March 1867.

The bridegroom was a son of Michael and Eliza Lyons, among the earliest settlers in the Western District of Victoria. He received a Catholic education at St Mary's College, Geelong, and then St Patrick's College, Melbourne. He learned his law articled to a Geelong solicitor, Mr G. Doyle, and in 1866 was admitted as a solicitor in Brisbane. How John's and Ellen's paths came to cross is unknown.

The venue for the marriage, performed on 13 February 1867 by Ellen's cousin Dr John Forrest of St John's College, was the weatherboard St Mary's Pro-Cathedral. This 170-feet long, sixty-feet wide building had been erected on a site opposite the charred remains of the former cathedral – in the garden of the archbishop's residence at the corner of St Mary's Road and College Street. The first services were held there in October 1865, within four months of the blaze that consigned the old cathedral to oblivion. Another fire consumed this edifice in January 1869, and a second temporary cathedral was ready for use the following June. This time, to guard against a further conflagration, iron was used for the interior framework and the walls were built of brick.

John and Ellen initially settled at North Quay, Brisbane, where their

Ellen and John Perry Lyons.

first child, Mary Agnes, was born on 12 November 1867. (Jerry placed a notice in the *Courier* announcing the arrival of his first grandchild.) The family must have moved soon afterwards to Maryborough, a port town 260 kilometres to the north first settled in the 1840s, because advertisements for John Perry Lyons, attorney, solicitor, proctor and conveyancer, began appearing on the front page of the *Maryborough Chronicle* in January 1868. A major gold rush had just started at nearby Gympie; the find there, said to have saved Queensland from bankruptcy, was notified to the Maryborough police in October 1867. Presumably confident that the influx of diggers would generate plenty of work for a lawyer, John set up his practice two doors from the post office in Bazaar Street.

Apparently, Jerry became ill while he was in Sydney for the wedding. He and a squatter neighbour, Samuel Barber of Bogalara, were in dispute over boundaries and two cases were listed for hearing by Judge Purefoy at the district court, Yass, on 28 February 1867. Jerry was claiming £50 damages for trespass by Barber, and in return Barber was being more ambitious, seeking £200 for trespass by Jerry. When the cases came up, Jerry's attorney, George Allman, applied for and was granted a postponement 'owing to the illness of Mr Lehane, now in Sydney.' Jerry was ordered to pay the day's costs – £9 18s 6d. By the time the court returned in June, the neighbours had settled their dispute.

The success of his Globe Hotel in attracting a string of distinguished visitors would have been pleasing news for Jerry in the first half of 1867. The *Courier* adopted the habit around this time of naming the hotel chosen by the VIPs passing through Yass. The Globe's main competitor was the Commercial Hotel in Cooma Street, owned and run by Thomas Colls.

At eleven-twenty on a Sunday morning in late January, James Martin – premier, attorney-general and member for the Lachlan – arrived at the Globe on his way to Melbourne, appearing 'in robust health and good spirits'. He departed at twelve-thirty. In early March, the Catholic bishop of Brisbane, James Quinn, stayed overnight en route from Bathurst to Goulburn. The following month, Mr Justice Cheeke, his associate, Crown prosecutor William Dalley and another lawyer made the Globe their Yass home for the night as they proceeded to Wagga Wagga for a court sitting. Next to call, just over a week later, was the most distinguished guest of all, the governor of New South Wales, Sir John Young. Attended by his private secretary and accompanied by the minister for lands and the colony's chief engineer, he spent a night at the Globe on his way to Albury.

Sometimes the visitors were more interesting than distinguished. One such in early June was Christian Frederick Schafer, 'a German gentleman who is accomplishing a tour through the world on foot'. According to the *Courier*,

> He is intelligent, courteous, and communicative, and his book of credentials, with the signatures and seals of the great in all parts of the globe, is an interesting record of what can be done through indomitable perseverance directed to one object. The range of his travels has been, even up to the present time, wide to a marvel, considering the mode of journeying he has adopted. The extremes of the American continent, the whole surface of Europe, the coast-lying parts of Africa, British India, the Celestial Empire, as well as the chief islands that stud the face of our seas and oceans, have been visited by him.

Presumably, the Globe was also home for Jerry on his visits to Yass. In August 1867, another cattle-stealing case brought him to town, this time as the key witness rather than the accused. Jerry was not at

Christian Schafer, the intercontinental walker who called at the Globe.

the first court of petty sessions hearing when Sub Inspector Brennan, head of the local police, outlined the prosecution case. Brennan told the magistrates that two men had driven four head of cattle to Coppabella and offered to sell them to Jerry. The offer was refused; instead the police were notified and three men – two named Barry and George Webster, a half-caste Aboriginal also known as Brown George – were arrested.

Coppabella stockman Black Jack, who appeared next, provided descriptions of the cattle. He said that, after Jerry had refused to buy them, the two men had taken them away. Later he saw three of the four cattle in a paddock on the station; these were later removed by the police. Black Jack confirmed that Webster was one of the pair who had wanted to sell the cattle to Jerry. However, he was sure the second man was not one of the Barrys. The magistrates discharged both Barrys.

Two farmers from Spring Creek near Young then gave evidence. The first, James Dwyer, had no doubt that two of the cattle held by the police were his, and the second, John Russell, claimed ownership of the third.

A week later, the case resumed with another man, John Francis Ryan, in the dock beside Webster. Jerry was the first witness, and the *Courier*'s apparently verbatim report of his evidence provides a feeling for how he spoke, presumably with a Cork accent somewhat tempered by twenty-eight years in the colony.

Jerry said that between ten and eleven on a Saturday morning Webster had come to his house and said there were four head of fat cattle in his stockyard for sale:

> I asked him where he had brought them from; he said from near Burrowa. I asked him who was with him; he said a young fellow from near Burrowa. I said I did not care for that, and asked him for the name. He hesitated and said the name was Gallagher. I told him I would go and see the cattle after I had done serving the rations. Accordingly I went to the yard and saw there a young man with him [the prisoner, John Francis Ryan, was identified as that person].

After describing the cattle and their brands to the magistrates, Jerry said he had told the two men that it would be a pity to kill such cattle as some of them were in calf and very young. He added that he had informed them he did not want the cattle as he had purchased some the previous day. Jerry continued,

> I asked the prisoner George what he might want for them. Ryan said £12. I said if I wanted them I would not give more than half that sum for them. I walked away from the yard. George called after me and said: 'Mr Lehane, is the big cow worth £2?' I said: 'She is George, she is worth £3.' He said: 'Will you give £3 for her now?' I said: 'No George, I do not require her.' When I said that I would not give more than half, Ryan asked George if he was satisfied; George said no.

Jerry said he did not know what the men subsequently did with the cattle, but later he had seen three of them in one of his paddocks three miles away. Both prisoners were bailed to face trial at the next Yass Quarter Sessions. Before the petty sessions hearing ended, Sub Inspector Brennan told the magistrates Jerry had received an anonymous letter related to the case, which the *Courier* recorded as follows:

> Mr Lehane there is a young man of the name of Ryan in Yass lockup for stealing those cattle that was offered to you for sail he is left for the identifycation of you and your blackfellow.
>
> You ought to caution the Blackfellow to be very cautious in describin him as several men resemble each other the man is an honest hard-working man. I hope this wil make an impression on your mind.
>
> BURROWA

In early September, police located the fourth cow offered for sale and a man claiming to be its owner, John Lee, also a farmer from Spring Creek. This cow was with a mob of bush cattle near Reedy Creek, a fact that the *Courier* thought odd:

> [This] would lead to the supposition that it had been drafted away from its mates, and had made its way into the bush mob. It is not probable that the beast would have, of its own accord, singled itself out and quitted the other three which had been taken with it off the same run at Spring Creek.

The paper did not indicate who it thought did the drafting.

At the trial of Webster and Ryan in October, Jerry repeated his account of the conversation at the stockyard. He said he had thought from the start that the cattle were stolen. Appearing for Ryan, lawyer George Allman asked Jerry and the two other witnesses from Coppabella, Black Jack and Robert Pearson, a cook, whether they had had any previous contacts with his client. Jerry doubted he had seen Ryan before, and Pearson was sure he had not. He added, 'I took particular notice of the parties because I did not think the cattle were right'. Black Jack said he had seen Ryan at Binalong, but had never spoken to him.

Allman asked similar questions of two of the owners of the cattle, Dwyer and Russell, who both said they had known Ryan for years and considered him a hard-working and, in Russell's case, honest, man. Then the lawyer called as a witness Catherine Mehaffee of Binalong, who claimed Ryan had been building a hut for her at the time he was allegedly at Coppabella.

'Mr Allman addressed the jury in a forcible speech, contending that there were a multiplicity of cases of mis-identity,' the *Courier* reported.

> He appealed to the jury whether it was not more likely that the identification of the prisoner was safer in the hands of Mrs Mehaffee, who had engaged him to do work for her, who had actually noted down in her memorandum book the date of her contract with him to build the hut, than of the witnesses who could easily be mistaken in contact with a person with whom they had but little to do.

The jury was not swayed; both Webster and Ryan were found guilty and sentenced to two years' hard labour.

Miles was also in court in October 1867, continuing a long-running battle before the Murrumburrah magistrates with John Wilson, the man he had appointed in March to run his flour mill. Wilson's time as miller was fairly brief; Miles suspended him on 6 June and sacked him a week later. The October case was over an anonymous letter, dated 24 May 1867, that Wilson's wife had allegedly written to a wheat-grower customer of the mill saying Miles was robbing people by not delivering all the flour they were entitled to. Miles claimed that this libelled him.

Wilson's lawyer, Anthony Freestone, told the court his client was not guilty, but he also pleaded justification in that the alleged libel was true and for the public benefit. Miles did not have legal representation, which was probably a mistake. The mill's engineer, Thomas Bishop, provided support, denying the letter's claim that he agreed that Miles was robbing the people who sent their wheat to the mill. However, Freestone had no trouble sinking Miles' case, arguing that it had not been proved Wilson's wife wrote the letter – and, even if it had been, evidence would be needed that Wilson authorised her to do so.

Freestone asked Miles during the hearing, 'Did you ever say that if you could get John Wilson convicted you would shout champagne?' 'Never,' replied Miles to a probably sceptical audience. Miles had first taken Wilson to court four months earlier when he sacked him; the claim then was that Wilson had made statements calculated to injure him in his business. This case was dismissed. Wilson responded in September, claiming £10 from Miles in overtime payments.

Wilson told the magistrates he worked twelve to fifteen hours a day, and Miles had agreed that overtime would be paid at 1s 6d an hour. Miles had also given him free use of a cottage, with wood and as much flour as he needed; these were not offered on condition that he work beyond normal hours. Appearing for the defence, Miles' son John denied Wilson had been promised the cottage free and claimed he had often expressed gratitude for having it in exchange for the extra work.

Bishop, the mill's engineer, was called next, prompting an objection from Wilson who claimed he was an infidel. 'Do you believe in God and a future state?' asked one of the two magistrates hearing the case. 'Yes,' replied Bishop. That settled, Bishop said he was present when Miles offered the house, wood and flour, and agreed they were provided in

Fire destroyed the old flour mill about eighty years ago and a new mill was built on the site. It ceased operations some years ago.

exchange for extra work. The magistrates accepted this, so Miles had a win.

The next case, also brought by Wilson, followed immediately – a claim for £8 allegedly owed for early termination of his six-months contract. Wilson and Miles gave contradictory evidence about altercations they had had about dirty wheat. Miles said that on one occasion Wilson had ordered him out of the mill; Wilson denied this. The big question, though, was: who cut the mill's 'silk-dresser', used to produce fine flour? In the *Courier* of 5 June 1867, Miles offered a generous reward for information leading to conviction of the perpetrator:

£100 Reward

Whereas, on or about the 1st June, some evil-disposed person or persons did cut up and destroy certain SILK in the Steam Flour Mills of the undersigned. Now, I do hereby offer the above reward of One Hundred Pounds sterling for such information as will procure a conviction against the party within three months from this date.

MILES MURPHY
Steam Mills
Murrumburrah.

Miles told the magistrates he thought Wilson had cut the dresser, which was worth about £21. This was why he had suspended the miller. He had not accused Wilson publicly of the vandalism because he thought, 'as the plaintiff was fond of law', this might result in an action for libel against him. Cross-examined by Freestone, Miles agreed that thirty or forty people had access to the mill during the weekend when the damage was done, because the Murrumburrah Races were on. He said these included 'the serenaders' – presumably part of the races weekend entertainment.

Miles also said, though, that the part of the mill that housed the dresser was locked over the weekend – the key was 'generally left on the chimney piece in the parlour', and he 'handed it out' when work started each morning. He could not swear that it was not Wilson who first told him of the dresser being cut – it was either Wilson or Bishop. He could also not swear that his receipt of a summons from Wilson for abusive language was not the event that precipitated the miller's suspension.

Addressing the magistrates, Miles' lawyer George Allman said Wilson's demeanour in ordering his master out of his own mill when found fault with for damaging his flour gave Miles strong grounds for suspecting Wilson had cut the dresser. And he said Wilson had accused Miles falsely of robbing people. Allman argued that the terms of Miles' original agreement with Wilson had not been fulfilled, so Wilson was not entitled to damages.

In response, Freestone claimed that only Miles' fancies led him to believe Wilson had cut the dresser. Freestone said the agreement with Wilson provided that he should be paid the coach fare to Sydney if his services were no longer required. The magistrates accepted this, and decided Miles should pay £6 3s.

Miles' response was to immediately launch the libel case that was thrown out in October. Then Wilson served notice of action against Miles for malicious prosecution and Miles threatened to prosecute Mrs Wilson, the alleged writer of the libellous letter. Perhaps, though, the *Courier* was correct in suggesting that 'both parties may be led to think it wiser to drop a litigation which has now been going on for four or five months', because the new actions do not seem to have eventuated.

For Miles, 1867 was, among much else, a year of cutting ties with

Binalong, the settlement where his rise to prosperity and prominence had begun twenty years earlier when he opened the first hotel and store there. By now, the early hopes for the village, reflected in the prediction of a *Goulburn Herald* writer in 1854 that it would 'take a prominent position among the towns of the southern interior', had well and truly faded. A *Sydney Morning Herald* reporter who passed through in August 1865 was far from impressed. He described Binalong as 'small and unimportant' – one of those places 'that lead one to wonder what on earth they were ever established there for'. The 1871 census put its population at 189, compared with 1,284 for Yass but only 182 for Murrumburrah.

Miles had put the Swan Inn on the market in 1858 and 1864 but was still the owner and publican at the start of 1867. In February, a *Courier* advertisement announcing the sale of the hotel's furniture signalled his departure. The goods to be auctioned by William Howard, manager of the Murphy store in Binalong, were

Hair-bottomed Chairs
Mahogany and other Tables, sets of Drawers
Cheffonieres, Meat Safes
Sofas, Beds and Bedsteads
Hair and other Mattresses
Pictures, Looking Glasses
Kitchen Utensils, &c., &c., &c.

Miles apparently retained ownership of the Swan but brought in a tenant publican, Timothy Ryan, to run it. According to an advertisement in the *Courier*, sale of the stock-in-trade and goodwill of the Binalong store was completed in May 1868. Miles' 'late assistant' Howard and second son Felix, who was then in his early twenties, were the buyers.

As a prelude to this sale, Miles placed an advertisement in the *Courier* advising customers with outstanding accounts that these would soon be handed over to a solicitor for enforcement. This ran in every issue from March to September 1867, presumably in the expectation that repetition would ensure the message got through. Probably to help Felix fund his share of the purchase, Miles advanced him £500 some time before November 1867. Miles' will, drawn up that month, provided that the £500 be deducted from Felix's share of the deceased estate.

Back in Murrumburrah, problems at the flour mill were not the only source of aggravation for Miles. In early September, a petition 'numerously signed' by residents of the town was sent to the minister for lands calling for the withdrawal of his lease of the Murrumburrah pastoral run because it was holding back progress. John Dillon of the town's Commercial Hotel, who two years earlier had hosted the party celebrating the laying of the flour mill's foundation stone, was the petition's instigator.

The *Courier* correspondent, clearly a supporter of the petition, wrote,

> ...the residents in the township of Murrumburrah who have invested their capital in the place feel that there is a great hindrance to the further settlement of the town and neighbourhood in the fact that the lessee of the run has the power to run his sheep and cattle all over the unfenced lands of the town, and to impound the stock of the townspeople if found outside the immediate township boundary. It is true, I believe, that he does not usually exercise this right of impounding; but still he *has* the right, and people do not like to speculate in a place where they are in this respect dependent on the favour of any one great proprietor. Now, the population boundary of the township extends even beyond the Murrumburrah run (which only pays £30 a year to Government), and what the petitioners aim at is the withdrawal of the lease and the proclamation of the land for sale, and for a town common. It is thought here that if this were done, persons looking out for profitable employment for their money would be disposed to invest the same in the township and on the neighbouring farm lands, a good deal of which was surveyed some years back.

Miles, predictably, was not impressed, and according to the *Courier* wrote to the government claiming all or most of the signatures on the petition were fictitious. 'This, I am satisfied, is a mistake', wrote the *Courier* correspondent. 'Possibly the 'wish is father to the thought'.' He claimed Dillon had shown the petition to everybody whose signature it carried, and all had signed it themselves 'with the exception of some three or four, who, not being able to write, requested Mr Dillon to do the needful calligraphy'. In these cases, Dillon had fully explained the nature of the petition. Before posting the document, Dillon had taken it to the Murphys' place. Miles was away, but his son John had read it through with all but one signature attached – 'that of Mr English, landlord of the Travellers' Rest Hotel, who also read it and signed it last of all.' The correspondent went on,

> I have heard that the lessee (Mr Miles Murphy), on learning the nature of the petition, began to cross-examine everyone at a great rate as to who had signed it, threatening to impound all stock belonging to any who had done so. He succeeded so far with one individual as to send him up to Mr Dillon's, post haste, before the petition was closed, to get his name scratched off, which was accordingly done. Possibly under the pressure of similar threats, some others may have been induced to deny their signatures, or that they had authorised their names to be used – poor people, I say. If the prayer of the petition be granted, they need no longer fear Mr Murphy's impounding power.

Apparently, the prayer was not granted. The *Courier* does not tell us whether the matter was on the agenda when the under-secretary for lands, Michael Fitzpatrick, visited the town in August 1868 with the engineer-in-chief and superintendent of telegraphs and put up at Miles' Criterion Hotel. Murrumburrah was still listed in the early 1870s as a pastoral run with the Murphys as its lessees.

In early September 1867, while this drama was occupying many of the townsfolk, the newly appointed first Catholic bishop of Goulburn, the Right Rev. Dr William Lanigan, paid Murrumburrah a visit. The Murphys would have been pleased that, after being escorted into town 'by some hundred people or more, in carriages of various kinds and on horseback', the bishop and his vicar-general, the Very Rev. Dr McAlroy, took up residence at the Criterion Hotel. Over the next few years – while St Mary's, the town's Catholic church, was being built – visiting priests conducted Mass alternately at Dillon's Commercial Hotel and the Murphys' Criterion.

With 'all those who had gathered in the town thronged up into the verandah of the hotel', John Murphy, who seems to have been the family member most involved in the church, read an address welcoming the bishop. 'We, the Catholics of Murrumburrah and its district, beg to come before you to bid you a hearty and affectionate welcome, and to give expression to the feelings with which we hail your lordship amongst us,' he began. He said the district was large and populous, and 'the increase of the worshippers of our holy faith is now becoming so great that it is absolutely necessary that some steps should be taken for the production of church accommodation and a temple for Almighty God.' He requested the bishop's sanction for the designs drawn up for St Mary's (chapter 7), and for his assistance in 'causing the erection of our church at Murrumburrah to be proceeded with shortly'.

Replying, the bishop said he was delighted and encouraged by the fine Catholic spirit he had encountered everywhere in his travels through the diocese. He observed that Murrumburrah had few houses, and it seemed from the numbers of people present that 'they had dropped from the clouds to meet him.' Referring to the Irish origin of the Murrumburrah Catholics, he said they were descendants of a noble race, 'especially noble for their adherence to that faith which had been kept by them under all circumstances of difficulty and danger'. He praised their determination to build a church in the town.

After hearing confessions and celebrating Mass, Bishop Lanigan departed next morning for Wagga Wagga, escorted by 'the principal people' of Murrumburrah. The *Courier* continued,

> At about four miles out on the road, the bishop addressed the numerous escort which had followed him, saying that he would not wish to take them farther, and bidding them farewell in a pious and feeling address, expressing and showing how much he was affected by the warm and affectionate reception he had met with.

The following month family tragedy again struck the Murphys; a strong faith may have helped Miles and Anne cope with the death on 25 October of their youngest child, James. The nine-year-old died at St Augustine's School, Yass, where he was a boarder. The cause of death was pneumonia following measles. Dr Morgan O'Connor attended, but there was nothing he could do. Dean Hanly officiated at the burial at Milora cemetery, near Binalong. James was the fourth and last of the nine Murphy children to die in their parents' lifetime. Only one – Patrick (1849–50) – was lost as a baby. Robert, born in 1846, reached his twelfth birthday. Joseph, born the following year and a contemporary of William Lehane at Lyndhurst College (chapter 8), lived to sixteen.

11
Sectarian passions rise

Memories of Ben Hall and his companions may have been starting to fade by the end of 1867, but bushranging was not yet dead. After receiving a visit from the solitary Robert Bourke in August 1866, Coppabella – which the Hall gang had apparently left untouched – was targeted by another of the new breed of bushrangers, Blue Cap, during October 1867.

With a companion named Duce, Blue Cap – real name Robert Cottrell – held Jerry at gunpoint at his Reedy Creek house and took £6, a revolver and a saddle. Then the pair stuck up two travellers on the southern road – Jerry's neighbour Richard Julian and Globe Hotel publican Owen Hilly. Next they visited George Bodkin's Five Mile Creek Inn, and were served nobblers of brandy by his wife. As they drank, Mrs Bodkin overheard one of the men urge his companion to stick up the place. 'This the latter resolutely refused to do, saying that he would not as there were only two women in the house,' the *Courier* reported.

> Mrs Bodkin thus discovering what their intention had been when they first came to the inn, was naturally anxious for their departure, which took place shortly after, without their having committed any depredation there.

Jerry provided details of Blue Cap's visit to Coppabella in evidence to the Young Magistrates' Court in November 1867. The life of crime of this bushranger had come to an end when three travellers he attempted to stick up turned out to be mounted constables. They arrested him without resistance. Perhaps his poor sight contributed to his capture; the name Blue Cap came from a blue shade that he wore to protect his eyes.

Jerry told the court he was 'close by the house at a well which some men I had employed were cleaning out' when Blue Cap came up and asked for him by name. 'I told him I was Mr Lehane; the prisoner then ordered all of us to go up to the house,' he said. 'I asked him if he belonged to the police force. He said, 'No, I am a bushranger'.' Jerry said Blue Cap was armed (he gave no details), and went on,

> He marched us up to the verandah of the house, where we saw an accomplice of the prisoner's. He was also armed, and called himself the 'White Chief'. I believe his name is Jerry Duce. The prisoner gave the men in charge of Duce, and then ordered me to accompany him to my private office. Prisoner then said he wanted a revolver I had. I gave it to him. He then ordered me to open a certain drawer in my desk, in which were several papers and a pocket book, the latter containing six one-pound notes. He opened the book and extracted the money. He searched about for more money, but found none. He took a double-barrel gun, which he returned as he was leaving. He ordered me to proceed with him to the stable. He took a saddle, but being told it belonged to one of the labourers he put it back, and took another belonging to my stockman. The whole of the articles stolen, including the money, I value at about £20 10s.

Blue Cap, described in one newspaper report as 'quite a youth, with none of the commanding bearing or ferocious appearance popularly associated with the leaders of this class of criminals', pleaded guilty to three armed robberies – including the Coppabella stick-up – at the Wagga Wagga Assizes in April 1868. Judge Faucett sentenced him to ten years' hard labour on the roads. He reportedly looked 'dreadfully ill' at the trial. Earlier, he had apparently confided to a reporter that 'the continual hunting about' that he had experienced, and the hardships endured from lack of shelter and rest, had 'so thoroughly sickened him of the highwayman's life that nothing would ever induce him to resume it on regaining his liberty'.

In mid-1867, this unlikely leader had at least four followers. The gang's bushranging activities included, during August, a visit by one member to Jerry's other station, Narraburra, where apparently he hoped to obtain a saddle and firearms. During this raid, according to court reports in October, the gang member, Black Jack (not Jerry's employee of that name), was an accomplice in the attempted rape by a man called Black Bob of the wife of a Narraburra stockman. Bob was sentenced to three years' gaol with hard labour for this crime. Jack and two other Blue

Cap gang members captured shortly after the Narraburra raid – 'as weedy scrubbers as could well be imagined', according to the *Courier* – received ten years' hard labour sentences for a string of armed robberies.

Twenty-year-old William Lehane, then managing Narraburra for his father, had another problem on his hands in early 1868. A seventy-one-year-old shepherd, Patrick Ringwood, had accused Walter Gaffney, a fellow shepherd with whom he shared a hut on the station, of committing an 'unnatural offence'. Gaffney, according to the *Courier*'s report of the Yass Magistrates' Court hearing in April, was 'apparently about 64 or 65 years of age'. Ringwood said the offence had been committed every night for more than three months, except for a week when the two shepherds were separately 'on the road'. He had not fled because Gaffney had threatened to kill him, but he 'had told Willie Lehane that prisoner had committed the offence'.

At the trial in Goulburn six months later, Ringwood told the jury Gaffney 'nearly choked me and beat me with a piece of bark' when he offered resistance. One night, after the two men had shared a bottle of rum,

> he beat me so seriously with a piece of bark that I did not know what was going on. After we had been in bed some time he got the spade to kill me. I ran out, and after some time I came back and found prisoner with all my things going to burn them.

The defence argued that Ringwood's claims were entirely uncorroborated, and the jury accepted this and acquitted Gaffney. Earlier, the prosecuting lawyer, the solicitor-general, had admonished spectators in the court. 'There was no necessity for so many persons voluntarily remaining in court, some actually making it a matter for laughter and jest,' the *Goulburn Herald* reported him saying. 'One would think it was the gallery of a shilling theatre rather than a tribunal of justice.'

The big popular diversion around this time was the visit to Australia of Queen Victoria's fourth child and second son, Prince Alfred, the Duke of Edinburgh. The twenty-three-year-old prince and his entourage stepped ashore at Adelaide from the royal yacht *Galatea* on 30 October 1867. The town was reportedly in a state of great excitement. Activities during the South Australian leg of the tour included 'a trip kangarooing' and a grand corroboree. The Aborigines who performed the corroboree,

Prince Alfred, Duke of Edinburgh.

'to the evident gratification of the Prince', carried a large red, white and blue flag inscribed in gold 'Goolwa blackfellow big one glad see him Queen piccaninny'.

The *Yass Courier* caught the mood, saying the prince's visit 'will be productive of a fresh assurance that British subjects were loyal to the throne, when occupied by virtue, in whatever part of the globe they may be sojourners'. However, it was not impressed by his reception in Melbourne: 'vulgar curiosity and obtrusiveness formed such a large element of the demonstrative loyalty there as almost to destroy the effect of the latter'. It feared the prince 'must be wearied with that vulgar flunkeyism which allows him no rest, and insists on trying to amuse him with that which must absolutely produce nausea'.

In Yass, as elsewhere in the colony, a holiday with stores closed and flags flying marked the prince's arrival in Sydney on 22 January 1868. A *Courier* leader predicted an 'unprecedented gala day' in Sydney and 'thousands of hearts joyous to receive the representative of a Queen who rules by the love of her subjects'. Early the following month, the paper carried an advertisement for an issue of the *Illustrated Sydney News* containing a two-page portrait of the prince and engravings of the *Galatea* and accompanying fleet entering the Heads, the Triumphal Arch and landing at Circular Quay, the Government Gate Arch, the South Head Road Arch, and fireworks in the Domain. In early March, *Courier* readers were treated to a little drollery:

> Why was his Royal Highness the Duke of Edinburgh when leaving his noble ship like the sentimental youth quitting the side of his sweetheart? Because he left his gal a tear. The inventor of the foregoing is to be handed over to Mr Sub-inspector Brennan [the local head of police] immediately.

Then, on the afternoon of Thursday 12 March, an assassin's shot rang out at a royal picnic at harbour-side Clontarf. Bystanders grabbed the assailant, Henry James O'Farrell, and immediately tried to lynch him. 'The police interfered, and succeeded in taking him away in a steamer,' the *Courier* told its readers. The prince was conveyed to Government House, where doctors attended the wound from a bullet that had entered his back two inches from the spine and lodged in the abdomen. He made a speedy recovery.

The next day in Sydney 20,000 people attended an 'indignation meeting' in Hyde Park. The *Courier* reported that 'the utmost excitement prevailed' when 'the painful news' reached Yass.

> There was a general feeling that the populace should have been permitted to have claimed their own law on O'Farrell, that they should have dealt with him as cruelly as they thought his crime justified. It was wisdom that they were not permitted to do so.

Among the most indignant in Yass was the Rev. Frederick Lillingston, rector of St Clement's Church of England. His name headed the list of those calling a public meeting at the courthouse 'to give expression to their most heartfelt sympathy with His Royal Highness, to their horror and indignation at the dastardly and cowardly attempt made upon his life, and their sincere hope of his speedy recovery'. This meeting, which attracted an attendance of 150 to 200, resolved that a suitable address should be sent to the Queen from the people of Yass.

Lillingston was a frequent writer of long letters to the *Courier*. One in September 1867 accused the Catholic Dr Morgan O'Connor of sounding like an agent of the Irish revolutionary Fenians when he told a meeting in Boorowa that the persecution of Irish Catholics had no parallels in the annals of civilised Europe. Lillingston, who disputed that the Irish were especially badly dealt with, was often in conflict with O'Connor, once accusing him of 'Celtic trickery' and claiming to be unable to contend with him 'in the use of language not generally heard among gentlemen'.

The disputes of these two prominent townsmen were perhaps symbolic of a growing Protestant–Catholic rift in the community. The two clashed frequently as members of the Yass Hospital committee, and Miles was at the centre of one eruption. He had guaranteed to pay the fee of a patient called Hooper, but the payment was slow to arrive. O'Connor undertook to obtain it, but Lillingston was not satisfied with his promise to do so. O'Connor responded, 'I suppose you would consider it sufficient to give your word in order to get a patient into hospital; and my word I suppose is as good as yours.'

Shortly afterwards, he responded in similarly mild tones to an anonymous letter to the *Courier* that claimed he had been party to an attempt to eliminate Protestants from the hospital committee, turning it 'into a tool in the hands of an ambitious priesthood'. O'Connor wrote, 'I would as soon see the hospital governed by Protestants as Catholics... Its interests would be equally safe in the hands of either.' Lillingston would have none of this, claiming in reply that the reason why the committee still had a Protestant majority despite Catholic attempts to stack it was 'the absolute impossibility of finding suitable men among their own body'. He said most of the Protestant members absented themselves from committee meetings because it was 'next to impossible for any gentleman of feeling to sit in the same room' as the Catholics.

News of activities of the Fenians, who were planning an armed uprising aimed at securing Irish independence, fanned the sectarian flames. An event that stirred passions in early 1868 was the execution in England of three men whose attempt to rescue Fenian prisoners resulted in the fatal shooting of a British policeman. Feelings ran hot even in the Australian bush. The *Courier* correspondent at Murringo, between Young and Boorowa, was distressed to hear 'much pro and con argument... during which many hot words have been used, and threats of personal violence uttered.'

In this climate, many saw the shooting of Prince Alfred as part of a Fenian conspiracy rather than the act of a deranged individual. Lawyer George Allman wrote the address that the Yass indignation meeting resolved to send to the Queen; as well as expressing sorrow and abhorrence for what had happened and loyalty to the monarch and government, he broached the Fenian issue. In words accepted by O'Connor and Father Richard Duigan of St Augustine's, as well as by Lillingston and other local Protestants, the address expressed 'our utmost hatred and detestation of that secret society, organisation or brotherhood commonly known as Fenianism' and pledged utmost endeavours, if called upon, to 'suppress and eradicate it from the land'.

For many Irish Catholics, the choice may have seemed to be: join the bandwagon of public indignation or keep a low profile. Church leaders were prominent among those adopting the first course. In Sydney, Archdeacon McEncroe told a congregation that no crime during his thirty-six years in the colony 'could be compared in wickedness and infamy' with the attack on Prince Alfred. At St John's College, University of Sydney, Dr Forrest prepared an address to the prince that was adopted by a special meeting of the college council. After expressing deep sympathy, and horror at the 'atrocious and cowardly attempt' made on his life, this assured Alfred,

> The gloom which this crime has cast over the whole colony will we fervently hope, by God's blessing, be soon dispelled by your speedy recovery and restoration to perfect health. We desire also to convey to your Highness the assurance of our attachment to the person of her most Gracious Majesty your Royal mother and the laws and institutions under which we live, and our warm appreciation of the kindly and estimable qualities which have won for you personally the affection and good-will of the whole community.

In Yass, plans were quickly made after the indignation meeting for a second public meeting, this time to express 'our satisfaction at the vigorous steps being taken by Government to crush Fenianism in New South Wales'. The seventy-two people who signed the advertisement calling this meeting, nine days after the first, included both the Rev. Lillingston and Morgan O'Connor. Three prominent Catholics headed the list – Dr Isidore Blake JP, Father Duigan and another priest, Father William O'Brien.

The principal anti-Fenian step taken by the government was a drastic one – incorporation of the British Treason Felony Act into the colonial statutes. A public notice signed by the premier, Henry Parkes, urged 'all loyal subjects' to inform the authorities

The old St Augustine's Church – now the Mt Carmel Convent chapel.

about people liable to prosecution under this Act. Such people included any who 'shall use any language disrespectful to her Most Gracious Majesty or shall factiously avow a determination to refuse to join in any loyal toast or demonstration in honour of her Majesty…' Those convicted faced two years' gaol, with or without hard labour.

The 'numerous' people who turned up for the Yass anti-Fenian meeting applauded fiery rhetoric from, among others, Rev. Lillingston and the minister of the Yass Presbyterian church, Rev. John Gibson. They adopted resolutions describing Fenianism as diabolically wicked and giving their 'entire approbation' to enactment of the Treason Felony Act. A further resolution moved by Lillingston, 'that we pledge ourselves to assist the Government by all the means in our power to crush out any, even the slightest, signs of Fenianism which may appear in the country', was carried by acclamation.

Lillingston told the meeting that some said there were no Fenians in Australia, or at all events no Fenianism, but 'he did not altogether agree with that'. John Paterson of Illalong went further, saying 'some people imagined that there were no Fenians out here. He knew of their existence himself (Hear, hear)'. At least one brave soul was prepared to publicly swim against the tide – a teacher, Henry Sullivan, who also defied convention by attaching his name rather than a pseudonym to a letter to the *Courier*. Sullivan was witness at the burial at Bookham nearly two years later of a thirteen-month-old child of John and Honora Vicq, and so presumably was a friend of that family, and possibly of Jerry's as well. He was a contemporary of William Lehane's at Lyndhurst College in the early 1860s. In his letter Sullivan challenged Paterson to either

> give up the names of *his* alleged Fenians to the authorities, as he ought to do as a loyal man and a magistrate of the territory, that they may be proceeded against under the lately passed Treason Felony Act, and by so doing relieve the community from the terror they must be living under now of being murdered (murder and Fenianism being synonymous terms according to several of the speakers); or expect to be looked upon as a person who, to pander to a vile and truculent excitement, has publicly stated a deliberate and wanton falsehood.

He added,

It may bring on me the imputation of being a Fenian, but I cannot help saying that all the speeches delivered at last Monday's meeting appear to me very pretty specimens of bunkum and blatherskite.

The editor of the *Courier* probably had some sympathy with this view. He wrote that public opinion had made strong laws against Fenianism necessary, whether or not it actually existed in the colony. But the time had come to calm down: 'The longer the agitation is kept on foot, the more disturbed will be society, and that which may be possibly a phantom may take the form of reality.'

At his trial at the end of March, O'Farrell was found guilty of unlawful wounding with intent to murder and sentenced to death. Prince Alfred departed on the *Galatea* in early April having, according to a press report, expressed a wish that his assailant not be hanged. Whether or not that was the case, the execution went ahead as planned a few weeks later. It was reported in the 25 April issue of the *Courier*, which also noted that news of the shooting would be reaching England about then – a reminder of how slowly news travelled between Australia and the other side of the world before the completion of the telegraph connection in 1872.

In late July, the colonial governor, the Earl of Belmore, ordered the publication of a Buckingham Palace despatch dated 1 May announcing that the Queen had been told of the attempt to kill her son. 'Although it is inevitable that her Majesty should have been greatly moved at intelligence so unexpected, the Colonists of New South Wales may be assured that it has not impaired her appreciation of the hearty and unanimous enthusiasm which has marked the reception of His Royal Highness in New South Wales and in all the other British communities which he has visited,' her spokesman advised.

In late June, three months after the indignation meeting in Yass, the *Courier* noted that the town's loyal address to the Queen had not been sent yet; the sheets left at the town's banks and stores for signing were still there. This prompted letters to the editor lamenting an 'aggravated insult to the Queen' and the 'supineness' of the people of Yass. The address was never sent.

Away from the big town excitements, in Murrumburrah, 1868 got off to a good start for the Murphys, first at the races. The refreshment booth they set up at the course for the New Year's Day carnival was 'pretty well patronised', as were those of the other two publicans, John Dillon and John English. John Murphy fielded two winning horses and Miles' Black Bess came first in the Ladies' Purse. Unfortunately, this mare succumbed to snakebite at the end of the year, before she could provide Miles with further champions.

Things were also looking up for the flour milling business. In early February, the *Courier* reported that the Murrumburrah mill had despatched large quantities of flour to Sydney over the past two months. Six weeks later, Miles placed an advertisement seeking teams to carry 100 tons of flour from the mill to the railhead at Mittagong. The ad also offered five shillings per bushel for wheat in any quantity and a higher price for 'very superior samples' – presumably to try to ensure that the mill could continue to meet the demand for its flour. In early April, the news from Murrumburrah was that

> during the past week this little township has worn rather a busy appearance from the number of drays, waggons &c. passing through. Many of these were engaged to take flour down to Sydney from Mr Murphy's mill, which has been working late hours for a long time past.

The previous month, Miles' tenders for supplying maize, oats, bran, hay and straw for the police horses at Murrumburrah and Binalong had been accepted. In April, work started on the erection of a quartz-crushing machine at Demondrille Creek near Murrumburrah, site of a minor gold rush. This followed an offer made by Miles, in company with rival hotelier John Dillon and storekeepers J. and G. Barnes, 'to guarantee a liberal bonus to any machine proprietor who shall erect the *first* proper Crushing Machine in any suitable locality near Murrumburrah.'

In July, Father Duigan made one of his regular visits to Murrumburrah. The Murphys' Criterion Hotel was crowded for his Thursday celebration of Mass, at which, the *Courier* reported, he delivered 'a very moving discourse'. Duigan stayed on until the following Monday when he performed the marriage ceremony for John Johnston, a bootmaker, and Winifred Murphy, daughter of local farmers Patrick and Mary Murphy.

Although the venue for this, and subsequent celebrations attended by sixty or seventy guests, was Dillon's Commercial Hotel, Miles chaired proceedings. According to the *Courier* correspondent, 'in a short but emphatic speech [he] stated his high opinion of the bridegroom, and of the beauty of the bride, sentiments which were warmly responded to by those present'. After an 'excellent' dinner, dancing commenced

> ...and was kept up with spirit till daylight. The house was thronged with visitors, many from a distance, and the fun produced was something tremendous. Guns were fired off at intervals all round the place, and had it not been so wet and stormy, a grand illumination in the shape of bonfires would have added to the general gaiety. Amongst other things a sonorous serenade of tin boxes, understood as 'kettling', formed no small element in the programme... From all I hear I should judge that there has not been such a wedding known in Murrumburrah before. ...the amount of animal life and spirit exhibited was certainly encouraging to such as might be disposed to lament the decay of the old British stamina in these usually sultry regions. ...one after the other the special favourites of the town were hoisted up to the ceiling, waving their hats amid enthusiastic cheers and laughter.

Three weeks later, 'a few of the congregation' of St Augustine's Church, Yass, met at the Globe Hotel to launch a testimonial fund for the thirty-year-old Father Duigan 'as a small acknowledgment of his services in the mission'. A healthy £102 was quickly raised, with another £10 to £15 expected by the time of the 8 September presentation. Apparently the real purpose of this collection was to pay off debts Duigan had accumulated through excessive alcohol consumption – perhaps the recent excitements in Yass and the long weekend at Murrumburrah had contributed to his problem. Historian Father Brian Maher records that Bishop Lanigan reprimanded Duigan for taking up a testimonial to himself while his mission still had a debt of £100.

Duigan was back in Murrumburrah at the end of September, this time in company with Lanigan. After celebrating Mass at Dillon's hotel, they proceeded to the hilltop site where St Mary's Church was to be built. There the bishop consecrated the foundation stone and exhorted local Catholics to subscribe to the building fund, which had about £140 – a quarter of the required sum – in hand.

Duigan was in trouble again in March 1870 after diverting to himself

£100 from £120 sent from Goulburn by the vicar-general for church purposes. His period in Yass was controversial for reasons besides his drinking and debts, but he seems to have had many admirers, including the Lehane and Murphy families. He makes further appearances in the story in chapters 13, 14, 15 and 16.

12

Black and white

Loyal fervour was still running strongly in Yass in July 1868, and the first visit to the town of the Earl of Belmore, colonial governor since late 1867, provided an opportunity to display it. A meeting of prominent townsmen, including Morgan O'Connor and the Rev. Lillingston, decided a triumphal arch should be erected. They also composed an appropriate welcoming address, declaring 'our deep-felt loyalty to the Queen and respect for the Constitution under which we live' and hoping the governor and the Countess of Belmore would enjoy their tour of southern NSW.

The arch, which cost £23 to build and was paid for by public donations (O'Connor gave £1 11s and Lillingston £1 11s 6d – no contribution from Jerry or Miles), spanned the main street at the entrance to the town. The *Courier* described it as 'really handsome and pretty':

The governor and his entourage enter Yass through a triumphal arch.

The centre arch had a span of fifteen feet, the two side arches of eight feet each: the piers were massive (eight feet) and tastefully decorated with foliage: across the top of the arch, on both sides, were painted (the letters ornamental and neatly formed) the words – 'Welcome to Yass'. Surmounting this line, and immediately under the curve of the main arch, royalty was represented by a crown, resting over a wreath: below this was a coronet, with the motto of the Belmore family – 'Virtus semper viridis' – supported on either side, and at a little higher elevation, by the escutcheon of his Excellency. The piers had flags, on the one side containing the rose, thistle, and shamrock, and on the other the Southern Cross. Projecting from the arches were a large number of red, white and blue flags, spearheads &c. The *tout ensemble* was effective, well designed, and creditable to the town.

On the afternoon appointed for the governor's arrival, a welcoming party of fourteen or fifteen carriages and about 150 horsemen assembled outside the town despite drenching rain. A 'party of scouts' was sent to the top of a nearby hill, and 'shortly after four o'clock a lusty hallo gave intimation that the expected visitors were in sight'. A 'loud and hearty cheer' greeted the governor, and a procession – two-horse vehicles first, then one-horse vehicles, with the horsemen following in twos – formed behind the official party, which also included the premier, James Martin. The procession 'proceeded at a rapid rate towards the town', stopping at Colls' Commercial Hotel (the Globe, the previous year's vice-regal residence in Yass, missed out this time). There, Cornelius O'Brien read the address of welcome before taking the earl on a tour in his carriage. The governor praised the courthouse, the gaol, and the Catholic and Anglican churches, but was disappointed by the hospital building and concerned that the town's drainage seemed defective.

In the evening, the arch was 'beautifully lighted up' and at the top of the town a 'huge' bonfire 'blazed up right royally'. Despite the rain, a large gathering congregated around the fire, and 'on more than one occasion the National Anthem was shouted with a will by probably more than one hundred Stentorian voices'. The *Courier* reported that the governor was impressed by Yass, and had remarked that

> if he had anticipated the gratifying reception accorded him by the inhabitants, and the importance of the town, he should have so arranged as to have been able to have remained a day at least.

Yass in 1868, looking over the river and up Cooma Street. St Clement's Church is on the left, St Augustine's on the right. The telegraph line runs up the right-hand side of the main road.

After an early start next morning, the Belmores stopped for breakfast at Thomas Drummond's (formerly John Vicq's) Bookham Inn at Bogolong, where Jerry's twenty-one-year-old niece Catherine, a daughter of Daniel Lehane, may have served them. The host and hostess had 'every requisite' prepared for the vice-regal party, the *Courier* tells us, and the countess expressed herself well satisfied with the arrangements. 'A number of the neighbouring settlers were in attendance to welcome his Excellency on his arrival', but they probably did not include Jerry and Hannah because two days later the couple's second child, Josephine, was born at their Reedy Creek home. The first, Jeremiah, was then nearly four.

Catherine's employment at the inn comes to light from reports of the inquest into the death of an elderly carrier, George Smith, who stopped there for the night two weeks after the governor's visit. He was on his way from Goulburn to Albury, 'carrying luggage for the nuns', according to the *Courier*. A man whom Smith drank with that night, Michael Murphy, admitted adding a patent medicine, Chlorodyne, to his last drink and was arrested on suspicion of causing the death. Murphy claimed he meant the Chlorodyne to ease Smith's pain and help him sleep. The question was: did he deliberately administer an excessive quantity?

Chlorodyne seems to have been one of the most dangerous of the medicines freely available in the 1860s. Like many others, it was advertised as offering miraculous benefits; a dose of Chlorodyne, newspaper readers were told, would immediately relieve consumption in all its stages, coughs, whooping cough, asthma, bronchitis, fever, ague, diphtheria, hysteria, rheumatism, diarrhoea, spasms, colic and renal and uterine diseases. The risks of an overdose were well known. A Yass druggist, C.C. Finch, told the inquest forty-five drops was 'the largest dose a man could take safely', and Dr Allan Campbell, who performed a post-mortem examination on Smith, said Chlorodyne was 'a poison of a very deadly kind'.

Catherine told the inquest that at about midnight she saw Murphy take one of the glasses of liquor Mrs Drummond had poured for the two men and go on his knees near the fire:

> He poured something out of a bottle; he did not put it in in drops, but put it in all together. He then gave the tumbler to the deceased and the deceased took it out of his hand. The deceased then drank it; he shook his head and said it was very strong...after the deceased had drank the glass he said he had pains in his inside...about half an hour after he drank the glass he went to bed.

Smith was found dead the next morning. On Dr Campbell's recommendation, his stomach and the remaining contents of the Chlorodyne bottle were sent to the government analyst in Sydney for examination. The analyst, Charles Watt, reported back that the composition of Chlorodyne, as a proprietary medicine, was kept secret by the manufacturer, 'but it is known to contain a considerable proportion of chloroform, spirit, extract of liquorice, and the active portion of cayenne pepper, with other substances to thicken the mixture.' He said some authorities had stated that Chlorodyne contains small portions of prussic acid [hydrogen cyanide] and morphia, 'but I did not detect either of these substances in the sample in question'.

Watt said a thorough analysis of Chlorodyne 'would involve a considerable amount of time and trouble, as it is evidently prepared so as to offer every difficulty in determining its exact composition.' He had not undertaken this. His examination of the stomach had yielded slight evidence of chloroform, and had suggested Smith vomited before death. Having considered this meagre additional information, the inquest jury concluded it had insufficient evidence to determine the cause of Smith's death. The *Courier* was most unimpressed by Watt's 'thorough incompetency'. People had known 'since Chlorodyne was first introduced into quack practice' that it could contain prussic acid and morphia, the paper commented. Watt 'leaves us still to grope in the dark. He absolutely thickens the fog.'

Another sad death occurred three months later, that of Coppabella stockman Black Jack. The *Courier* was not sure of the circumstances, saying the death of the Aboriginal, who was 'not more than 23 or 25 years of age', was variously accounted for.

> It has been said he became insane under the influence of a sunstroke, and procuring a horse at Reedy Creek he galloped off in the direction of Binalong; however, he was some days absent, and when found in the bush by the police was shouting out as many a maniac would do.

The paper added,

> It is scarcely probable that his malady was caused by a *coup-de-soleil* as the skulls of the aboriginals are proof against such disasters. It is stated that he had been drinking at Binalong; whether this is true or not we cannot say.

Having conveyed Black Jack to the Binalong lock-up, the police sent word to Coppabella. As Jerry was in Yass, Hannah received the message and 'ordered a cart to be taken at once to Binalong to bring Black Jack home'. The stockman was still alive when he arrived, but died about an hour later.

When the news reached Jerry at Yass, 'that gentleman expressed his deep regret', the *Courier* reported. He described Black Jack as a 'valuable and faithful servant' and 'directed that a funeral should be furnished commensurate with the good feelings he had always entertained for the deceased'. Intriguingly, the paper went on to say Jerry had reared Black Jack 'from almost infancy'.

Earlier reports provide a little more information. One, from July 1864, quotes evidence Black Jack gave at the trial, in Gundagai, of an alleged cattle thief who left a bullock at Coppabella. He told the court he had been 'stockman for Mr Lehane' for eight or nine years, which suggests Jerry employed him soon after moving to Coppabella in 1854. He must have been very young – perhaps eleven or twelve years old – when first taken on. When he was called as a witness, the defendant's lawyer 'thought it necessary that the Christian doctrine of the witness should be tested' before he was sworn. 'His Honor put some questions as to his religious belief,' the *Courier* reported. 'He said he went to chapel, and often heard Dean Hanly. This being considered sufficient, he was sworn.'

Black Jack's next court appearances followed Jerry's arrest for allegedly stealing a bullock from John P. Sheahan (chapter 8). He told the initial magistrate's hearing in October 1865 that he had 'lived with Mr Lehane about ten years', which seems to confirm that he joined the household after the move to Coppabella rather than having been raised by Jerry from almost infancy. When called to give evidence the following month after the arrest of Jerry's nephew Jeremiah, he was again first questioned about his religious beliefs. The *Gundagai Herald* reported him saying,

> I am a Christian. I never have been baptised. Sometimes I go to church at the Roman Catholic church at Jugiong. Miss Lehane [presumably Jerry's daughter Ellen, then aged twenty-one] taught me all I know. I don't know the name of the book I have been sworn on. I have heard talk of the Bible, but don't know anything about it. I have never heard of people being sent to gaol for not telling the truth. Have heard (laughing) that there is such a place as hell, but don't know anything about it, whether there is or is not. I never pray. I have heard people say there is such a place as Heaven. I don't know (laughing) whether there is or not.

The *Herald* commented sanctimoniously,

> We think that it is to be deplored that benighted beings, such as this, should be sworn…the administering of oaths to such persons must naturally have a bad moral effect on bystanders, and tend to turn a very solemn act into a farce.

Presumably the paper saw nothing incongruous in expecting that the young man it condemned, only about twenty years old, should behave like a true Englishman in court, an institution that could scarcely be more alien to his people.

We will never know what caused the apparent fit of madness that led to Black Jack's death. But however well he was treated on Coppabella, and however highly regarded for his skills as a stockman, such an outcome should perhaps not cause too much surprise. The squatters first entered the region with their sheep and cattle only about forty years earlier and, despite sporadic resistance, the Aborigines were soon driven from their land. Black Jack was one who found work and sanctuary under the new order, but what happened to his family? He witnessed the depredations of disease and alcohol on his people, and saw them treated with disdain and much worse. He was probably aware of the prevailing educated view, even among the charitable, that the Aboriginal race was a low form of humanity destined to die out soon.

A lecturer at the Yass Mechanics Institute in May 1866, the Rev. W. Ridley, was applauded for his 'feeling remarks on the claims of our black brethren upon us' and disputed that 'it was an 'ordination of Providence' that the Aborigines 'should be exterminated'. He contended that they were a very ancient race, with languages that in many respects 'bore an affinity to the Latin and Greek', and that this showed that 'at some remote period they had been a civilised people'. Unfortunately, 'their forgetfulness of God and neglect of civilisation' had led them to sink into barbarism.

The liberal-minded *Courier* was also charitably inclined, but had no doubt that the Aborigines were doomed. Noting in April 1873 that settlers now occupied, 'in permanency', their ancient hunting grounds, it went on,

> The white race has subverted the vital conditions of the aboriginal's existence. He has deprived him of his old habits in parts; and in part superadded to them the worse 'white' habits. It is impossible for the black race to be raised. Individuals of it may burst their 'birth's invidious bar' and climb to some eminence above their kin; but the race, as a race, is doomed.

The *Courier*'s response was to advocate that a benevolent colonial government provide an 'adequate supply' of material comforts for the remaining Aborigines. 'Let the blacks be fed. They will not trouble us much longer. They are fast dying out; soon will their places know them no more.' It called for something much more generous than the long-established annual distribution of blankets on Queen Victoria's birthday, an event whose Yass manifestation it had chronicled annually since its launch in 1857.

That year the blankets arrived two months late, in July; the *Courier* condemned the government's failure to keep faith with 'those poor half-naked creatures'. The following month, 'a very large number' camped near town and 'several of the townsfolk visited their camp for the purpose of witnessing a 'corobora''. Some of the blacks were later seen drunk, 'a circumstance little to the credit of those who supplied them with liquor'. In 1858, the blankets were late again, and Aborigines lingered around town waiting for the handout. 'From their present condition one would imagine that the blacks must have sadly degenerated – both in bodily strength and appearance,' the *Courier* observed.

> They have become an indolent, inactive, and miserable looking race, and it must now be a somewhat difficult matter to work themselves up to the necessary pitch of excitement to enact a 'corrobora' with anything like the violent and singular gestures adopted in former times.

In 1860, only eight adults and five 'piccaninnies' turned up for the blanket distribution, compared with twenty-six adults and eight children the year before, leading the paper to conclude that, 'as in other thickly inhabited parts of the colony', extinction was approaching rapidly. In 1867, it again reported that the number claiming blankets was fast diminishing, and those who remained were chiefly half-castes. A corroboree near Yass a few months later was

> a miserable representation of ancient greatness... A few years more and these once powerful tribes will have dwindled into insignificance; and later still, all that will be known of a corroboree must be gathered from the records of the past.

The blanket distribution in May 1868 attracted 'very small numbers indeed' compared with a decade earlier. Two months later, on the evening that the governor, the Earl of Belmore, was in residence, King Andy, self-described king of the Yass blacks, turned up at the Commercial Hotel and, according to the *Courier*, presented his 'card' in an envelope.

> His Excellency left his room to see the sable monarch; and the Hon. the Premier presented Andy with half-a-crown, and it is said with his own hands placed a 'crown of laurel' upon his dusky brow – at any rate, he placed a number of laurel leaves round the rim of Andy's hat.

The previous year, Andy, whom the *Courier* described as 'of a lazy disposition and, like many others of his tribe...frequently seen the worse of drink', claimed he had gone to Sydney to see the Duke of Edinburgh and been spoken to by him.

Possibly the pain of separation from his people, and of observing the life most Aborigines now led, the humiliations they suffered and their lack of hope for the future, lay behind Black Jack's fatal flight. It's good to know that Jerry mourned him, and that he had apparently been well treated and respected by the Lehane family. A week before Black Jack took off, Mary Matthews, owner of a hotel at Boorowa, made a similar unexpected flight into the bush near Coppabella. She was on her way to Jugiong, but near Bogolong 'sprang from the coach and made for the bush', the *Courier* told its readers.

> She was too fleet for the driver, and in the absence of any person to take charge of his horses, he was obliged to allow the unfortunate woman to pursue her insane course through the wild bush.

Her naked body was found beside a creek two months later. Perhaps the weather precipitated both events. The *Courier* reported in early November that 'scorching heat' had prevailed for some time. One afternoon a high wind raised a dense column of dust, 'darkening the atmosphere for some fifteen minutes'.

Perhaps the heat also contributed to a dispute in Murrumburrah in November 1868 over where a 'grand ball and supper' planned by the town's newly formed cricket club should be held. The *Courier* correspondent noted with surprise early in the month that Miles' offer of his flour mill as the venue had been accepted despite the availability of an 'abundance' of suitable accommodation. 'I decline to comment further on this subject, only just mentioning that the above decision does not seem to have given general satisfaction,' he wrote, hinting that something fishy was going on.

Thomas McMahon, the club's honorary secretary, responded with a letter in the next *Courier*. He claimed there was 'an unanimous feeling throughout (with the exception of one party) of the greatest satisfaction' with the decision to hold the party in the mill.

> I presume there is no further proof required than to submit to you the result of votes, recorded by ballot, as to whose house should provide the ball, viz.: Mr Miles Murphy, 12; Mr John Dillon, 5; Mr John English, 4.

The rejoinders this attracted from both the first reporter and the *Courier* correspondent at the nearby settlement of Coramundra (now

Cootamundra) made it clear that another Murphy–Dillon spat was in progress. The Coramundra correspondent, obviously well briefed by the Dillon camp, claimed the Commercial Hotel had offered the ball, supper and drinks to the cricket club on 'terms to be decided by itself'. He found it hard to understand how this 'liberal' proposal – which would have given the club the use of 'two fine rooms, one of which is much larger (30x18) than the space available at the mill' – could have been rejected. He thought the mill floor would make 'a very queer dancing room as…the posts or supports to the upper storey would be very much in the way'. In addition,

> There is another evil to be apprehended, namely – that as soon as the Terpsichoring commence, they will most likely bring upon their devoted heads any amount of dust flour &c, which their performances will shake through the floor above. All I hear from Murrumburrah leads me to believe that the public (*ie*, not the club) is rather disappointed to find that such bad arrangements have been made, and it is thought extremely shabby that, after enjoying so many free balls and suppers at the Commercial, the club, when it has money, should spend it elsewhere. Such thoughts as these are, I think, very likely to affect the sale of tickets, as, in the days of comfortable ball-rooms, few respectable people will go to a place like that at which the Murrumburrah cricket club intends to hold its first ball.

In an equally long article (about 600 words), the Murrumburrah correspondent defended his claim of an apparent lack of general satisfaction with the decision to hold the party at the mill. Mounting his high horse, he said he 'avoided all personality' in his reporting, and confined himself 'simply to stating facts', which he did not commit to paper 'until I am pretty sure that they are correct'. He noted that there were nine votes against Miles' offer and twelve in favour: 'So much for unanimity.'

Next came a letter to the *Courier* from a Murphy supporter signing himself 'Amicus justitia', who said he expressed the views of 'at least nine-tenths of the community'. Without naming Dillon, he claimed the Coramundra correspondent had 'been drilled by a person whose feelings have suffered extremely by the decision of the Murrumburrah Cricket Club'. He pointed out that the mill had been used for a ball and supper before – at its opening two years earlier: '…some 150 persons or more of the most respectable order were present, and did not find the least inconvenience.' He considered the correspondent

> should be ashamed of acting as a tool of another whose sole motive is spite, for it is well known that on the result of the ballot being made public the party named compelled his own son to withdraw from the club, and also ordered two of his employees not to be present at the ball, one of whom, a most valuable assistant to him in his business for years past, at once gave him warning to provide himself with one in her place.

Dillon replied in the next issue. He denied that he had colluded with the Coramundra correspondent, but did not respond to the other claims of 'Amicus justitia'. Implying dark undercurrents, he said he was loath to lay bare 'the whole matter from beginning to end, and the expedients adopted in the various stages of this precious business'. The reason? 'There are several members of the club for whom I entertain a great respect, and it is due to a feeling of courtesy towards them, and not wishing to mix them up with others of not equal respectability, that has kept me silent.' Dillon wrote after the ball was over, and regretted,

> I can only say that the expectations of numerous visitors belonging to high circles in Young, Grenfell, and elsewhere, brass bands, &c. were not fully realised. I do, however, give Mr Murphy every credit for the supper he prepared, but that would be needless on my part when his well known energy and generosity to push matters he takes in hand is considered.

The last letter on the subject was signed 'A cricketer'. This reported that the day of the ball had been observed as a holiday in Murrumburrah as most of the town's businessmen were cricket club members. 'In order to give zest to the ball' a match was played first – single members versus married. While their prowess was not very great, their 'quiet and orderly behaviour was very generally remarked' and 'hopes were freely expressed that perseverance and practice would enable us at no distant time to 'take the field' against more formidable opponents'. Singles scored 129; married ninety-three.

After allowing sufficient time for the 'fatigue and excitement' of the game to subside, wrote 'A cricketer', the players turned their attention to the evening's entertainment:

At an early hour of the night we assembled in the ball-room, and very little delay occurred before the musicians went to business. The sound of the 'sole'-stirring music and the sight of the numerous fair ones only waiting to be led through the 'maze and whirl of the dance' could not be long withstood, and dancing commenced in real earnest until twelve o'clock, when we retired to do justice to a splendid supper – one which, whether in point of taste, or from the nature of the supply, could be scarcely surpassed... The meeting throughout was characterised by cheerfulness and good feeling, and the light jest and merry laugh was echoed from all parts of the board. After supper we again visited the ball-room, where dancing was kept up with great spirit until the grey dawn, when a general separation took place, and thus ended as pleasant a meeting as could occur within any walls...

13

Out together

The story of Miles Murphy contains many surprises, and his patronage of cricket is not the least of these. Probably his sons can take the credit, because the game was played at their old school in Sydney, Lyndhurst College. According to the *Freeman's Journal*, a distinguished visitor to the school in April 1866, His Royal Highness Louis of Orleans, Prince de Conde, 'particularly admired the old English game of cricket, in which the students were engaged at the time'.

Miles was again the busy host when the Murrumburrah cricketers took on their first out-of-town opponents on the colony's Anniversary Day holiday, 26 January 1869. The visiting team, from Yass, lodged at the Criterion. After the match, 'one of the finest dinners ever got up in the neighbourhood was provided'. Then the party repaired to the ball-room and danced till midnight, when they partook of a supper 'which far excelled the dinner'. Throughout the proceedings 'there was nothing but the height of good feeling and merriment', wrote the *Courier* correspondent.

Yass had won the cricket game, scoring twenty-three in its first innings and twenty-two in its second, compared with Murrumburrah's nineteen and twenty-four. The top individual score for both teams was seven. Miles provided a refreshment booth at the ground, 'so that the thirsty might satisfy themselves'. Perhaps there was a connection between this and the low scores, because 'the tent was completely crowded throughout the day'. According to the correspondent, 'the good feeling that prevailed was most remarkable, and not a single case of dispute arose amongst any of those present'.

In the *Courier*'s next issue, another writer, who admitted to knowing much more about hurling and football than cricket, described the action.

'If two men standing at the wickets jumping out every now and then and poking at the ball, and a lot more rushing after it and clustering about it like a swarm of bees, denote fine playing, the play of both teams was excellent,' he wrote.

Thirteen days after the cricket, on 8 February 1869, Miles' wife Anne died at their Murrumburrah home at the age of fifty-two. According to the *Courier*, she had suffered a short though severe illness. Dr O'Connor had attended, as had two Catholic priests. The death was not registered as the law required, so there is no certificate that might provide more information about the cause. The Murphys failed to register many of the births and deaths in the family; perhaps they objected to such bureaucratic record keeping.

Anne's funeral was held on Wednesday 10 February. The procession set out at eight a.m. on the twenty-mile, four-hour journey from Murrumburrah to the cemetery at Milora, near Binalong, where young James Murphy had been buried sixteen months earlier. A 'very large and respectable concourse of mourners' followed the coffin, the *Courier* reported, and numbers 'largely increased' as the cortege neared Binalong. Most likely Jerry was among those who accompanied Miles and his family on this sad journey.

We know little of Anne's life, other than that she bore nine children between 1843 and 1858 and had to cope with seeing four of them die. There can have been few dull moments with Miles for a husband and so many children. A younger sister, Sarah, followed her to the colony in 1862 – perhaps a sign that she had sent positive reports about life in the Australian bush to relatives in County Antrim. Sarah and her husband Archie Stewart settled at Murrumburrah, and Archie initially worked for Miles.

Anne presumably played an important part in many of the dinners, dances and other celebrations that Miles hosted. From the story (chapter 7) of the man 'of very respectable appearance' who in May 1865 stole blankets and a pillow from the Swan Inn, Binalong, it appears that she was in charge of the hotel at the time. She was in the news earlier in 1865 after an employee on Kalangan was badly injured in a cart accident and brought to the Swan to recuperate. 'I am glad to say through the unremitting attention of Mrs Murphy he is progressing favourably,' the *Courier*'s Binalong correspondent reported.

Its Murrumburrah correspondent wrote with feeling after Anne's death,

> Were it the death of one of the sterner sex, one might advert to his business-like habits, his enterprise and zeal in promoting the interests of the community, and his success in life, possibly after a severe and up-hill struggle with mighty and all but insuperable difficulties. None of these things have to be recorded of Mrs Murphy, who was known and prized, and is now and long will be remembered, for her motherly kindness to all who stood in need of assistance. Her unostentatious kindness and warm sympathy towards the necessitous will long be cherished in the memory of her late neighbours.

The *Courier* reported that in Yass the morning on which the funeral was held was very sultry, and in the afternoon 'rainfall swept the streets as if they had been visited by a tidal wave'. The paper was confident that the drought ravaging the region, which 'called forth a recollection of the great drought of 1837–9', was finally over. A week earlier an article reprinted from a Wagga Wagga newspaper had described conditions west of Murrumburrah, saying many stations were completely dry, with all stock removed. Narraburra was among those thought to be losing their water fast, 'and report says the stock was to be removed at once'.

This prompted Jerry's first and only letter to the *Courier* – at least the only one bearing his name:

> I see by a paragraph in your last *Courier*, taken from the *Wagga Wagga Advertiser*, that my run at Narraburra is short of grass and water. I have just returned from that station, and am happy to say that there is still abundance of grass and water for the stock, namely 12,000 sheep, besides some cattle and horses. Will you kindly contradict the paragraph alluded to, and that the informant of the *Wagga Wagga Advertiser* has been misinformed.

At Murrumburrah, the drought, whatever its severity, broke with a vengeance. The day after Anne's funeral the town experienced 'a fearful storm of rain and hail', the *Courier* reported. An approach to the bridge over Murrimboola Creek was swept away, 'and a vast amount of damage done to Mr Miles Murphy's garden'.

This is the last news we have of Miles until 9 April 1869, when the paper announced that he had died the previous day 'after an illness of

Mary Anne Murphy, who married John the day before his father's death.

a few weeks duration'. Again there is no death certificate and so no record of the cause of death. A certificate does exist, though, recording the marriage in Murrumburrah the day before Miles died of his eldest son John to Mary Anne McNamara – daughter of Michael McNamara, a teacher, and Susan O'Hehir, a sister of Hannah Lehane's first husband. One can only speculate on the circumstances, but most likely the wedding was brought forward so Miles could see it, and was performed at his house. Father Duigan officiated having ridden out from Yass, and John's twenty-four-year-old brother Felix and sixteen-year-old sister Sarah signed the marriage certificate as witnesses. Presumably Duigan also performed the appropriate Catholic rites over Miles, and probably all the Murphy young – eighteen-year-old Thomas and fourteen-year-old Miles as well as John, Felix and Sarah – were at his side when he died.

The *Courier* accorded Miles a substantial black-bordered obituary, which was reprinted in the Sydney *Freeman's Journal*. This recalled Anne's death just two months earlier and noted, 'The husband has not lingered long after the much-mourned and affectionate wife'. It continued,

> The deceased was fifty years of age, and for more than one-half of that period he has been a resident of Yass or of the surrounding districts. His career as a colonist was an enterprising and successful one. He arrived in the colony, we understand from Dublin, six or seven and twenty years ago, and shortly afterwards came to Yass. After having been engaged in building affairs for some time, he commenced business in this town as a wheelwright in conjunction with a smithy. He was highly successful in these undertakings, and subsequently removed to Binalong, where he built an inn and store, which

he kept for a number of years. While following these occupations, he became the purchaser of the well-known Kalangan station, near Murrumburrah. Of the latter township he may almost be said to have been the founder. He erected an inn there, and at a later date several other buildings, including one of the largest and best-fitted flour mills out of Sydney. As his family grew up he placed members of it in charge of these several businesses. At the time the diggings were discovered at Burrangong, Mr Murphy built and opened a large store on what is now the Main-street of Young, and this establishment was successfully conducted by his son, Mr J.A. Murphy, until, on the rush to Forbes taking place, the 'Flat' became almost deserted. Mr Murphy then determined to transfer the business to Murrumburrah, at which place it has since been successfully carried on. Since the establishment of the flour mill and opening of the store at Murrumburrah, the deceased has resided almost continuously there; and as he possessed a considerable quantity of land in the township, he occupied himself in its improvement as well as in superintending his station and other affairs.

The *Courier* went on to note, in something of an understatement, that Miles 'possessed an enterprising and active disposition', and said he would be 'much missed by his neighbours and numerous friends'. It understood that 'several of our townsmen' intended travelling from Yass to attend the funeral, which, like Anne's, was to involve a morning procession from Murrumburrah to Binalong and interment at the Milora cemetery.

In his will drawn up in November 1867, three weeks after the death of his last-born child James, Miles had appointed Anne and their oldest son John executors. So following the granting of probate on 29 April 1869 administration of the estate fell to John. Miles provided that after the youngest child (Miles junior, born in 1854) reached the age of twenty-one (in 1875) the whole of the estate should be sold and the proceeds divided equally between the surviving offspring (except for a deduction from Felix's share of the £500 already advanced to him). Alternatively, the property could be divided into portions of equal value, and then lots drawn to determine who received which items (again, allowance would be made for the advance to Felix).

In the meantime, income from the estate was to pay for the education and maintenance of the three children who were not yet twenty-one – Thomas, Sarah and Miles – and if necessary to help place the boys in a profession, business or employment or be otherwise applied for their 'benefit or advancement in the world'. The children's shares were to be adjusted after division of the estate in accordance with what had been spent on them. Sarah's portion was to be 'for her sole and separate use so as to be independent of the debts or control of any future husband or husbands', and was to be conveyed to her 'in such manner as strictly to carry out this intention'. Perhaps Miles had a premonition of the financial troubles that her husband from 1872, William Lehane, would get himself in to.

The will listed Miles' principal assets as follows: about 1,500 acres of purchased land and 120 allotments in and near Murrumburrah; the flour mill, hotel and store at 'Shoemaker's Corner', Murrumburrah; the hotel, store and various allotments in Binalong; and about 6,000 sheep, 1,300 horses and 500 head of cattle. When probate was granted, the value of Miles' goods was sworn at £4,000, but his estate was surely worth much more than that.

The *Courier*'s Murrumburrah correspondent referred briefly to Miles' death two weeks after the funeral. He wrote that the recent rain, while much wanted, had rendered the town's bridge unfit for traffic:

> and before this could be remedied the remains of an old and enterprising resident were escorted to their final resting-place. So in a few lines you have a record of two losses, one of which can be repaired, the other cannot.

The rains also disrupted traffic through Binalong. They turned the main road into a quagmire – 'it was only the other day that a dray became bogged opposite the stores of Messrs Murphy and Howard, and had to be dug out,' the *Courier* reported in late June – and damaged the town's bridge. The paper recalled that Miles had built the bridge at his own cost, and thought 'surely the government should not now begrudge to keep it in a crossable condition'. Whether or not repairs were done, it finally succumbed to nature's force when floodwater destroyed it in April 1870.

The bridge, built in less than six weeks at a cost of about £200 (chapter 4), withstood the heavy Yass to Lambing Flat traffic of the early 1860s and lasted nearly sixteen years. It must have been well made. Seeing it swept away, old Binalong residents may have cast their minds back to the October day in 1854 when around 100 gathered for the convivial celebration of its opening. They probably recalled the 'tables loaded with viands equally substantial and palatable', the many toasts drunk 'with a becoming degree of enthusiasm', and the 'bursts of hearty acknowledgment' of Miles, the 'hospitable founder of the feast'. Perhaps some proposed a toast to the memory of this remarkable colonist and his beloved wife Anne.

14

Life goes on

In Murrumburrah, the newly married twenty-six-year-old John Murphy wasted little time in making his own mark on the family businesses. His first project – begun the month Miles died, so possibly instigated by him – was a large addition to the Criterion Hotel. This required 60,000 bricks, and John advertised in late April and early May for men to make them at Murrumburrah.

Perhaps the fact that John Dillon had just opened a 'new and fine addition' to his Commercial Hotel prompted this work. The *Courier* correspondent thought the Commercial's new bar 'presented an appearance far superior to anything that would be looked for in a small country town like this'. He added that when the Criterion's additions were completed 'our town will afford ample facilities both for accommodation and amusement, and that to an extent unthought of by those who remember Murrumburrah as it was a few years back'.

The long-standing rivalry between Dillon and the Murphys was on full show when Murrumburrah hosted a cricket carnival on the Queen's birthday, 24 May 1869, and the day after. The first match, during which Felix Murphy took to the field as an umpire, was between Boorowa and Murrumburrah. Boorowa won. On the second day, Murrumburrah took on Cootamundra, with Felix part of the batting line-up. He scored two ducks, but his team was victorious.

Each of the town's hotels – the Criterion, the Commercial and John English's Murrumburrah – turned on entertainments for the cricketers. The *Courier* correspondent noted that the Criterion provided a 'sumptuous repast' and the Murrumburrah a 'well-furnished board'. Unfortunately he neglected to praise the Commercial's offering, apparently offending Dillon deeply. The correspondent was duly apologetic, perhaps with tongue slightly in cheek:

I had consoled myself with the belief that as the landlord of that establishment never neglected an opportunity of entertaining guests at his board, it would be understood he contributed no small share to the comfort of the numerous visitors at that festive time; but from circumstances that have come to my knowledge casually, I find that I have been mistaken, and hasten to remedy my neglect. To a man who ever since he came to this town has laboured hard to improve its condition and give general satisfaction I feel this apology due, and state explicitly that the Cootamundra cricketers, who were his special guests on that occasion, with a numerous and respectable company of townspeople and others sat down to a hot, substantial and comfortable dinner, got up under his special supervision, and, I need hardly add, did ample justice thereto. While confirming my report respecting similar entertainments at the other hotels, I hope that their proprietors will not misunderstand me in giving merit where merit is due, and paying the tribute due from one old townsman to another.

The extensions to the Criterion were in use by early August, when John Murphy hosted a group of visiting singers and actors, the Foley Troupe, there. A 'neat stage' was erected, and the performers – led by Miss Foley, who sang sweetly, and Master Johnny Foley, who possessed 'astonishing ability and genius' for a child of eight years – attracted full houses for each of their three shows. In November, the *Courier* praised the additions in its report of the Murrumburrah spring races; 'for neatness and elegance', it noted, the new bar 'may rival any out of Sydney'.

In the lead-up to the races, both Murphy and Dillon advertised their intention to set up booths at the track. Murphy's ad appeared first and assured patrons they would 'receive every attention, and may depend upon being supplied with Refreshments of the finest quality.' Dillon promised his patrons every attention to their wants and comforts, and trumped Murphy by also offering a free ball and supper at the Commercial after the races. In the event, both hotels staged balls, and two correspondents supplied reports to the *Courier*. One said dancing was conducted with great spirit at both hotels, but especially at the Commercial, 'where the services of a first-rate violinist were provided, and the presence of a numerous band of dancers amply rewarded the host's exertions'. The other mentioned only the Criterion, where dancing in the new 'long room' was 'kept up with zeal until the light of the morning sun warned the reveller that the holidays were over, and that another working day had commenced'.

The races themselves did not live up to the standard of earlier years, wrote one of the correspondents: 'I do not think that genuine lovers of racing as a sport could view them with any exceeding delight.' Perhaps he was missing Miles. Another journalist looking back nostalgically around this time was the writer (probably J.J. Brown) of the *Courier* obituary for Cornelius O'Brien, proprietor of Coppabella in the 1830s and '40s, who died at the age of seventy-three in early July 1869. 'The ranks of the early pioneers of the district around Yass are rapidly becoming thinned by the hand of Death,' he observed.

Jerry, though, was showing no sign of slowing down. He became a father again on 17 August 1869, when Hannah gave birth to her second son, John Thomas, in Yass. A month earlier, he had stepped into the publican's role at the Globe Hotel following the departure of Owen Hilly who, the *Courier* noted, had 'succeeded in gathering around him many warm friends and supporters through his excellent management and obliging manners'. Jerry was able to relinquish his publican's licence and return to the farm in October after employing Richard Hassett to run the Globe. Hassett came from another Yass hotel, the Fortune of War. Earlier, he had been a police constable in the town; Jerry's nephew James

The Globe Hotel and its Rossi Street neighbours, 1870.
The Courier *building is on the Globe's left.*

Lehane appeared in the magistrates' court in 1858 charged with assaulting him (chapter 3).

As through much of the 1860s, business was far from brisk in Yass in 1869. In June the *Courier* noted that three large stores were unoccupied, and in October the Braidwood Store, next to the Globe, advertised that its prices were the lowest in town 'because the landlord [Jerry] has reduced the rent 20 per cent'. A *Courier* leader in June suggested that part of the problem was that businesses did not advertise:

> Issue after issue and week after week the paper may be examined, and by its advertising columns it would be impossible to discover that a store, hotel or other business establishment existed in this town.

It complained that local advertising support for the paper was 'far from what we had and have a right to expect' and foreshadowed ceasing publication in a year's time if things did not improve.

A development that some feared would send business in Yass further into the doldrums was the completion of the railway from Sydney to Goulburn. The grand opening of Goulburn station took place on 27 May 1869. One of the four trains that arrived that day brought the governor, the Earl of Belmore, and his entourage. Another comprised two locomotives pulling nineteen well-filled passenger carriages. A banquet was held in the evening in the 'tastefully fitted up' goods shed; Terence Aubrey Murray, now president of the legislative council and a knight, sat next to the governor at the top table. According to the *Courier*, nearly every house in the 'very gaily decorated' town flew flags and streamers.

Agitation began immediately to try to ensure that Yass was not bypassed when the railway advanced further south. One *Courier* letter writer foresaw Yass coming to be recognised as 'an emporium of business, a sanatorium of health, and a little Eden of beauty' and urged townsfolk to 'give the Government no rest' until the 'iron-horse' was heard there. All speakers at a well-attended public meeting were pro-rail. Then an anti-railway letter appeared, claiming to reflect the majority view:

> All who dislike the rush and bustle so characteristic of the period, and of which the hissing, snorting locomotive is an apt emblem – all who dislike running into debt nationally or individually – will abstain from joining the movement.

Not surprisingly, this provoked ridicule from another correspondent:

> That humbug, Stephenson, should have been crushed under the first locomotive... Watt should have been boiled in his steam-kettle.

The *Courier*'s mid-year gloom began to lift in late July. It noted that a 'shoal' of auctioneers had commenced business in Yass, raising the prospect that the town would become an important centre for livestock sales. A major store was expanding its premises. Most importantly, new mineral discoveries promised to bring renewed prosperity to the region. 'This district bids fair to become famous for the extent and variety of its mineral wealth,' the paper commented in early August.

> Let the railway once reach Yass, and we predict that we shall soon after have furnaces smoking and blazing all around, with stalwart miners by the thousand ready to purchase all that our agriculturalists can produce.

Production seemed likely to begin soon at the Woolgarlo lead and silver mines fifteen miles south of Yass, and a new lead find on the Milora grazing run near Binalong looked very promising. John Vicq, still postmaster at Bogolong, discovered this lode, which the *Courier* expected would prove rich in silver as well as lead. Vicq had earlier dug for gold at the Muttama reef, north of Gundagai, and was later joint holder of a copper lease near Binalong.

News from Milora in October 1869 was that a shaft to test the dimensions of the lode was being sunk and a visiting team of experts had found the ore very rich in lead but deficient in silver. In November some 'exceedingly rich' ore from the find was put on display in Melbourne, with a sample to become a permanent exhibit at the city's Mining Museum. Apparently intending to develop the lode, one of the men who had assessed the ore, C.L. Throckmorton, obtained a forty-acre mining lease covering the site, but this was cancelled in June 1870 due to non-compliance with lease conditions. The *Courier* reported further interest in mining the ore in 1872 and 1874 but, as with many other mineral finds in the region, early hopes of 'furnaces smoking and blazing all around' were not realised.

Farming and grazing remained the area's economic mainstay, and in early August the *Courier* was pleased to see a revival of the local Pastoral and Agricultural Association, defunct since the first Yass stock and produce show held in March 1863. Jerry attended the public meeting that re-established the association, and was appointed to a large committee formed to canvass the district for potential members. Another meeting, in October, heard that 130 members had been recruited and elected a committee of thirty, again including Jerry, whose first task was to draw up rules and regulations for the society.

The *Courier* thought this meeting had committed some 'grave errors', notably setting up such a large committee. J.J. Brown, proprietor and editor, was an influential man, and congratulated the association after it decided at its next gathering to convene a special meeting to select a new, smaller, committee. That meeting, in late November, appointed one of the town's medicos, Dr Allan Campbell, president of the association and elected six other office-bearers and fifteen committee members, who did not include Jerry. They got on with the task of organising the second Yass Show, which was held successfully on a North Yass paddock on Thursday 24 March 1870.

Jerry was almost certainly not among the eighteen members who turned up for the special meeting, as continuing heavy rain was causing him major problems at Coppabella. Sheep washing and shearing were scheduled to start in the first week of October, but did not get under way then or for some time afterwards. The *Courier* reported in mid-October that floodwaters had washed away a newly constructed dam with sluices on the station. Jerry had been about to wash his flocks at the dam, which had cost him a 'considerable sum of money'.

In Yass, one effect of the rain was to make the road to the town's cemeteries impassable. On a hilltop to the west of the town, these were (and are) reached by Rossi Street, so patrons of the Globe would have been among those who doffed their hats as funeral processions passed. When Hassett took over as the Globe's publican in mid-October, he won the *Courier*'s praise for, at his own cost, filling 'the numerous ruts' in Rossi Street between the main road (Cooma Street) and the hotel, a distance of more than 100 yards. Further up the hill, though, as a public meeting called in mid-November to consider the problem heard, traffic could not get through in wet weather.

Those at this meeting included Father Duigan of St Augustine's, the

Anglican Rev. Lillingston (now an archdeacon), and the Presbyterian Rev. John Gibson. Lillingston moved and Gibson seconded a resolution that a committee composed of the clergy of the district and various lay townsmen be formed to collect subscriptions for the necessary road repairs and arrange the work. This was carried unanimously, and those present immediately put in £33 11s (including £5 5s from Duigan and £2 2s each from Lillingston and Gibson.

The question then became: how should the rest of the required funds be gathered? Lillingson proposed that subscription lists be forwarded to the town's banks and stores, but Duigan had a better idea – that 'as the work belonged to the clergy' they should take on the task. In an ecumenical gesture, Gibson said he hoped they would go collecting together. Duigan declared he had no objection to being seen with Gibson, and Lillingson, after noting that it was 'awfully hot', said he was 'quite game'. One of the lawyers at the meeting, George Allman, said the effect of the three going round together 'would be quite pleasing' and another, Christopher Dease, thought 'the proceedings would resemble that related of the three fat single gentlemen who were rolled into one. He hoped the time would come when such junction would be practicable.' Rev. Gibson suggested that the committee secretary accompany the clergy 'to take care of the cash', to which Lillingston responded, 'What, no confidence in parson or priest!'

It seems that the jollity and good intentions were not followed swiftly by action. A letter writer to the *Courier* noted two months after the meeting that 'this remarkable display of brotherly love seems to have led to no result':

> The three rev. gentlemen have not yet been seen perambulating the streets arm in arm, calling at every house with a common object, and bearing a common purse. Such an edifying spectacle of clerical unity has not yet been exhibited – Peter, Jack and Martin have not yet amalgamated, and probably never will.

The November 1869 public meeting had another issue to consider, the choice of a suitable candidate for Yass Plains at the coming legislative assembly election. This was the first item on the agenda, and a resolution asking Thomas Laidlaw, a wealthy retired Scottish storekeeper, to stand was quickly adopted without dissent. But then George Allman arrived with news that he had already put the proposition to Laidlaw, and the answer had been a 'decided refusal'.

Spirits were high when discussion returned to the election after the cemeteries road issue had been dealt with, but the ecumenical sweetness and light dissipated rapidly. Duigan proposed that Allman stand for election; if so, 'he would support him heart and hand'. But if neither Allman nor Laidlaw would stand, 'why it rested with the Catholic party to return the member'. Allman declined and 'begged leave…to dissent from the reverend gentleman's proposition that no one but a Roman Catholic had a chance for Yass'. A riled Duigan claimed he 'hardly deserved that such an insinuation should be thrown in his teeth' as he had come to the meeting in good faith to support either Allman, 'a Church of England gentleman', or Laidlaw, 'both of whom he highly respected'.

Inevitably, Duigan's suggestion that the Catholic Church might choose the district's MP prompted a spate of letters to the *Courier*. One correspondent burst into verse:

> If Laidlaw, according to Allman refuses,
> As M.P. to be our representative man;
> Never mind take the *angel* that Providence chooses,
> Through its resident agent, great Father Duigan.
> Oh, Father Duigan, dear Father Duigan,
> The Papal tiara for Father Duigan.

Duigan wrote to the paper saying he had gone to the meeting not 'with any sectarian motives' but to sign a request to the Protestant Laidlaw to represent the Yass Plains constituency. He continued,

> Living as I have always done on the most intimate terms of friendship with members of every denomination, nothing would more deeply grieve me than that I should, even in a moment of surprise or excitement, say ought that would lessen those friendly feelings that should exist between all Christian communities. As to the correctness of the report made of that conversation, or the right of making public what was then said, I will leave to the consideration of the gentlemen who were then present. There are occasions, and an election is especially one of those occasions, when a few individuals, for ends best known to themselves, take occasion of even an

incautious word or sentence spoken, to raise such word or sentence as a party cry, ignoring altogether the many evil consequences which may follow from such a proceeding.

In an editor's comment at the foot of the letter, J.J. Brown rejected the notion that Duigan's remarks were made in a private conversation and should not have been reported: 'If unpleasant consequences ensue from remarks incautiously made, the speaker – and he alone – is responsible.' Brown had a lot more to say in a leader in the next issue after Duigan wrote to the *Sydney Morning Herald* claiming his comments had been made in a spirit of banter rather than seriousness, and 'any accidental expression that could serve a party purpose is carefully noted, and, I think I may say, rather unscrupulously used'. The editor obtained confirmation from others present – including Dr Campbell, Lillingston and an unnamed prominent Catholic – that the meeting was still in progress when Duigan spoke, and claimed, 'we are almost hourly in receipt of evidence that the language made use of by the rev. gentleman is warmly and keenly resented and repudiated by his own people'.

The last word on the episode goes to John Shaw, the *Courier*'s reporter at the meeting. He wrote in a letter to the editor that, when making his remarks, Duigan had risen to his feet, addressed the chair, and adopted 'that conventional political gesticulation of table thumping so painful to a reporter whose desk happens to be the thumped table'. As it turned out, a Catholic did become the sole candidate for Yass Plains – Michael Fitzpatrick, head of the colonial government's Department of Lands and Works. He supported free selection, public schools and federation, and enjoyed, initially, strong backing from the *Courier*. He remained the local member until his death in 1881.

At the end of November 1869, Fitzpatrick took part in ceremonies associated with one of the biggest events in Yass for some time, the opening of the town's Mechanics Institute building in Cooma Street. He was apparently one of few Catholics to do so. Another was Dr Morgan O'Connor, who served as a steward at the celebratory public ball – 'one of the happiest assemblages in Yass' according to the *Courier*.

The institute, established in 1857, occupied borrowed accommodation until the completion of its 'truly elegant' building, dominated by a sixty-

The Yass Mechanics Institute.

seven by twenty-nine feet hall suited to events ranging from public lectures to balls. Like its counterparts established in cities and towns around Australia in the mid-1800s – and their forerunner, the Glasgow Mechanics Institute founded in 1823 – the Yass Mechanics Institute operated a library and reading room and put on public lectures. Its purpose was 'the diffusion of science and other useful knowledge'. In a speech in 1860, George Allman, the institute's president, said, 'we have endeavoured as far as possible to remove all forms of dissension amongst the members by excluding the ever dangerous practice of discussing religious or political subjects'.

The widow of the Catholic Henry O'Brien laid the new building's foundation stone in October 1868, and told the gathering the institute's establishment 'was ever an object of deep interest to my lamented husband'. However, Father Duigan apparently had a different view of it. He did not allow children from St Augustine's School to join the 150 from the Church of England, Presbyterian and Wesleyan schools who participated in the ceremony. In fact, according to a letter-writer to the *Courier*, the Catholic clergy now forbade the faithful from joining the institute – in accordance with their practice of discouraging associations 'not more or less under their supervision and control'.

When the town's children were invited to take part in the opening ceremony, and to assemble in the hall a few days later 'to hear a few pleasant words of advice and to receive something in the way of more pleasant confectionery', Duigan again said no on behalf of the Catholics. From the letter he wrote to the organisers it seems he felt no obligation to explain why:

> I only returned from Murrumburrah on yesterday, when I received your letter asking my permission to allow the children of the Catholic school to be present at the opening of the Mechanics' Institute. When the foundation-stone of the Mechanics' Institute was being laid by Mrs O'Brien, of Douro, I refused to allow the Catholic children to be present, and I can see no reason why I should deviate from the course I then adopted.

The new MP Michael Fitzpatrick spoke at the children's gathering, saying he was 'no disbeliever' in the advantages of mechanics' institutes. One 'great object' they helped achieve was blending classes and making members of communities 'more sociable and kindly' in their relations.

> With reference to the absence of the Roman Catholic children, or to the possible motive which actuated Father Duigan to refuse them permission to attend, he would say nothing.

While Duigan may at times have been a divisive influence in Yass, he seems to have been assiduous in attending to his flock in the bush. Murrumburrah, forty miles away, was a frequent destination, and the Murphys welcomed him in good times and bad. Shortly after Christmas 1869, he rode out to Coppabella and officiated at the burial of five-month-old John Thomas Lehane, who had died following thirty-six hours' diarrhoea on 27 December. Morgan O'Connor apparently went with Duigan as he is recorded as a witness, with Jerry, at the baby's interment at Reedy Creek.

The death of John Thomas was the first of three tragedies that struck the family in quick succession. John and Honora Vicq lost a thirteen-month-old son from convulsions associated with teething just three weeks later, on 19 January 1870. Then on 21 January chronic diarrhoea killed a ten-month-old daughter of John and Ellen Lyons. The death of this infant, who shared her mother's name, occurred in Sydney; apparently Ellen had brought her there from Maryborough in the hope that Dr James Gilhooley, brother-in-law of Dr Forrest of St John's College, could help. Jerry was with his daughter when the child died, certifying the death and, with Dr Gilhooley, witnessing the burial.

Five months later, on a dark and stormy June night, Jerry accompanied Father Duigan as he headed from Yass to Jugiong to conduct mass at the village church. At about nine-thirty, Jerry arrived at the Bodkins' house – no longer an inn – at Five Mile Creek, having ridden ahead to ask Mrs Bodkin if she could put the pair up for the night. She was happy to do so, and two men who were on the premises set out with a lantern to escort Duigan the last half mile to shelter. 'He was very wet, and I immediately got him some tea, took off his wet boots and socks, and put his feet in hot water,' Mrs Bodkin wrote in a letter to the *Courier*.

> When he retired to bed, he requested me to put plenty of clothes on his bed. I gave him the best bed in the house, and put over him, besides the sheet, two pairs of double blankets and a counterpane. I took his wet clothes, and sat up the whole night myself drying them, and gave them to him in the morning perfectly dry, when he proceeded on his journey in company with Mr Lehane.

Duigan performed his duties in Jugiong and returned to Yass on the mail coach. Two days later he died. The *Courier*'s obituary upset Mrs Bodkin as it claimed that, after arriving at Five Mile Creek 'drenched and weary' on his way to Jugiong, Duigan had 'remained in his wet clothes, and to this may be attributed the origin of the fatal illness which has deprived the Catholics of Yass and surrounding district of a warm-hearted and zealous priest'. The letter was her response. 'If the accommodation was not equal to what might have been expected at an hotel,' she wrote, 'I at least did the best I could with the materials at my command, and was not destitute, as your informant would make it appear, of the common dictates of humanity.'

The *Courier* was full of praise for the 'respected, energetic and much beloved' young Irish-born priest; past disagreements were forgotten. He had 'laboured assiduously in the performance of the duties of his sacred calling':

> ...and in all states of the weather, whether by day or by night, in storm or sunshine, in town or in the solitary bush, the reverend gentleman was at the call of his parishioners, on occasions even when a due consideration of his own health – at all times delicate – might well have justified him in deferring

many long, weary, and lonely journeys, often in dreary weather and by night, in the bush, even though for the purpose of affording the consolations of religion to the sick or dying.

The funeral service, a High Requiem Mass, was conducted at St Augustine's by the church's former priest and now vicar-general of the Goulburn diocese, Dr McAlroy. It attracted an 'immense crowd', the *Courier* reported; the rest of Yass appeared deserted. The church's 'gallery, nave, and chancel were filled to overflowing', with all eyes on the coffin 'standing as it were in the very centre of the edifice, covered with candlesticks ablaze with light, and surrounded by the priests who had arrived to take part in the proceedings'.

Jerry was one of eight pall bearers; two of the others had also come from distant parts of the parish – John Murphy from Murrumburrah and John Sheahan, Jerry's accuser in the 1865 cattle-stealing episode, from Jugiong. McAlroy 'had to beg those present' to make room when the procession formed to escort the coffin from the church, and as the pallbearers lifted it, 'a great number…burst into tears, many being violently affected with grief'. The *Courier*'s report continued,

> Before the coffin, in order, two and two, headed by the Rev. Father Finnegan bearing a massive cross of silver, marched the priests present on the occasion, chanting the customary office. On reaching the door the procession turned to the north, and made the circuit of the church ground until, having reached the site selected, a spot some few feet distant from the south-eastern angle of the sacred fabric, the coffin was deposited on the edge of the grave. Those present were then asked to kneel and say together the Lord's Prayer, a request complied with by all; and it was, the sad occasion apart, no unpleasing sight to witness so many, of conflicting opinions as to doctrine, bending uncovered in the wind and rain beside the open grave of the departed pastor, before his and their God. The ceremonial being finished, the body was lowered into the grave amid the sorrowful wailing of many present – indeed, when the heavy sound of the clay clods was heard as they fell on the coffin lid, the weeping of many was loud and bitter. When the excavated earth was all replaced above the coffin, and a mound formed to indicate the spot, until a fitting monument can be erected, the meeting gradually and sorrowfully dispersed.

15

The skies open

Most issues of the *Yass Courier* carried weather reports, but these were descriptions of what had been happening rather than forecasts. In February 1869, the paper devoted a long leading article to meteorology, calling for the appointment of competent people across the colony to make daily observations of changes in wind direction, atmospheric pressure and temperature. The readings could be used to construct meteorological charts that 'in time would become of value to science'. Confident in scientific progress, the *Courier* expected the day would come when 'we shall be able to calculate with something like a certainty when we are to suffer from drought, and when we are to undergo the penalties of a flood'.

Long and deepening drought – the Yass River had stopped flowing two months earlier – prompted the editor's observations. By the end of the year, it seemed that an equally extreme period of wet weather had set in. During September, the *Courier* described the current season as the most remarkable within the recollection of the colony's oldest inhabitants, with stormy nights and 'rapid transitions from the warmth of an equatorial climate to the frigidity of the North Pole'. It reported in October that the river was alive with leeches, and in December that storms had flooded houses in Yass and turned much of the main street into a rapid stream.

A correspondent noted that the eminent geologist the Rev. W.B. Clarke had suggested an unusual quantity of icebergs breaking off from Antarctica and drifting northwards might be bringing the rain-bearing clouds. Whatever the cause of the wet weather, the timing could hardly have been worse for the people of Yass and for travellers and transport on the main road south. A new iron bridge, with its roadway eight feet above the level of the great flood of 1852, was under construction over

The old wooden Yass bridge, and workmen starting on its iron replacement, 1869.

the Yass River but completion was some way off. As the work continued, all but foot traffic was banned from February 1870 on the increasingly shaky old wooden bridge, which had been built in 1854. This meant that, until the new bridge was opened, the only river crossing for horse riders, buggies and wagons would be a ford.

In late February, the *Courier* reported that several bullock teams had become bogged on the ford's approaches. Fortunately, the weather cleared for the first Yass agricultural show since 1863, held on 24 March in a paddock in North Yass, over the river from the town centre. Out of town exhibitors who managed to make their way in over the sticky roads included John Murphy, who won a £1 prize for best hackney in the horses section and a ten-shilling prize for first quality flour. Evidently pleased by the prospect of an annual show in the district, he donated his winnings, plus another £2 2s, to the Pastoral and Agricultural Association. The post-show dinner was held at the Globe Hotel; Archdeacon Lillingston proposed the toast to the association, saying events such as the show tended to elevate the character of a community.

The next month brought a renewal of heavy rain. The *Courier* dispatched on the morning of 26 April reported that a number of drays were 'stuck up' between Yass and Reedy Creek and would not be able to move until the weather cleared. By the end of the day, as rain continued to pelt down, much of the town was under water. Even worse, the well-advanced new bridgeworks, and the old bridge, had been washed away.

After the flood – the old bridge has been washed away and girders of the new one rest on the riverbed.

The *Courier*'s description of the great flood of 1870 is vivid and detailed. Apparently one of its compositors was the first to raise the alarm; on his way home at four a.m. after the day's paper had gone to press, he noticed that water was starting to encroach into James Ritchie's store in the main street, and immediately roused the people who worked there. They lifted most of the store's goods on to the counters – 'out of reach as they imagined of all danger'. But the water kept rising, and by mid-morning Ritchie had decided his stock should be moved to another store on higher ground. A band of volunteers gathered for the task, working up to their waists in water. 'It was very pleasant to witness the neighbourly good feeling displayed... all classes went at the work with right good will, Archdeacon Lillingston's clerical appearance from the waist upwards being especially conspicuous,' the *Courier* observed. Around this time, as 'the rain continued to come down in torrents', the water was rising at about twenty inches an hour.

> The view of the river from the precipice opposite the pound was indescribably grand. Through its rocky tortuous passage it came in tumultuous spasms, seething and yeasty.

A large portion of the old wooden bridge 'went with a crash' at 12.40 p.m. At one-twenty-five, the river reached the level of the 1852 flood; by then the water was up to the windowsills of the Commercial Bank and damage included the nearly total destruction of the town's flour mill. By two p.m., the water had reached the iron girders of the new bridge and was still rising fast – at two feet six inches an hour according to a calculation made at two-forty. By then, 'the general aspect at the lower end of the town was very sad – furniture, stores, and live stock all floating about in immense confusion'.

At two-fifty, the water was within twelve inches of the eaves of Ritchie's store, the remainder of the old bridge was breaking up fast, and 'ominous cracks' had started issuing from the new bridge. Shortly after four p.m., the bridge's girders 'went with a sad melancholy crash, leaving nothing visible of man's work save the heads of the four cylinders on which they had rested'. This 'calamity' had been expected, but 'as soon as it was known that the girders had sank into the stream and that Yass was placed, so far as communication northward is concerned, in the same position it had occupied before 1854, lament was general; it seemed somewhat as if the news had arrived of the death of a friend well-known and beloved by all.'

By five p.m., the river was five or six feet above the 1852 flood level, the rain showed no sign of easing, it was getting dark, and 'people hardly knew what to do for the best'. At eight p.m., 'nothing could be seen through the dark, in the direction of the river, but the reflection of lamps and lanterns on what seemed a sea of waters'. Then at last, around nine-thirty, the weather began to clear and the water stopped rising. By ten p.m., the rain had stopped; 'the stars began to shine – it was felt in earnest that even a little light is a blessed thing.'

Many houses had been washed away or submerged, and the *Courier* was pleased by the readiness with which shelter was provided for all, 'poor as well as affluent'. It noted that at the Globe (well above the flood on the Rossi Street hill), Commercial and other hotels, 'bed-rooms were at once provided'. The churches and many townsfolk offered accommodation, and some people were 'made as comfortable as circumstances permitted' by Mr Bourke, the lock-up-keeper. The scene the next morning was 'a very sad spectacle':

> The whole of the lower end of the town was a heap of ruins, and looked as if it had just sustained a siege. The streets were covered with thick alluvial

slime, and in all directions along the high water mark left by the flood, could be seen traces of wreck and desolation, in the shape of crates, furniture, doors, hay, casks, bedding, &c., &c. From measurements we ascertained that the waters reached to about nine feet higher than the spot pointed out to us as the flood level of 1852; yet if the blacks' testimony, as given to Mr Hamilton Hume forty years ago, is to be believed, floods have been known by them to have reached to a level of two feet higher than that attained on Tuesday evening.

Looking on the bright side, the *Courier* noted that no lives had been lost. It feared that, if the main flooding had occurred at night, 'our labour of chronicling its disastrous effects would have been made infinitely more sorrowful by the vast amount of loss of life which under such circumstances must have been inevitable'.

Although the water fell quickly, there was no possibility of crossing the river the day after the deluge. As 'parties on either side' were anxious for information, some ingenious means of communication were devised. First, blackboards were set up on both sides of the river. Through messages written in chalk and viewed through opera glasses, 'lengthy conversations were held' during the afternoon. Then, at about four o'clock, 'a rather amusing incident' occurred:

> The Venerable Archdeacon Lillingston, anxious to originate some better mode of communication than the two boards and glasses permitted, procured a ball of string and a rocket. The string was attached, the stick with the rocket placed in position, and the rocket ignited. Amid great laughter it was speedily discovered that the rocket had been placed point downmost, and of course it darted with a splutter into the slime at the feet of the pseudo-pyrotechnists. Ultimately the cord was fastened to a stone, and after several futile attempts, success crowned the praiseworthy efforts. A connection was formed, a clothes-line followed the cord, and by this means the Murrumburrah, Young, and Binalong mail-bags were got across.

The following day, some residents of North Yass managed to cross the river by clambering over one of the fallen iron girders. Then the girder sank further into the stream, preventing a return journey. The river fell rapidly over succeeding days, and within a week its rocky bed was visible again. By then, a firm footpath of boards had been built across the girders.

In the region, other bridges lost in the floods included the Murrumbidgee crossing at Jugiong and the one Miles Murphy built at Binalong. Near Coppabella, the approaches to the bridges over both Reedy Creek and Five Mile Creek were swept away, but the bridges themselves survived. Jerry's losses on the property, the *Courier* reported, were 'a couple of dams' and 'a deal of fencing'. In Yass, the paper brought science to bear to determine precisely how fast the river had risen. The clock hanging in the Commercial Bank stopped at four-twenty-five p.m., 115 minutes after that on a mantelshelf in the manager's private apartments.

> As the difference of the respective levels at which the above time-pieces were suspended is exactly forty-five inches (reckoning from their pendulums) it becomes a mere question of long division – rise of forty-five inches in one hundred and fifteen minutes; or, about, twenty-two inches an hour.

Storms continued in the region, bringing further fluctuations in river levels, and reports of perilous river crossings and dire effects on business began to appear regularly. Squatter and JP Henry Brown had a narrow escape as he was being driven into town in a spring-cart and pair to catch the mail coach to Sydney two weeks after the flood. One of the horses stumbled on the ford, resulting in both horses and the cart being swept away in the strong current. 'Mr Brown jumped out and succeeded in saving his portmanteau and in reaching the bank; and his groom was equally fortunate.' All types of business in Yass were suffering – for example, saddlers and shoemakers had to close their operations for lack of leather supplies – and forage for horses was extremely scarce.

At the end of May, the *Courier* reported a series of near disasters on the ford and complained of the 'unaccountable and highly censurable' neglect of the authorities in failing to make the crossing safe: 'All that has yet been done is to pitch a few loads of stones in a narrow line across the bed of the flooded river.' When around this time the government sent the 'jolly-boat' *Emily* to provide a link between the town and North Yass (which, confusingly, is on the road south) the paper was scathing. 'As was expected, it proved utterly useless, and was speedily hauled up the bank of the river, where it now again lies high and dry.'

A week later, after more heavy rain, the *Courier* conceded it might have been wrong about the *Emily*, which had rendered good service in bringing the mails and many people over the river. In late June it was 'in constant requisition' and 'of great service'. In one incident, a boatman jumped into the river and saved a man from drowning. A few days later, the *Emily*'s cargo included the Anglican bishop of Goulburn's carriage. On the other hand, there were frequent complaints about the operators being drunk and unhelpful. In July, a woman and her young children had to scramble over the girders one evening, with 'the water running in torrents and nearly touching our feet', after the boatmen declared that the *Emily* had been locked up for the night. Early in August, another woman described 'the Blondin-like acrobatic feats' she and others had been obliged to perform over the prostrate girders, 'with the seething waters beneath our feet ready to engulf us'.

Her immediate complaint in a letter to the *Courier* was that the boatmen had left 'between two and three dozen' people, mostly females, waiting in 'pelting rain and sleet' to cross the river; for half an hour 'they kept grinning at each other in exultation over our hapless condition'. The group's destination this Wednesday morning was St Augustine's Church, where special services involving more than ten priests were to be held in memory of Father Duigan, five weeks after his funeral. Despite the weather, the church was crowded for this event, and according to the *Courier* many of those present had come from considerable distances. Most likely they included Lehanes and Murphys, who perhaps were among those who had to cross the river on the *Emily*.

Father George Dillon from Sydney delivered a long and eloquent panegyric, which the *Courier* published in full. He described his friendship with Father Duigan, which had developed when they studied together for the priesthood at All Hallows College, Dublin – an institution established to provide priests for foreign lands, 'especially those where the millions of Irish exiles were now to be found'. He spoke of 'the greatness of soul of the Irish missionaries who left 'home, country, friends, and every worldly prospect to devote themselves to the obscure, painful life and lonely death so certain to be their only earthly portion'. Duigan was an 'earnest, humble, saintly' prelate who had chosen to endure

>...the weary journeying to meet the scattered flock, the weeks, and often

months, spent far from the slender rest of even a missionary's home – the dangers from floods, drought, from the scorching summer's sun, from the miasma of the marsh, the days without rest, the nights without shelter – all borne with uncomplainingly, all unregistered upon this earth. What matter, provided the scattered sheep are fed with the bread of life – what matter, providing grace comes to souls needing it – what matter if one, even one soul reconciled to God, it will abundantly repay all.

Three months had now passed since the flood, and the *Courier* was becoming increasingly concerned for the future of Yass. The town had once been among the most flourishing and prosperous in the colony; now it threatened to become, if it was not already, 'a petty roadside village, where a passing waggon will soon be an object of curiosity to the inhabitants'. In earlier years,

> teams by the dozen might be seen loading and unloading at the stores in town – station supplies were dispatched by dray-loads daily, almost the whole year round, and in the season tons upon tons of wool were received by our storekeepers for dispatch to Sydney or to be forwarded to England for sale. Now, the trade of the town appears to the looker-on to have dwindled down to petty retail transactions, and customers even in this small way are few and far between. Our hotel-keepers, with one or two exceptions, participate in the prevailing dullness…

Making matters worse, the 'dilapidated' condition of the lower end of the main road and the 'wretched state of mud and slush existing in all the streets and by-ways' gave the town a 'very forlorn aspect'.

In early September, a delegation of leading townsmen including J.J. Brown and Archdeacon Lillingston travelled to Sydney to meet the minister for public works, Mr Sutherland. They told him the loss of the bridge had almost completely destroyed trade in Yass and asked for work to be sped up on a new one. The local MP, Michael Fitzpatrick, supported their case, arguing that delay in building a new crossing could result in traffic being diverted permanently around the town. The delegation was assured that a new iron bridge would be completed in seven to eight months (in the event, it took ten).

The *Courier* argued that one of the main lessons from the flood was the need for the people of Yass to take charge of their own affairs through a municipal council. As well as dealing with matters such as dangerous ditches and uplifted culverts, an elected council would help build a more self-reliant spirit in Yass, J.J. Brown wrote in his first post-flood leader. A week later, he expressed confidence that 'the necessity of having the streets made passable' was persuading waverers of the benefits of incorporation. Under the law of the time, a town that sent the government a petition signed by large numbers of potential ratepayers could expect to be granted municipal status.

The *Courier*'s support for incorporation dated back at least to July 1865, when Brown claimed it would enhance the importance of the town and increase property values. An 1866 article noted that in the absence of municipal by-laws 'throwing refuse of all kinds on the roadway, much to the annoyance not only of households close by but also of pedestrians' was common practice. A letter to the editor in 1869 attributed much of the sickness in the town to 'bad drainage, bad water, and the accumulation of refuse, &c', problems that the writer was confident a municipal council would remedy.

When in mid-May Brown, storekeeper James Ritchie and lawyer Christopher Dease took a petition for incorporation from door to door few people declined to sign. All but three or four of the town's large property holders supported the cause, the *Courier* reported. At the end of the month the petition, bearing 155 signatures, was sent to the local member, Michael Fitzpatrick, for transmission to the colonial secretary's office.

But then the opposition emerged, led by Richard Hassett of the Globe Hotel. He and his supporters prepared a petition objecting to incorporation partly on the grounds that 'the population are few, and with few exceptions unable to bear taxation'. They obtained 184 signatures, including that of Jerry, Hassett's employer. While most prominent townsmen supported incorporation, Jerry was in good company; the no petition also bore the signature of Hamilton Hume, now a frail seventy-three-year-old. The *Courier* was scathing, claiming a paid collector had spent weeks obtaining the anti-incorporation signatures, many of the signatories were unknown in the district, and sixty or seventy people had signed both petitions. 'How persons supposed to have arrived at the years of discretion can so trifle with their signatures is utterly beyond

*The Sydney Intercolonial Exhibition, 1870.
A visit by Globe publican Richard Hassett caused a stir in Yass.*

comprehension,' J.J. Brown lamented. In November, advice arrived from Sydney that, because the anti signatures outnumbered the pro, 'the municipality prayed for cannot be proclaimed under the present petition'.

At the end of August, shortly after he circulated the anti-incorporation petition, Hassett was one of numerous Yass residents who set off for Sydney to visit the Intercolonial Exhibition near Redfern railway station – staged to mark the centenary of Captain Cook's arrival at Botany Bay. 'Yass is desolate, nearly all heads of departments, establishments, sects, &c being in the capacious maw of the hungry metropolis,' reported the *Courier*. 'Were an invading fleet to enter Port Jackson any time during the ensuing month, they would make a good haul.'

Hassett's trip to Sydney caused quite a stir, which first surfaced in the *Courier* in a titillating item headed 'Town Talk' on 18 October 1870. 'For many weeks past a very unpleasant and scandalous topic has been the current conversation of the townspeople, in which the name of an old resident, a married man, and *père de famille*, a hotelkeeper in Yass, and that of a young woman, the wife of a warder in the gaol, a native of the town, and the mother of several young children, have been mixed up,' it began. Although both parties denied that there was any truth 'in the statements floating about', they had 'had the bad taste to feed and increase the scandal by their acts – the two having, for instance, recently returned from a visit to the late Exhibition – the journey there and back having been performed in each other's company, and in the hotelkeeper's buggy'.

More details emerged the next day, when Hassett appeared in the Yass Magistrates' Court claiming to have been assaulted by a young man named William Martin. After this case was dismissed on a legal technicality, the accused and defendant swapped roles. Martin claimed Hassett had struck him with a bludgeon after he had approached Hassett and begun a fistfight. Explaining the events, Martin's lawyer George Allman told the magistrates,

> The complainant is the son of a very old man who is blind, and is the brother of a young woman… There are certain duties not laid down in the law books, and it became necessary to protect this young woman's character. The defendant had…for months past made this unfortunate woman's name (the complainant's sister) a by-word and a scorn throughout the town of Yass. It was impossible that his client's ears could be shut to these disgraceful and scandalous proceedings, and believing the truth of them, was it likely he should stand by and tamely permit their continuance… The whole thing culminated in…this old man leaving the town for Sydney, and taking complainant's sister along with him… This lad having been told and believing it to be true that Hassett and his sister had represented themselves to be man and wife at the hotel where they were staying, was it to be expected that he would stand coolly by, and permit such a state of things to continue?

At the conclusion of evidence, reported the *Courier*, one of the JPs hearing the case, Dr Isidore Blake, expressed the view that Hassett might have deserved to be hit. He said the magistrates 'by no means desired to stamp their approval on the conduct of either [Martin or Hassett], but they were bound to look at the justice of the thing'. After they found Hassett guilty and announced their decision to fine him a shilling and award costs against him, 'there was unanimous and loud applause throughout the court…which the magistrates did not attempt to suppress'.

While these events were unfolding, Hassett sank into debt, and a meeting of his creditors was held at the Globe the day after the court hearings. Between nine and ten that evening, the *Courier* told its readers under the heading 'And Yet a Lower Depth', Hassett and the 'person described by Mr Allman as the complainant's sister' were discovered together in the dark in the Globe's laundry.

> Hassett's two daughters, his son-in-law, and one or two other persons were present, and before a light was procured the 'complainant's sister' made a bolt for it, but had not gone far when she was laid [hold] of – we do not see why we should hesitate to mention the name, having full permission to do so, and also having been requested to give the circumstance publicity in order to check the rash continuance of the misconduct, and moreover the action was rather creditable than otherwise – laid hold of by Miss Hassett, whose temper was so roused at the unbearable indignity thrust upon the family, that she succeeded in administering a good beating to the shameless person referred to, and the yard being sloppy from the heavy rain, 'the complainant's sister' got pretty well rolled in the mud in the transaction.

Clearly, Jerry had a problem on his hands at the Globe. The timing was hardly ideal, because on 7 November 1870 Hannah gave birth to another child at home at Reedy Creek. Perhaps because he was rather busy, Jerry did not get around to registering the arrival of Gertrude at Boorowa until 28 December. In the meantime he had undertaken another stint as publican of the Globe, officially taking back the licence on 16 November and then relinquishing it to his new tenant, Patrick Macnamara, a local builder, on 14 December.

While Jerry was publican, 'the whole of the furniture and stock-in-trade' of the Globe, evidently owned by Hassett, was put up for auction. The list of items on offer covers more than two columns of the *Courier*, with the contents of all rooms – including thirteen bedrooms, five parlours, the bar, bagatelle room, cellar, kitchen, pantry, laundry, bath-house and stable – enumerated. For example, the laundry housed a twelve-gallon boiler, three wash tubs, a patent mangle and four smoothing irons, and the bath-house a plunging shower bath and pump. Items for sale from the cellar included jars of salt, cases of curry powder and Worcester sauce, and five cases of champagne. The sale went well, attracting a large crowd and spirited bidding, and bringing in nearly £700. Probably Macnamara was the major purchaser, because the hotel's business does not seem to have been disrupted.

16

The biggest of all

Other visitors from the region to the Intercolonial Exhibition at the end of August 1870 included John Murphy. Apparently Murrumburrah did not follow Yass's example in sending a large contingent; the *Courier*'s correspondent knew of no others from the town who had made the trip. John may have been in a celebratory frame of mind. The paper reported earlier in the month that, after his mill's flour won a prize at the Yass Show in March, a Yass storekeeper had placed an order for regular supplies of 'a considerable quantity'.

This would have been a happier trip to Sydney than one the previous November for an appearance at the Supreme Court. John was being sued by a wholesale grocer for failure to pay for goods ordered by the Murphy store in Murrumburrah. Despite demands from the wholesaler, John had refused to pay until the order, delayed for months on the road, was received. When it eventually arrived, he found that ten bottles of brandy had been opened and the spirits substituted with dirty water. John sent a cheque for the sum owing, £53 6s 10d, minus 13s 4d, the value of the lost brandy. The wholesaler, however, had already launched legal action and refused to call it off unless John paid the full sum plus £6 6s costs. The court found in favour of the wholesaler.

John's first child, Annie, was born on 14 February 1870. A week later, an advertisement over his signature appeared in the *Courier* promoting a major advance in grain farming technology – a steam threshing machine 'capable of threshing and dressing, fit for market, 700 to 800 bushels per day'. It was to be on show for ten days in Murrumburrah and then proceed to Yass. Those wanting further particulars were invited to apply to John or to the machine's proprietor, Thomas Denny.

The following June, Felix Murphy and William Howard dissolved the partnership they had entered into to run the store Miles built at Binalong in 1847. This appears to have been a sound move from Felix's viewpoint because Howard, who retained the store, went broke three years later. In September 1873, the insolvency court accepted a claim by John Murphy that Howard owed him the large sum of £1,210 6s 4d. John followed his younger brother out of storekeeping in August 1870, renting the Murrumburrah premises to a James Dawson.

At the Criterion, Mass continued to be said frequently – until March 1871 when St Mary's Church was finally completed, consecrated by Bishop Lanigan and opened for divine service. Father Finnegan from Yass held services at the hotel in early October and November 1870, and then on 17 November a priest who was touring the colony to raise funds for Ireland's Catholic University celebrated a special Mass there. The committee organising the annual Murrumburrah race meeting, which included Felix Murphy, met at the Criterion on the same day. Earlier in the week, a meeting to relaunch the Murrumburrah Cricket Club had been held there. This elected a seven-man committee, including Felix, and decided to challenge Burrangong's cricketers to a match on the coming St Andrew's Day, 30 November. Having accepted the challenge, Burrangong won by 146 to 102. Felix still showed little cricketing aptitude, scoring ducks in both Murrumburrah innings. A list published by the *Courier* of seventeen players and non-players who had signed up as members of the cricket club included John, Thomas and Felix Murphy, and William Lehane. In a display of multiculturalism unusual for the time, it also included a young man named James Sing Quong.

Back in Yass, readers of the *Courier* over preceding months may have received a jolt when they saw a long article in the 13 January 1871 issue extolling the go-ahead nature of the town and region. Gone was all the gloom. Instead, Yass was 'a large and thriving town' in the centre of 'a most important and thriving' district. It was a case of tailoring the message to the audience; the article had been prepared at the request of the commissioners of the international exhibition to be held in London later in the year, and naturally aimed to give exhibition goers a good impression.

There was good news to report locally, though. Work was proceeding rapidly on the new bridge, and in late January a 'driving of the first rivet' ceremony was held, followed by a gathering at the Globe at which 'several toasts were proposed in sparkling champagne'. In mid-February, 'one of the most spirited and unanimous' public meetings held in Yass 'for a long time past' started planning the bridge-opening festivities. It decided the structure should be called Hume Bridge after the explorer, that Henry O'Brien's widow should be invited to officially name it, and that the town's banks, government offices, stores and other places of business should close for the day.

The atmosphere at another meeting in Yass three weeks earlier was very different. Held at the St Augustine's schoolhouse, it had been called to decide what to do about debts totalling at least £150 found to have been owed by Father Duigan at his death. Those present were Father Patrick Dunne from Goulburn, who had been delegated by Bishop Lanigan to call the meeting, two more priests and about twenty prominent Catholic laymen including Jerry; Dr Morgan O'Connor took the chair. The *Courier* carried a detailed report.

Father Dunne proposed that money Catholics had subscribed to build a monument to Duigan should be diverted to help clear the debts, and donations that had come from Protestants should be returned 'with sincere thanks for their generosity and their charity'. He thought it would be an insult to put the money received from Protestants into the debt fund, even if they offered to contribute. His estimate of the debts due was £197 12s. On the other side of the ledger, Duigan's bank account contained £93, but this could not be touched yet. A list published in the *Courier* the previous month showed donations for the monument then totalled £172 19s 6d.

Dr Isidore Blake, treasurer of the monument fund, disputed the need to divert money from that project; he said a separate debt fund, restricted to Catholics, had already been established and donations of £101 promised. The temperature of the meeting rose sharply when he added that he had been told Duigan's personal debts amounted to no more than about £150 while a letter he had received from Father Dunne suggested the figure was some £240. He feared Church debts had 'been saddled on' to Duigan's memory, and the people of the district were being asked to subscribe 'not to pay off personal debts alone, but the debts – he only repeated what he had heard, and did not say it was correct – the debts that ought to fall upon the heads of the Church, the Bishop and his Vicar-General'. He had no doubt that if people knew precisely what Duigan's debts were they would 'come forward and liquidate [them]'.

Blake refused O'Connor's request to name his source for the suggestion that the debts were not all Duigan's, but claimed it was 'a person he could believe'. He said he had been told debts relating to church construction or repair at Murrumburrah, Binalong and Yass had been added. 'Dr Blake is giving you rumour,' replied Father Dunne. 'I am happy to say it is entirely without foundation.'

The meeting became even more heated when Blake criticised O'Connor and lawyer Christopher Dease for earlier backing plans for the monument but now wanting to use the money collected for it from Catholics to pay off the debt. An interruption from Father Dunne provoked an angry response: 'If the rev. gentleman likes he can burke what I have to say, but otherwise he will listen to what I have to state.' O'Connor objected to the term 'burke' – nineteenth-century slang for smother or hush up – and Blake offered his regrets and withdrew the remark. 'At many meetings the use of such an expression would have caused the party to be turned out,' O'Connor said. 'Pitch him out of the window!' called Michael Conlon, another supporter of diverting money from the monument fund.

When a motion was put backing Father Dunne's plan to return the monument fund donations received from Protestants and ask Catholic donors to transfer their contributions to the debt fund, Blake moved an amendment. His proposal, that a public meeting of subscribers to the monument fund be called to decide what to do with the money, was carried nine to six. An annoyed Dunne said he would wash his hands of the matter. 'The affair might now go into the Insolvent Court. Would the Catholics of Yass allow that to be done? He would let them take the responsibility of disgracing themselves and their religion.' Apparently unmoved, the meeting then rejected a further amendment proposed by Conlon – that the money subscribed by Protestants be returned to them. 'It would be a most outrageous, most uncourteous act to the Protestant gentlemen who had subscribed to ask them to take back their money,' Blake argued.

Jerry spoke up late in the meeting, saying he did not see why so much reference should be made to Protestants. 'They had subscribed towards the fund willingly and their subscriptions had been taken with pleasure,' the *Courier* reported him saying.

> That having been done he did not see why distinctions should be drawn as to whether the subscribers were Catholics or Protestants. The Chairman: That is the sense of the meeting. Mr Lehane: I did not hear it. It was proposed to hand Protestants back their subscriptions, and he thought that was a very mean thing to do.

At Young the resident priest, Father Riordan, could not contain his anger when he read the *Courier*'s report of the meeting. He dashed off a letter to the editor signed 'A Catholic, not of a clique':

> Why wake the dead? Why rake up the ashes of the departed? Why tear from the red sacred soil the roses and flowers of all descriptions planted by affectionate hands? Why desecrate the grave and memory of poor, affectionate, kind Father Duigan, so many months dead and passed away?
>
> This train of vexatious thought occurs to me because of the trifling reason for which the name of the almost adored Father Duigan is bandied about for the merriment of every printer's devil in the land, to the sincere sorrow and distress of the people – the whole people – of Yass, who in a day would gladly subscribe and wipe out the few grocers' bills, or other liabilities that may be against him.

Riordan was distressed that 'the foul, filthy distinction of creeds' had been introduced into the discussion, and 'our kind, friendly Protestant neighbours' insulted. He commented on all the lay speakers at the meeting. Morgan O'Connor was 'Signor Pomponioso, very large in dimensions, but extensively larger in self-conceit... This Esculapius or Hippocrates, or hypocrite if you will, had the coolness to rule as out of order Dr Blake, than whom there is not perhaps a more honest man or more sterling magistrate in Australia.' Dease was 'a pious impecunious stalking attorney'. Conlan, 'that brave muscular man who would pitch Doctor Blake through the window', was fit only for Tarban Creek lunatic asylum. The performance of these men reminded Riordan of 'the Fair of French Fuize, near the Curragh of Kildare, where I saw about a dozen donkeys kick each other fiercely to settle which of them should have the first bite of a tempting thistle'.

He nominated four 'men of honour' among the participants. The first three were Dr Blake, Michael Cassidy, who had seconded Blake's amendment to Father Dunne's proposal, and police Sub Inspector Brennan, who had expressed confidence that the people of Yass could pay off Duigan's debts without touching the monument fund. Fourth was Jerry:

> ...the proudest, ablest, and biggest of them all, Mr Jeremiah Lehane, stood like a tower of strength against the face of the enemy.

'Let all Catholics honour and praise these four men,' Riordan added.

In the same issue, the *Courier* commented that 'a formidable mountain appears to have been made of a most insignificant molehill' in dealing with the debt. It understood that fifty to sixty Catholic subscribers to the monument fund had requested that Bishop Lanigan approve a separate subscription list to meet Duigan's debt, with the monument money being kept for its original purpose. The paper published a balance sheet it had compiled which suggested available funds already exceeded the debt. These funds comprised the money in Duigan's bank account, collections made in Yass, Gunning and Sydney, and a further item: 'Subscription, Mr Lehane', £5. Clearly, Jerry wanted to help finalise the matter with minimum fuss.

News of the Duigan affair was spreading beyond the region, including to Deniliquin, where he had been posted before coming to Yass. The local paper there, the *Pastoral Times*, noted that the young priest had been 'not very worldly in regard to money matters; we hear that he gave largely and secretly'. It added that he was greatly esteemed in the town, 'and probably some who were his friends here would like to aid in freeing his memory from any illiberal remarks respecting his indebtedness'.

The public meeting, proposed by Dr Blake, of subscribers to the monument fund went ahead two and a half weeks after the St Augustine's schoolroom gathering. Blake took the chair, and prominent Protestants present included Archdeacon Lillingston and George Allman. Blake's stand at the first meeting seems to have had unanimous support; resolutions carried by acclamation insisted that the money donated for the monument be used for that purpose. Allman objected strongly to the idea of returning the Protestant subscriptions, saying this would be offensive and likely 'to destroy the good feeling which, he was happy to think, had hitherto existed for so many years between the Catholics and Protestants of the district'. Allman added that there had been a time when he and many others had greatly misunderstood and wrongly judged Father Duigan's motives and actions, but they 'had lived to know him better before he died'. They had subscribed to the monument fund to show their feelings of respect for him.

Father Riordan's letter had a sequel a month later, when the *Courier* reported that Morgan O'Connor had launched a libel action against the paper, but dropped it after the priest willingly admitted that he was the letter's author and apologised. 'The conduct of the rev. gentleman who wrote the letter and of Dr O'Connor has been worthy of all praise,' commented the *Courier*.

> We are much pleased to find that the writer of the letter – written at a time when he was annoyed and vexed at certain proceedings having reference to a deceased and warm friend – so honourably and straightforwardly authorised his name to be given up, and immediately on being asked tendered a gentlemanly apology for what was written hastily and without due consideration.

The *Courier* offered its own apology – for publishing a letter that was 'somewhat coarse and scandalous'. So we have J.J. Brown's error of judgement to thank for the survival in print of Father Riordan's glowing tribute to Jerry.

The final clearing of the debts seems to have taken about a year. An advertisement in the *Courier* on 1 March 1872 invited those who had proved their claims and still had money owing to contact Father Dunne. He was now 'prepared to settle all demands in full'.

Back on the farm, Jerry set about renewing his sheep folds, advertising in mid-March 1871 for hurdle makers – 'none but competent hands need apply' – to make 400 five-bar hurdles. Hannah placed an advertisement in the same issue of the *Courier* seeking 'a married couple, without encumbrance' – the man to cook 'and otherwise make himself useful' and the woman as laundress and to assist with children. Young Jeremiah was now six years old, Josephine nearly three and Gertrude four months.

The following month, Jerry was required again in Yass, this time as a judge at the annual Pastoral and Agricultural Association show. With fellow graziers Thomas Turner and William Macansh, his task was to select the prizewinners in eight categories of fine-woolled, coarse-woolled and fat sheep. The number of entries was disappointingly low – only twenty-six – and, reported the *Courier*, with the exception of William Wotton's pen of fine-woolled ewes 'they were not considered to be first class by the judges'. One decision proved controversial; Wotton lodged a protest after the judges awarded the prize for fine-woolled rams to Frederick Hume rather than himself, 'the judges having perhaps not taken into consideration the question of the date of shearing'. Jerry and his colleagues were unmoved, upholding their previous decision.

The day's proceedings on the North Yass showground got off to a bad start, with rain falling in the morning and many intending exhibitors having to be refused entry after arriving late. Nevertheless, according to the *Courier*, the show 'passed off most successfully'. The sun came out about ten a.m. and the number of visitors was very large; more than 400 paid for admission and 'very many avoided payment by entering the ground over the fence'. The Burton's Circus band played from one to three p.m. and Patrick Sheekey's refreshment stall was well patronised. Despite the problem with late arrivals, the number and quality of exhibits was generally a 'vast improvement' compared with the previous year. The *Courier* nominated three lessons learned for future shows: shed accommodation needed to be greatly increased, the fence to be strongly paled, and the public and members more strictly excluded while the judges were considering their awards.

John Murphy did not come over from Murrumburrah this time; instead, he was an exhibitor at the closer Burrangong (Young) Show held shortly afterwards, taking prizes for best hack and best pony. Earlier he had been appointed to the committee of the Burrangong Pastoral and Agricultural Association, which organised the show. John's second child, another Miles Murphy, was born on 3 May. Two days later, he attended a public lunch at Binalong's Swan Inn to honour Edgar Beckham, who had retired after nearly thirty years as Crown lands commissioner and was leaving the district. John was given the task of collecting the 'purse of sovereigns' for Beckham's testimonial presentation.

The *Courier* marked the anniversary of the Yass flood on 26 April with renewed gloom. Rain was now needed badly again; if it did not come soon, many farmers would be unable to plough their land and any crops that were planted might not germinate. In town, the Braidwood Store next to the Globe planned to close. Business in Yass had fallen off 'in a remarkable and unaccountable manner' over the past year or two, the paper commented. 'The want of a bridge over the Yass River perhaps explains in part this decrease in transactions, but we are afraid that much of the slackness arises from the poverty of the surrounding population, occasioned by a succession of unfavourable seasons.' Data from the latest census, published in the next issue, appeared to confirm that Yass was stagnating. The town's population had grown from 1,123 in 1861 to 1,371 in 1871 – an increase (eighteen per cent) that was far below the forty-three per cent gain, from 351,000 to 503,000, for the colony as a whole.

A new cause for concern had emerged soon after the flood – suggestions that the planned railway extension south of Goulburn might not pass through Yass. This fear took concrete form in October 1870, when railway surveyors produced a map of their favoured route, which skirted the town. Its nearest point was two and a quarter miles from the courthouse. The *Courier* warned that if Yass property owners responded to this news with indifference and apathy they could blame only themselves for the losses that a terminus well away from the town would cause them. Its calls for protest prompted the creation towards the end of 1870 of a Permanent Railway Progress Committee, which spent the three years the government took to make a final decision agitating for a change of plans. Jerry was among those who contributed to the effort, which proved fruitless, to bring the railway close to town (chapter 18).

The engineering work of most interest to the people of Yass early in 1871 was, of course, construction of the new bridge. On 11 March, just six weeks after the ceremony marking driving of the first rivet, another was held to celebrate driving of the last. Watched by a crowd of fifty or sixty, three prominent townsmen – storekeeper James Cottrell, publican Thomas Colls and J.J. Brown – were presented with red-hot rivets to insert. Cottrell and Colls 'stripped off their coats, set to work with a will and performed the job capitally for amateurs', wrote Brown, modestly neglecting to describe his own contribution. Then about thirty gentlemen, including the head of the contracting company for the ironwork, Mr Bartholomew, retired to the Commercial Hotel for a round of champagne toasts. Brown was full of praise for the efforts of Bartholomew and his men, whose only remaining tasks were painting the bridge and removing scaffolding. Jobs still to be done by others were the laying of the bridge's wooden floor – the Globe's new publican Patrick Macnamara had the contract for that task – and building the approaches. The *Courier* was confident that all would be complete within about two months, allowing a Queen's Birthday (24 May) opening.

Unfortunately, this work proceeded 'at a snail's pace', for which the paper blamed the government officials in charge. 'The public have to behold the noble structure spanning the river, at an unapproachable elevation, minus flooring, and regret the incapacity, blundering ignorance, or stupid negligence of those paid, and well paid, out of the public funds for mismanaging the public works in a way that no private firm would tolerate,' it noted a week before the Queen's Birthday. At the end of May, Mrs O'Brien pulled out of the opening ceremony, unable to further delay a planned visit to Sydney. Two more months passed before all was in readiness.

In the meantime, a series of meetings was held to organise the celebrations, including a public luncheon, a ball and a gathering of the town's schoolchildren at which sweetmeats – cost £5 – would be distributed. One of the last of these, on 10 July, heard that the town's Catholic, Anglican and Presbyterian clergy had agreed to arrange for the bells of their churches to be rung on the opening day. The organising committee applauded when J.J. Brown announced that Jerry had donated five guineas to help cover the costs of the celebrations. In the next day's *Courier*, Cottrell's store advertised attire for the celebration ball – including 'splendid grenadine ball dresses', 'white and other tarlatans', 'ribbons, feathers and flowers', and 'ladies' and gentlemen's white kid gloves'.

At last the great day, Tuesday 25 July, arrived – greeted by that morning's *Courier* as the day

> the weary, dreary, bridgeless time of grumbling, entreaty, and remonstrance is at an end... So here's to the new bridge, and may it carry our friends and ourselves safe over many a long day to come.

The paper reported that visitors had come from far and wide for the

*The new Yass bridge – a sketch from the 1880s.
It gave more than 100 years' service.*

celebrations, the bridge had been decked out with green bows and wattle branches bursting into bloom, flags and bunting were set to fly from the town's main buildings, and a bullock had been spitted ready for roasting over a large fire.

Although the day turned out gusty, cold and wet, 'the ceremonial passed off in a highly satisfactory manner', said the *Courier*'s next edition. Events started with a procession of more than a thousand people from the courthouse to the bridge. The Goulburn City Band led the way, followed by 300 children behind the banners of the Catholic, Anglican and Presbyterian schools. Next came the organising committee headed by Dr Allan Campbell, followed by members of the Yass and Goulburn Oddfellows lodges in full insignia and carrying 'numerous very beautiful banners'. The 'general public' made up the rear.

When they reached the bridge, 'the crush was very great'. At the site selected for the opening ceremony, a bottle of champagne, 'gaily decorated with ribbons', had been suspended. Dr Campbell commenced proceedings by introducing Emily Allman, wife of lawyer George Allman, who had been invited to perform the opening in place of Mrs O'Brien. After he handed her the bottle and 'begged to request her to name the bridge,

Mrs Allman, on the cessation of the cheering, remarked, in a distinct voice: 'On behalf of the inhabitants of Yass, and at their request, I name this bridge the Hume Bridge, and I sincerely hope that its services to the colony may be as great and lasting as those of the illustrious explorer whose name it bears.' These words were no sooner uttered than smash went the bottle, and the cheering which followed was something astounding. The wind was blowing so strongly that a considerable number of those in the vicinity were besprinkled by the sparkling liquid, and Mrs Allman herself shared in the baptismal drops. The school children, band, and most of those present then joined in the National Anthem, which was most excellently rendered, after which hearty cheers were given for Mrs Allman, Mr Hume, Dr Campbell, and others. The church bells also struck up a merry peal, and the din altogether was unusual in Yass.

The procession then headed up Cooma Street to the Mechanics Institute, where cakes and sweetmeats were handed to 'the little folk' who again sang the national anthem 'very nicely'. Across the river, a large gathering 'mustered in the vicinity of the roasted bullock', where bread, ale and wine as well as beef were distributed to all comers. 'The fun at this part of the proceedings was hearty and frolicsome', the *Courier* reported.

Inside the Mechanics Institute, between forty and fifty ladies and gentlemen sat down to the official luncheon, presided over by Dr Campbell. He was greeted with loud cheers when he proposed a toast to Hamilton and Mrs Hume, who had declined the committee's invitation to attend the ceremonies because of ill health. John K. Hume from Boorowa responded on behalf of his uncle and aunt. In the evening, about 170 gathered at the Mechanics Institute for the ball. 'It was really pleasant to perceive that all classes mingled without distinction in the various dances,' noted the *Courier*.

> The ball was kept up till nearly six a.m. on Wednesday. The Goulburn city band occupied the orchestra and gave satisfaction, although many of those present would have preferred a string to a brass band.

17

Transitions

Two weeks before the bridge opening, Bishop Lanigan visited Yass to conduct a confirmation service for about 140 young men and women. The Catholics of Yass made quite a celebration of the visit, which came only months after the bishop's return from a journey to Rome. Lanigan had attended Pope Pius IX's First Vatican Council, which ran from December 1869 to October 1870. The *Courier* reported that large numbers of people, in vehicles and on horseback, greeted him four miles from town and escorted him in. When the procession neared Yass, 'the sonorous peals of the large bell at St Augustine's gathered together a congregation of about two hundred to meet the bishop'. A floral arch had been erected for him to pass under as he entered the church.

As a prominent member of the St Augustine's congregation, Jerry was most likely among those who welcomed the bishop. The timing of J.J. Brown's announcement of Jerry's contribution to the bridge opening fund – the day after the confirmation service – suggests that he was in town then; perhaps he had paid Brown a visit at the *Courier* office, next to the Globe. Jerry's election the following week to the committee of the town's newly formed Jockey Club, of which Morgan O'Connor was president, is further evidence that he was spending some time in Yass. Possibly he stayed on for the bridge opening.

If he was among the 200 at St Augustine's when the bishop arrived, he would have heard O'Connor deliver a lengthy welcoming address, mainly on the subject of the Vatican Council's controversial adoption of the doctrine of Papal infallibility. O'Connor said the Yass congregation received the new dogma with 'joy and unhesitating faith', and added,

> We believe that that dogma is a special inspiration of the Holy Ghost to meet

the exigencies of our troubled and disastrous times, now that the powers of darkness, more than ever, appear to have thrown open their flood-gates and let loose the dark waves of error and dissolution, now surging with such wild fury through the world and threatening to engulf, in one common ruin, truth, religion, and civilisation. Ah! Fortunately for truth, fortunately for religion, fortunately for civilisation, there is one power still on earth against which the gates of hell shall never prevail. The barque of Peter sits securely moored on the Rock of Christ, changeless and unchangeable amid all change – the fountain of truth, the source of all Christian civilisation, and the fount in which again the apostate world must lave or she will assuredly revert to her former barbarism, from which heretofore the Church redeemed her.

On reading the address, the Anglican Archdeacon Lillingston wasted no time in tackling his old adversary (chapter 11) in a long letter to the *Courier*. He made fun of some of O'Connor's imagery – for example, 'while barques may sometimes be moored to rocks, they are not generally moored on them, as...that experiment would usually result in foundering'. His more serious point was to wonder how a change in church dogma that had caused so much debate 'throughout the length and breadth of Europe' could 'so easily and so quietly' be accepted by the Catholics of Yass without their having heard or read all the arguments advanced on both sides of the question.

The letter attracted many responses, both calm and strident. Probably the one most to the point, signed 'Old Catholic', wondered whether Lillingston had read all the arguments that had been advanced for and against every element of his own beliefs. Catholics chose to be guided 'by the expressed essence of the theological wisdom and learning of the Christian world' rather than by 'their own defective judgement or any authority less profound, sublime, or holy', Old Catholic wrote. He added that he was sorry to see the 'well-conducted and useful' *Courier* being used for such polemical discussion 'as it invariably leads to sectarian animosity, which it is the duty of every thinking man to discourage'.

While this controversy proceeded, J.J. Brown focused on another target in his continuing campaign against sectarian division. Long leaders in two mid-July issues attacked the rise of anti-Catholic Orange associations, although Yass did not have one yet. The first article drew a response from Lillingston, who thought the associations had a legitimate role in 'mutual self-defence from a common, an ubiquitous, an active, and an unscrupulous enemy'. The *Courier* would have none of this:

> We object to Orangeism because it seeks to enflame ignorance rather than to teach it – to drill souls to a united hatred rather than to seek to elevate them to charity.

Nevertheless, Brown had a lot of time for Lillingston, who returned to England at the end of the year. The *Courier* praised him for having 'so thoroughly identified with the people of Yass, their interests and affairs'. He had denounced sin and wickedness 'with conscientious boldness', but 'was yet withal so tender'.

A more down-to-earth matter that would have attracted Jerry's attention around this time was a gold discovery beside Reedy Creek. The *Courier*'s first report, in September 1871, said about sixty people were already working the find 'and great hopes are entertained that the ground will prove rich'. Large amounts of tea, sugar and flour had been purchased in Yass to provide for the expected rush, and a butcher's shop 'is also said to be in course of erection'. A week later, the outlook was much dimmer. About twenty holes had been dug, but in only a few had 'the 'colour' of gold' been found. All the diggers were expected to leave within days.

In October, Jerry obtained a new tenant in Yass, the Post Office. The *Courier* reported that he had made a building adjacent to the Globe Hotel available at a very moderate rental. A month later, the first public sign appeared that, once more, all was not well at the Globe. An advertisement headed 'Notice and Caution' signed by Jerry 'imperatively' cautioned 'bankers, storekeepers, hotelkeepers and the public generally against giving credit in his name or acknowledging orders drawn upon him for any purpose whatsoever', unless authorised by Hannah or him personally. That the warning related to Patrick Macnamara, publican of the Globe for the past year, became clear in January 1872, when Macnamara followed his predecessor, Richard Hassett, into insolvency.

Like Hassett's, Macnamara's incumbency at the Globe began with good publicity generated by public-spirited work. Hassett performed major road repairs in Rossi Street (chapter 14). Macnamara's contribution was a large culvert at the corner of Cooma and Rossi Streets over an open drain running down the side of Cooma Street. Known as the 'government ditch', this stormwater drain, which doubled as a sewer, received frequent mentions in the *Courier* as an eyesore and a hazard to both health and traffic. Because Cooma Street was part of the colony's main southern road, its maintenance was the government's responsibility – hence the drain's name. Nevertheless, the roads department contributed only £10 towards building the culvert; the rest had to be raised from public subscriptions in Yass. The completed structure was 'broad and substantial', the *Courier* reported, and Macnamara deserved 'great credit for having succeeded in removing a great hindrance to traffic'.

In August, Macnamara attended a public meeting called to initiate a new push for municipal incorporation, and his signature was one of 120 – Jerry's was not among them – on a fresh petition sent to the government in October. As before, J.J. Brown was a prime mover for the cause. A reported comment by the commissioner for roads strengthened the case; until Yass had a municipal council, he warned, the only repairs made in Cooma Street would be those absolutely necessary to allow traffic to proceed through the town. No counter-petition emerged this time, but incorporation was again denied, in April 1872, because the area proposed for the municipality exceeded that allowed under the legislation. An annoyed Brown began his campaign for a third attempt (this time successful – the municipality was proclaimed in March 1873)

Cooma Street, Yass, in 1872. The 'government ditch' running its length had to be bridged to allow access to buildings.

by publishing a news item about 'the vilest and most abominable odours, sufficient to originate a pestilence in the neighbourhood', polluting part of Cooma Street. In the absence of a municipal inspector of nuisances, asked the *Courier*, 'who's business is it to trace the cause, and compel a removal?'

In January 1872, Macnamara reported to the insolvency court that his liabilities exceeded his assets by about £450. Jerry advertised for a new tenant for the Globe at the end of the month. Despite the upheaval and a new auction sale of the furniture and fittings, the advertisement claimed the hotel was 'in full trade' and 'amply furnished'. It was 'well worth the attention of parties on the look-out for a genuine concern'. Joshua Shipway, a tailor and frequent participant in local theatricals (chapter 7), took up the challenge and was granted the publican's licence in early March. He had already had an experience of insolvency, in 1865. In an advertisement placed in every issue of the *Courier* from mid-March to June, he begged 'to acquaint his old friends and the public' that he was now running the Globe and hoped 'by keeping everything of the best brands to merit a share of patronage'. He advised that 'Baths and other conveniences have been added to the establishment. The stables are large and airy, and the forage the best that can be procured in the Southern District.'

Macnamara's insolvency court hearings began in mid-February. Debts proved at the first creditors' meeting included £199 1s 11d owed to Jerry, and the second meeting two weeks later found John Murphy was owed about £63. Explaining his predicament at that meeting, Macnamara said he had lost money on various building contracts entered into with churches and the government. Asked about his takings as publican of the Globe, he said they had averaged £20 a week in his first six months there – scarcely the makings of a large profit. The next creditors' meeting, in April, heard that Macnamara owed Jerry £75 for six months' rent, so he, too, was not making much money from the hotel, which had probably seemed a much better investment in the boom times of the early 1860s.

In late February 1872, Jerry was back in Yass to again judge sheep at the annual pastoral and agricultural show. The event was most successful, the *Courier* reported. Twelve to thirteen hundred people attended, 'a very considerable number of whom were ladies'. A band from Sydney provided entertainment, playing favourite airs through the day. Stock exhibits were 'numerous and generally of a very fine description', and the displays of farm produce, fruit and vegetables were 'really excellent'.

Jerry and his four fellow sheep judges – William Macansh, who was also on the previous year's judging panel, William Allan from Young, Henry Broughton, and George Eason from Boorowa, who makes further appearances later in this chapter – found the sheep exhibits unusually excellent. According to the *Courier*, they had much trouble in arriving at decisions in several classes. Part of the problem was that only some of the sheep had been shorn; the judges 'were unanimous in stating their opinion that all the sheep should be either full-fleeced or shorn'. They suggested that late summer was not a suitable time for judging sheep as it was too close to shearing. The Pastoral and Agricultural Association agreed, and in later years held a separate sheep show in July.

Andrew Hamilton Hume of Everton near Boorowa, a grazier-relative of the explorer, was the main prizewinner for fine-woolled sheep. John Murphy, who had again decided that the journey from Murrumburrah was worth the effort, received an honourable mention for his exhibit of two merino ewes. Charles Massy from the Gundaroo district won prizes in the Southdown and fat sheep divisions. He was an old associate of Jerry's from his days as overseer for Terence Aubrey Murray (chapter 2). In 1868, both Jerry and Massy gave evidence in support of Murray in a Goulburn court case over the disputed ownership of two blocks of land. They were asked to recall discussions that had taken place more than twenty years earlier; their recollections helped persuade the jury that Murray's claim to the land was legitimate.

Murphy had a highly successful show, winning prizes for flour, ham and bacon, and an honourable mention for his thoroughbred stallion, Mormon, as well as for his merino ewes. His success with ham and bacon came just over a year after he placed a wanted to buy ad in the *Courier* for two to three hundred pigs; his piggery enterprise at Kalangan, like his flour mill, was evidently turning out top quality product. The following October, he advertised the stud services of Mormon – £5 for one mare, plus five shillings groomage. The large advertisement noted that the stallion had also won a gold medal at the 1872 Burrangong Show and spelt out his illustrious pedigree – he was related to a winner of the

Epsom Derby – and racing history. Mormon came second to Archer in the first Melbourne Cup, run in 1861, and second again in the 1863 Cup. His race winnings over five years totalled £6,990. He had since, John advised potential customers, 'proved himself a sure foal-getter' over four seasons at Lancefield, Victoria.

On Friday 19 April 1872, the *Courier* noted the arrival in Yass two days earlier of the Very Rev. Dr John Forrest and Dr James Gilhooley, and their departure the following morning for Reedy Creek on a visit to Jerry. 'We understand that tomorrow (Saturday) Dr Forrest will celebrate the marriage ceremony between Mr W. Lehane, of Narraburra, and Miss Murphy, daughter of the late Mr Miles Murphy, of Kalangan, near Murrumburrah,' the item went on. 'The ceremony is to take place at Reedy Creek, the residence of the bridegroom's father.' Whether Dr Gilhooley's wife Mary Ann, sister of Forrest and hence also a cousin of William Lehane, was with the two men is not recorded.

Sarah Murphy was nineteen and William twenty-five. Since taking charge of Narraburra for his father six years earlier, William had probably made fairly frequent visits to Murrumburrah, which is just past the halfway point on the most direct route to Coppabella. He was a steward at the Murrumburrah races in 1867 and joined the Murrumburrah Cricket Club in 1870 (although there is no report of him participating in any of their matches). Earlier, he had boarded at Lyndhurst College in Sydney with Sarah's brothers Felix and Joseph. Miles and Jerry had known each other

Jerry (seated), William Lehane (left), John Murphy (standing) and Felix Murphy.

at least since 1859 when they both attended the great St Patrick's Day dinner in Yass (chapter 3). Jerry's place at the top table at the opening of Miles' flour mill in 1866 is a sign that these two successful Irishmen were good friends. The happy photo that has survived of a seated Jerry flanked on one side by William and on the other by John and Felix Murphy, with a small dog, suggests that the families remained close after the death of Miles in 1869.

Most likely, the wedding was a big and cheerful affair. Accounts of the life of John Forrest speak of his hospitable nature and fondness for socialising, and his benevolent disposition, liberal outlook and humorous, good-natured manner. He was assisted in the religious ceremonies by the Very Rev. Dr John O'Connor who, if he was anything like his brother Morgan O'Connor, would also have enjoyed a party. This distinguished priest was on an extended visit to the colony after, according to the *Courier*, successful tours of Europe and America. His trip to Reedy Creek for the wedding came at the end of a stint as parish priest at Boorowa. Before returning to Ireland, he headed to north Queensland; newspaper accounts of his preaching there praised his non-sectarian approach and liberality.

Sarah Lehane.

Guests at the wedding included Nicholas Besnard junior, son of the master of ceremonies at the 1859 St Patrick's Day dinner; we know this because he signed the marriage certificate as a witness. The other witness was Mary O'Hehir, Hannah's sixteen-year-old daughter from her first marriage. Presumably, Sarah's brothers John, Felix, Thomas and Miles were there, and John's wife Mary Anne. Five days after the celebration, some of the party visited the Royal Hotel, Boorowa, for a farewell presentation to the Rev. Dr

O'Connor. The local paper noted that, as well as many of the town's leading residents, those present included visitors from Reedy Creek (that could only be Lehanes) and Murrumburrah (probably Murphys). In keeping with the non-sectarian spirit in the air, the chief organiser of this event was an Irish-born Anglican, George Eason, Jerry's fellow sheep judge at the Yass Show.

William and Sarah presumably settled at Narraburra after the wedding. Early in August, however, Sarah accompanied Jerry and his seven-year-old son Jeremiah on a buggy ride from Yass to Reedy Creek; according to the *Courier* report, Jeremiah had been brought to town for medical treatment. A nasty accident occurred as they neared home, and Sarah's quick thinking probably saved the child from serious injury. 'It appears that Mr Lehane was driving a pair of spirited horses at a leisurely pace, and was approaching his own place when the off wheels of the buggy dropped into one of the many deep and dangerous ruts on that portion of the main southern road,' the paper reported.

> The unexpected jolt caused Mr Lehane to lose his seat and let the reins slip, when Mrs Lehane, junior, unfortunately screamed, causing the horses to bolt. This young lady threw her nephew, fortunately without accident, on to the roadside, and afterwards succeeded in getting clear of the buggy herself, with very trifling injury. The buggy, however, was smashed to pieces, and almost entirely destroyed. Under the circumstances it is almost miraculous that serious injuries were escaped.

Plans were in hand to improve the road. A government report in early 1871 estimated the cost of metalling the twenty-seven miles from Yass to Reedy Creek at about £23,000. Tenders were called for the job, to be undertaken in five sections, in May 1872. It is doubtful, though, that much progress had been made by mid-September, when Jerry again set off for Yass, this time to visit lawyer George Allman's office to make his will. Probably the buggy accident had jolted him into action, not before time for a man of sixty-one or sixty-two with a much younger wife and three small children.

Jerry nominated Hannah and George Eason, whom he described as 'my friend', as executors. Perhaps the friendship developed during the sheep judging; no information on any earlier association with Jerry has come to light, although Miles Murphy was acquainted with him from at least as early as 1860 (chapter 6). Eason was an interesting character. He ran Gegullalong station near Boorowa for many years, and then in 1874 launched the weekly *Burrowa News*. He had long been a prominent citizen in the region, serving as a JP and taking a leading role in community activities, including theatrical performances; according to one report, a rendering of Byron's 'Address to the Ocean' showed 'a purity of expression and a distinctness of utterance indicative of an elocutionary training which few could excel'. He gave two lectures at the Yass Mechanics Institute during 1872. The first, in June, was on tariff protection, which he opposed. His second topic, in October, was 'The land, what shall we do with it?' He argued that most of the colony's rural land should be made available as freehold, with blocks sold at a low price to small farmers.

Jerry's will provided for Hannah, the three children of their marriage, and the daughter of his first marriage, Ellen Lyons. Jerry had already looked after William, transferring the lease of Narraburra to him. Under the will, Coppabella was to be valued when young Jeremiah turned twenty-one (in 1885), and he was to have the 'option and privilege' of then taking on the station provided his mother and two sisters each received payments of a quarter of its value. Hannah was to retain the Yass real estate until her death or remarriage. Then it was to be sold, with £1,000 going to Ellen and the rest in equal shares to the three children. All Hannah's entitlements depended on her remaining unmarried.

Jerry evidently had second thoughts after returning home because a month later he was back in Yass preparing a codicil. Perhaps it occurred to him that Jeremiah could find it very difficult to make the required payments to Hannah, Josephine and Gertrude on taking over Coppabella. The codicil made this easier, providing that the Yass holdings would go to Jeremiah when Hannah died or remarried. His sisters would receive shares only if he died 'without leaving lawful issue'. None of the proceeds would now go to Ellen; maybe Jerry had heard that John Perry Lyons' legal practice in Maryborough was doing well.

By odd coincidence, George Allman died the day the codicil was signed. The news may have reached his Rossi Street office by telegraph while Jerry was there; he died in Sydney, having gone to the city two weeks earlier in search of medical help for his heart and liver condition. Jerry must have known Allman well. The lawyer helped him win two important law cases – the Coppabella boundaries dispute of 1860 (chapter 3) and the action for cattle stealing brought by John P. Sheahan in 1865 (chapter 8). And Allman was a prominent figure at many gatherings that Jerry attended in Yass – including the 1859 St Patrick's Day dinner and the 1865 public meeting to begin fundraising for the new St Mary's Cathedral (chapter 7). He was one of the Protestant subscribers to the Father Duigan monument fund whose donations Jerry thought it would be very mean to return (chapter 16).

The forty-eight-year-old Allman had lived in Yass since the mid-1840s. 'His honourable life will…be embalmed in the memory of the townspeople, and ever afford an example that may beneficially be followed by all,' wrote the *Courier*. 'No public movement for the benefit of the town or the advancement of the district occurred in which he did not take a leading part.'

Confirming that nature abhors a vacuum, two young lawyers – Louis Adam Windeyer and Edward Arthur Iceton – set up practices in Rossi Street, near the courthouse, within two weeks of Allman's death. Both were welcomed by the Yass magistrates at their 13 November sitting. Windeyer, an unmarried thirty-two-year-old who had previously practised in Goulburn, took up lodgings at the Globe and immediately became an active member of the Yass community. Before year's end, he had been elected vice-president of the Jockey Club and umpired a cricket match between teams from Yass and Goulburn. Soon afterwards he was elected secretary of the Pastoral and Agricultural Association and a member of the hospital committee.

The week in which the new lawyers were made welcome ended with a public holiday throughout New South Wales. This celebrated a major step in the development of today's 'global village' – the linking of Europe and the colony by telegraph. The first messages from the other side of the world were actually received in mid-1872 following completion of the Adelaide to Port Darwin overland telegraph; Java and Darwin had been connected by an undersea cable six months earlier. The *Courier* published its first London telegram from Australian Associated Press on 5 July; the rather dull news it conveyed was that '*The Times* suggests that the colonies should petition the Crown for the repeal of the Act against differential duties.' The first private telegram from Yass to the UK was sent on 23 November 1872 – cost for twenty words a somewhat startling £9 12s 6d.

The *Courier* marked the holiday with a brief leader expressing the hope that, in an era noted for verbosity, the international telegraph would teach the value of condensation of thought and speech:

> Now that we are *en rapport* with the universe, it is evident that time is doubly precious. Reuter and other press agents have to compress into a brief sentence the pith and marrow of big events. Talky-talky and undue efflorescence on the surface of ideas cannot be tolerated at the rate of several shillings a syllable. May public speakers, especially honourable members during the present session, take the hint, and strive after that *cablegramic* brevity which is so essential to business! Politicians used to study how to utter little meaning in many words. Let the modern telegram teach them the converse – how to say much in a few words. Then would today be blessed to many ears. How happy for reporters the time when orators, both in rostra and pulpit, will yearn to be ranked as *telegrammatic!*

18

Farewells

A gold discovery at Nanima, about fifteen miles south of Yass, generated great excitement in the town in the second half of 1872. The local clerk of petty sessions issued more than fifty miners' rights within a week of the *Courier*'s first report of the find in late July. Prominent townsmen who joined the rush included Dr Allan Campbell, storekeepers James Cottrell and James Ritchie, Thomas Colls of the Commercial Hotel, and Joshua Shipway, licensee of the Globe. Even J.J. Brown of the *Courier* became a partner in a claim there.

A little earlier, a promising gold find had been made even closer to Yass, on the Hardwicke estate just out of town. Hardwicke's owner and Yass auctioneer Arthur Remmington launched a company to work it, and Dr Morgan O'Connor and Shipway were among prominent locals who took up shares. Catching the mood, Remmington presented a lecture – 'a masterly elocutionary effort' according to the *Courier* – on 'Gold!' at the Yass Mechanics Institute at the end of July. The audience of about a hundred interrupted him frequently with 'loud and hearty applause' as he waxed lyrical:

> What a wonderful panorama floats before our imagination when we contemplate the magnificence and power of gold – the heroes it has made – the miracles it has wrought – the cities it has built – the Empires it has laid in ruins…

A month later, gold was discovered in Yass – 'a couple of pretty little nuggets' in gravel taken from the riverbank in a public recreation reserve. The *Courier* reported that a prospecting area had been marked out immediately. 'We should not be at all surprised if the spot proves to yield gold in payable quantities,' it added.

All the finds proved disappointments. Nanima was the biggest, and in October the *Courier* was impressed by 'several very fine specimens of auriferous stone' that Joshua Shipway brought in to Yass – 'one or two of the pieces of quartz were literally peppered with the precious metal'. The same report noted, though, that tests on quartz samples sent to Sydney had given disappointing results and some holders of claims were contemplating abandoning them. While small-scale mining continued at Nanima, little more was heard of the Hardwicke field and nothing more of the Yass discovery.

Another gold find, west of Yass, stayed in the news longer with a correspondent submitting reports to the *Courier* through most of 1872 and 1873. This was Kangaroo Reefs, around Cumbamurra Creek just north of Coppabella. In a dispatch at the end of July 1872, the correspondent noted promising results from shaft and creek bed workings despite recent heavy rains and flooding. Sadly, a 'hard-working, honest, and inoffensive' miner, George White, had drowned in the flood; a boy employed by Jerry found his body. Perhaps this was the same Coppabella 'shepherd boy' who the following November, while 'following his flock', made another discovery, a promising copper lode. Copper had been found earlier nearby, and in late October John Vicq and three other men were granted a lease over that area. Initial indications were that the new lode was richer: 'The sample of surface ore surpasses anything yet obtained in this district,' reported the *Courier*.

The news from Kangaroo Reefs often extended beyond mining matters. In his 20 November 1872 dispatch, for example, the correspondent noted that shearing had begun at Coppabella a week earlier. His 3 May 1873 report informed *Courier* readers that the autumn weather in the district was 'all that could be desired' by a farmer: 'The late rain has made the ground soft, so that the plough is now doing its work on the different selections.' Unfortunately, though, cattle on local properties were dying from a disease thought to be 'dry pleuro' – presumably pleuropneumonia, which was introduced into Australia in 1858 and not eradicated nationally until 1968.

Jerry's view of conditions at the time was somewhat different – more rain was needed – and it seems he was not having problems with pleuro. A letter he wrote to a friend named Molly – we have no other identification

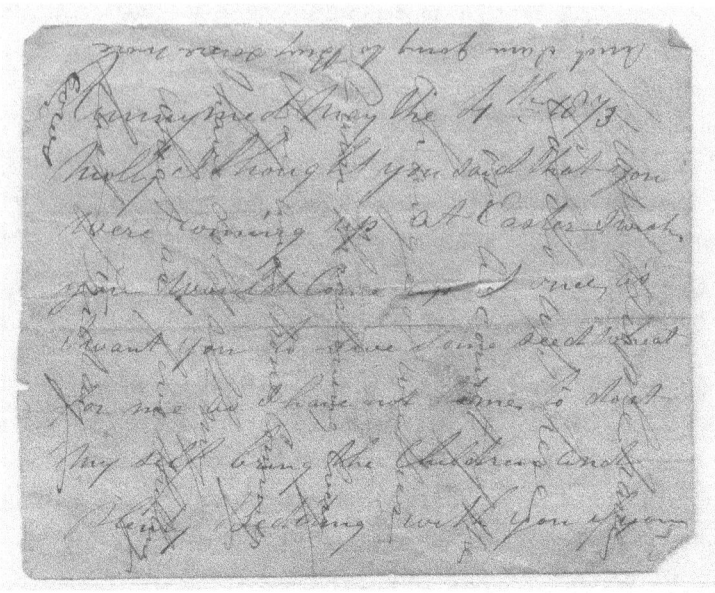

Above and opposite: Jerry's letter.

– on 4 May provides this information, as well as glimpses of a brusque but generous nature. Written, as was common practice in the nineteenth century, both across and down both sides of a small square of paper, it is the only known surviving document in his hand; how it came to be passed down in the family is a mystery. Jerry comes straight to the point:

> Molly I thought you said that you were coming up at Easter. I wish you would come up at once as I want you to sow some seed wheat for me as I have not time to do it myself. Bring the children and plenty bedding with you if you can come and do not encumber yourself with drink or anything else. The weather up here has been cold and dry lately. I cannot get on with ploughing my new land for want of rain. I have about 26 acres ready to put in so if you are all well come up for a while a week on Sunday while I am putting the seed in. Most people have colds up here on account of the change of weather. Rain threatening every day and none coming. I have sold all my wheat at five shillings last Friday and I am going to buy some more cows. Drop a note and chance my getting it stating the day you mean to come. Otherwise you may have to walk from the Railway Station to [indecipherable].

The terminus of the southern railway was still Goulburn; it sounds as

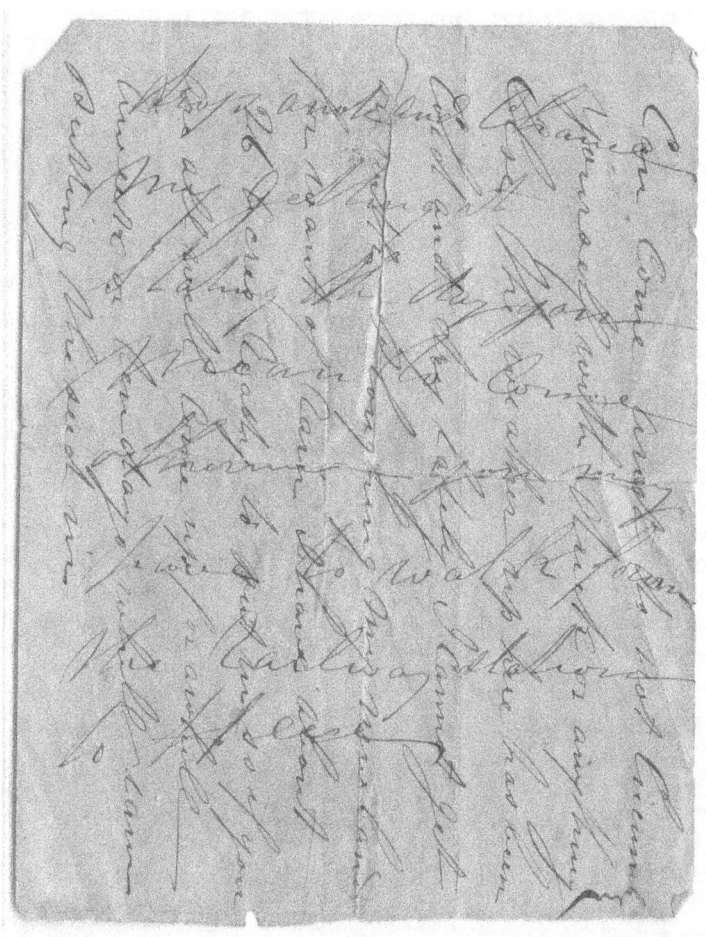

if Jerry intended to collect Molly and her family there if he heard from them in time. Failing that, they presumably would have had to catch a southern coach and alight at Reedy Creek. The homestead was near the main road.

The earlier rains apparently led to good pasture growth over summer, allowing Jerry to place an advertisement in the *Courier* in March offering 2,000 'very ripe and sound' fat sheep for sale. The previous month he had again been a sheep judge at the Yass Show; he was also one of fourteen Pastoral and Agricultural Association supporters offering special prizes – silver cups or cash – for exhibits. The one guinea he offered for the best two-year-old ram was the most parsimonious of the special cash prizes, which ranged up to five guineas.

The show had vice-regal patronage in 1873, a sign that it was now firmly established as an annual event. The *Courier* reported in July 1872 that the governor, Sir Hercules Robinson, had accepted the association's invitation to become its patron, and that it was the first country show society to win this honour. In October, photographs of the medal to be presented to prizewinners were forwarded to Sir Hercules, and the following month the *Courier* published engravings of the design – a rare departure from its usual text-only format. It described the medal as very beautiful:

> The obverse shows the words 'Yass Pastoral and Agricultural Association' surrounded by a wreath of native flowers, arranged in this order: The Christmas Bush (Ceratopetalum gumniferum); White Hibiscus (Hibiscus hererophyllus); Waratah (Telopea speciossima); Moreton Bay Bignonia (Bignonia jasninoides); Natroc (Xylomelum pyriforme); Sturt's Desert Pea (Dianthus Dampierii). The reverse carries a blank centre (for the necessary inscription), surrounded by a laurel wreath, round which runs the legend 'Palmam qui meruit ferat.' (Let him who deserves the laurel wear it.) The size of the medal will be $2^1/_2$ inches in diameter. As a work of art we venture to say… it will be unique in the colonies.

The *Courier* declared the show a decided success:

> The exhibits were unusually excellent, the attendance of visitors very numerous, the awards gave general satisfaction, and the weather was highly favourable throughout.

The sheep entries were much more numerous than the previous year and 'very superior'; Jerry and his two fellow judges had 'no little trouble to decide between the merits of the various pens, so nearly equal were they in quality'. Charles Massy and Frederick Hume, a nephew of the explorer, were the main prizewinners, and Hume took Jerry's special prize.

Shortly before the show, Yass bade farewell to Morgan O'Connor, a doctor in the town since 1860 and throughout his stay one of its most prominent citizens. The *Courier* announced the impending departure of this 'estimable and much respected townsman' on Christmas Eve 1872.

His destination was Wagga Wagga, to take over the practice of a retiring doctor. J.J. Brown lamented this 'serious loss', saying it would be felt particularly by 'the sick poor':

> By night or by day – however great the distance he might be required to go – he was always ready to attend to the call of the sick, and to his praise be it said – what can be noted of very few in his profession – he never higgled as to the payment of his fees before attending to the requirements of suffering humanity. Fee or no fee, Dr O'Connor never hesitated, and in addition to his eminent services as a medical man, he was equally liberal, when the need was apparent, with the contents of his purse to alleviate distress of which he was frequently an eye-witness. During his residence in Yass he proved himself to be a large-hearted, liberal-minded, able and skilful physician, while in the ordinary walks of life he was valued as a useful, energetic, and public-spirited townsman.

A public meeting in Yass early in the New Year decided a farewell dinner should be arranged, and an illuminated address presented to O'Connor. Jerry, who had known him at least since January 1861 when he attended the dying Mary Lehane, was a member of the thirty-eight-man organising committee; John Murphy and George Eason were other committee members from distant regions on the doctor's rounds. Probably their main job was selling tickets for the dinner (twenty-one shillings each). All came to town for the event; they were among fifty or so men who assembled at the Mechanics Institute on the evening of Wednesday 15 January and seated themselves around an 'elegantly laid' table that extended the length of the hall.

O'Connor's speech, which followed many toasts, was long and emotional. Being able to relieve pain and suffering was the real reward for a physician's life of devotion and labour, he said. He had been honoured to serve the people as a magistrate 'on one of the best benches in the colony', and had taken a special interest in the Pastoral and Agricultural Association because improvements to farming practices increased 'God's gift to man'. 'If I have interested myself in the various movements for the good of the town and district, it is only what every citizen ought to do,' he added. 'We are all, gentle and simple, dependent upon one another, and neither can be safe or sound but in the other's weal.'

More toasts followed and the party, 'a particularly happy one' according to the *Courier*, continued until two or three in the morning. Sixteen months later, when O'Connor was established in Wagga Wagga, news came through that the Pope had created him a knight of the order of the Golden Spur of St Sylvester, a high acknowledgement of his services. In November 1874, nearly two years after the dinner, he at last received the illuminated address from the people of Yass (he had been given a copy of the text at the dinner). In a letter of thanks he praised its 'artistic beauty' and said it recalled 'many many happy days' and 'true and valued friends'.

That was not the end of the story, unfortunately. The *Courier* reported in April 1875 that the address had not yet been paid for, and that a meeting called to remedy the situation had lapsed for want of a quorum. The news five months later was that four more meetings had been called without result, and that O'Connor was offering to pay the bill, about £20, himself 'if it is not paid for by the Yass people'. Further fund-raising efforts in Yass resulted in a progress payment of nearly £13 being sent in January 1876; two years later, Louis Steffanoni, maker of the address, placed an advertisement in the *Courier* saying he was still owed £10. It seems he was never paid in full.

On 21 April 1873, three months after Morgan O'Connor's departure, Yass farewelled Hamilton Hume following his death at Cooma Cottage at the age of seventy-five. Between thirty and forty carriages and nearly a hundred horsemen joined the funeral procession that took the remains of this pioneer and patriarch of the district to the town's hilltop cemetery. The *Courier*'s lengthy obituary noted that Hume had discovered the Yass Plains in 1821, in company with his brother John, his brother-in-law George Barber and W.H. Broughton. It praised his efforts as an explorer and strongly supported his side in his protracted and bitter dispute with William Hovell over their respective contributions to the famous 1824 expedition from Lake George to Port Phillip. 'No honours were bestowed upon him by the Crown, though others with less claims for distinction reaped ribbons and crosses,' the paper commented. 'History, let us hope, will determine more justly.'

Days after the death of the old man who, fifty years earlier, had opened the region to settlement, news arrived of a decision that the *Courier* declared 'will simply ruin the Yass of the present'. The government had finally decided where the town's railway station would be built – more than two miles out of town. 'Years of industry will be ignored,' wrote J.J. Brown. 'Hard-earned money will be turned to dry leaves, as in the fairy tale. And for what? To save between thirty and forty thousand pounds!' Continuing the theme, he reprinted, under the heading 'What Yass May Become', an article from the Melbourne *Argus* about post-gold-rush Castlemaine:

> Reposing tranquilly amidst its hilly surroundings – rather picturesque than otherwise as to its situation – rather forlorn and ruinous as to its buildings – rather somnolent and apathetic as to its inhabitants – stands the township of Castlemaine. Silent and neglected now, it lives on the memory of the good old times…

The decision was a victory for the chief railway engineer, John Whitton, who for more than three years stood firm against pleas from Yass and half-promises from politicians to take the line through or close to the town. He argued that engineering problems and the resulting extra costs made this untenable. The *Courier* claimed several railway surveyors had said privately that bringing the line into Yass would not create difficulties.

> Mr Whitton's adverse opinion was, however, too well known for these gentlemen to risk their positions by reporting otherwise than favourably to the Engineer-in-Chief's crotchet or foregone conclusion.

According to J.J. Brown, Whitton had failed to honour a commitment made during a visit to Yass in December 1871 to arrange full surveys of both his preferred route and one through the town. This provided the opening for the Yass railway committee to launch a final effort to reverse the government's decision. It won permission to organise a private survey, and then an extension from six to ten weeks in the time allowed for the work. A civil engineer, Francis Grundy, was selected for the job and the necessary funds – just over £400 – were raised quickly. Two contributors – retired storeowner Thomas Laidlaw and the Commercial Banking Company – put in £100. Jerry, who gave £8 8s, was among the most generous of the other fifty or so donors.

Grundy's report, presented in late July 1873, agreed with its sponsors' opinion that running the line close to the town, with a station at North Yass, was perfectly feasible. At first, the *Courier* was confident that the battle had been won:

> The struggle made by the people of Yass has been a protracted one, and it must be eminently satisfactory for them now to find that their efforts to prevent the destruction of the town are likely to terminate successfully.

But the tide turned quickly. In November, the paper conceded that Grundy's cost estimates appeared 'immensely understated'. Then, in March 1874, the legislative assembly voted overwhelmingly in favour of the proposal to bypass the town. When the government agreed the following June to locate the railway station a little closer to Yass than Whitton had intended, the *Courier* urged acceptance of this small victory: 'We think now that the matter ought to be allowed to rest.'

The April 1873 decision on the railway was soon followed by another event of major interest to civic-minded citizens, the first elections for the newly proclaimed municipal council. In mid-May, Joshua Shipway advertised his intention to hold a public meeting at the Globe Hotel 'to take into consideration who will be the coming Aldermen and Auditors'. 'All electors attend!' he urged. 'Working men Attend! The time is short! You must be careful! Yass expects every man to do his duty!' Nearly forty people turned up, and seventeen names were put forward as contenders

The Globe in Joshua Shipway's time as publican.
A large upstairs veranda was added later.

for the nine council positions. When nominations closed on 26 May, the list had grown to twenty.

Some candidates advertised their credentials in the *Courier*, including Shipway, who seems to have been a whimsical fellow. 'Vote for Shipway and Fair Play!' he urged. 'Shipway's the man for Galway! Vote for Shipway and every man's rights! Vote for Shipway and no Humbug!' His efforts went unrewarded. The *Courier* was pleased with the voters' choices, which were announced to 200 cheering spectators at the courthouse on the afternoon of polling day. 'All are men whom a lengthened experience has guaranteed to be honest men,' the paper assured its readers. Storekeeper James Cottrell was elected mayor.

Disillusion set in fairly quickly. In July 1874, the *Courier* summarised the council's activities over its first year and concluded it had done 'next to nothing'. Three months later, the paper, which had strongly supported municipal incorporation, declared the council had drifted into a

> semi-chaotic state of almost hopeless muddle… They have done scores of things which they ought not to have done; and he would be a bold man who would undertake to assert that since incorporation of the town they have done any one thing which they ought to have done.

A news item that appeared shortly before the council elections may have interested Jerry. This concerned George Miller, the 'inoffensive' young coach driver whom he allegedly assaulted ten years earlier in a fit of temper after losing an arbitration case connected with his purchase of the Globe (chapter 7). The *Courier* reported that a drunken passenger had tried to stab Miller, 'the best known and most civil of all the civil drivers on the various coaches to and from Yass'. Miller managed to throw the miscreant off the coach 'and very properly drove on and left him where he fell'. A few months later, Miller's coach was damaged when a woman, 'who appeared to be tipsy at the time', stood in its path and forced it off the road. Possibly these events convinced the driver that eleven years on the Yass to Young mail coach run was long enough. He retired soon afterwards and was honoured with a testimonial presentation recognising his services 'as a careful driver'.

Jerry certainly would have been interested, and saddened, to learn in June 1873 of the death of Terence Aubrey Murray, his employer for his first twelve years in the colony. Murray had sold his pastoral properties in the 1860s but continued his political activities. He was president of the legislative council when he died, and had earlier served as speaker of the assembly. The *Courier* noted his reputation 'for dignity and impartiality in maintaining the due decorum of debate'. It also praised his contributions to discussion of social issues, particularly his opposition to capital punishment. The *Sydney Morning Herald* described him as 'one of our leading personages' and 'decidedly a popular man...devoted to literature, amiable in disposition, and courteous in his manners'.

In early August, Jerry was a committee member, and therefore a ticket seller, for two big events at the Mechanics Institute in Yass – a public ball in aid of St Augustine's School and a dinner to honour the premier, Sir Henry Parkes, and four other visiting politicians. Whether Jerry actually attended either event is not recorded. Perhaps he brought Hannah to the ball; if so, a £1 double ticket would have given them entry. Any other members of the family who came would have been admitted for 7s 6d on a family ticket.

The ball was a 'gratifying success', reported the *Courier*. Nearly 150 ladies and gentlemen attended, and danced 'with much spirit until the break of day'. There was just one problem:

> ...at times during the night the whole of the large hall was enveloped in a dense cloud of dust, which settled on hair and headdresses, altering their colour, and converted the black dress coats of the gentlemen into drab or grey. If the hall of the institute is again converted into a ball-room, it would be well to have the floor properly prepared, and thus prevent a renewal of what was actually a 'dust storm', not a pleasant visitant at any time and much less so on such an occasion as that referred to.

The party of politicians, who called at Yass as part of a tour of the region, comprised the ministers for public works (J. Sutherland) and lands (J.S. Farnell) and the local members Michael Fitzpatrick (Yass Plains) and James Watson (the Lachlan), as well as the premier. As was the custom, they were greeted and escorted into town 'by a number of gentlemen in buggies'. Then they received two deputations.

A group led by Dr Campbell tackled Parkes and his ministers on the railway route issue. Campbell said their lobbying had been 'actuated simply by a sincere and earnest wish to relieve the community from utter, irretrievable ruin'. Parkes responded coolly to this proposition, assuring them that the government had 'no desire to injure Yass or any other place' but had to avoid 'detriment to the general interests'. The second deputation comprised the town's mayor and aldermen. Issues raised included the 'government ditch' down the side of the main road (chapter 17), which one alderman claimed was six feet deep in places. Parkes insisted that the problem was one for the council to solve. The mayor, Alderman Cottrell, chaired the dinner held that evening at the Mechanics Institute. According to the *Courier*, nothing was said in any of the addresses 'exceptional to usual after-dinner speeches on similar occasions'.

On 28 August, the feast day of St Augustine, the grandson of Jerry destined to pass on the family name was born at Narraburra. The *Courier* carried a birth notice for John Augustine Lehane, the only child of William and Sarah, nearly three weeks after the event. Perhaps Jerry placed it in the paper on a visit to Yass. John Augustine was grandchild number six. John and Ellen Lyons, living far away in Maryborough, Queensland, had already produced five offspring – Mary Agnes (born 12 November 1867), Ellen (born 25 March 1869, died 21 January 1870), Frank Joseph (born 20 August 1870), John Perry (born 2 March 1872) and Elizabeth Augusta (born 17 June 1873).

John Augustine's birth was not the only good news as 1873 drew to a close. At the end of October, the *Courier*'s Kangaroo Reefs correspondent reported that lambing in the region had been 'exceedingly good', shearing had commenced on most stations and 'I think the squatters in general have reason to be proud of the harvest they will reap this year'. Earlier in the month, Jerry had placed two ads in the paper. The first announced: 'Shearing to commence at Coppabella on Monday, 20th instant. Expert hands wanted. One pound per hundred for such.' The second sought people to cart the wool away: 'Carriers wanted next week at Coppabella, for wool. Highest rates of carriage given.'

In early December, Jerry took ill. Dr Blake visited him the day before Christmas, but had no means of countering the 'inflammation of the lungs' that was bringing his life to an end. Perhaps the clouds of dust at the St Augustine's School ball in August had caused damage that set the scene for pneumonia to develop. Jerry died at home on New Year's Day 1874. Father John Gallagher, a young Irish priest who became Bishop of Goulburn (1900–1923), performed the religious rites at his burial at Yass cemetery two days later.

The only newspaper report we have of Jerry's death is from the *Burrangong Chronicle*, published at Young:

> Death of an old resident – It is with regret we announce the death of Mr Jeremiah Lehane, of Reedy Creek. He died at noon yesterday, at his residence. His age was 63. He will be buried in Yass, on Saturday, when we have no doubt that his funeral will be largely attended.

The *Chronicle* named the *Yass Courier* of 2 January 1874 as the source of this report. Sadly, that edition of the *Courier* is one of the few that apparently have been lost forever, so we will never know whether J.J. Brown had more to say about Jerry then. Possibly he did, because he remembered Jerry a year later in his New Year's Day 1875 leader reflecting on the events of 1874. This recalled three 'faces once familiar that the past year has taken from us'; Jerry was top of the list.

Jerry's son William and John Murphy are recorded on the death certificate as witnesses to the burial. As they stood at the graveside, these two young men – William was twenty-six and John thirty – probably reflected on the enterprising and successful lives of their fathers and pondered their own futures. These should have been bright. Their fathers had set them up well, and both had married and begun raising families. William had run Narraburra for many years and John had proved himself in various Murphy businesses. Perhaps their relatively privileged upbringing, including an education that emphasised Greek and Latin rather than more worldly subjects, proved a hindrance rather than a help in a colony that was changing very rapidly. Census figures illustrate the rate of change – the European population of about 100,000 when Jerry and Miles arrived from Ireland had grown to well over 500,000 by 1874. Whatever the causes, the remainder of the 1870s proved far from propitious for William, John and other Lehanes and Murphys.

19
Fun and games

Just four days after Jerry's funeral, the telegraph brought news of the death of John Perry Lyons, husband of his eldest daughter Ellen. John died in Geelong where, according to the report in his hometown newspaper, the *Maryborough Chronicle*, he was transacting business connected with the settlement of family property. The doctor who attended him at Geelong's Union Hotel recorded that he had been ill for only four days and died of peritonitis and rapid exhaustion.

The *Chronicle* said the thirty-year-old lawyer had built a large legal practice and won a prominent position in the community in the six years since he and Ellen settled in the booming Queensland port town. 'He was a hard worker before being admitted [as a solicitor], and we all know how hard he worked afterwards, and during the last twelve months he became aware that his excessive devotion to his profession had materially affected his health,' the paper reported. Under medical advice, he had left his practice for some months at the beginning of 1873 'to recruit himself in the neighbouring colonies'. He had been very much better when he returned, and the news of his death was received 'with general surprise'.

When the Maryborough Police Court next sat, tributes were paid to John's contributions. A competing solicitor, Henry Walker, recalled that he and John had fought many a hard legal battle, but 'their private friendship had always been unshaken, and his ability was fully acknowledged'. Walker asked the police magistrate to convey 'the profession's deep regret and sympathy' to Ellen who, having lost both her husband and her father in the first week of 1874, faced the prospect of bringing up – alone – four children aged from six months to six years.

Back at Reedy Creek, Ellen's stepmother Hannah Lehane had three children, aged between three and nine, to bring up, Coppabella to run,

*Lyons family:
Frank and Mary (top), Elizabeth and John.*

and the Globe Hotel and Jerry's other Yass properties to look after. She wasted no time in beginning the task of settling his affairs. A notice quickly appeared in the *Yass Courier*, dated two days after the funeral, requesting those with claims against the estate to send them forthwith to her or to Edward Iceton, her solicitor. Those indebted to the estate were similarly asked to pay up quickly.

Another advertisement a month later was possibly a sign that neighbours were causing problems. Headed 'Notice and Caution', this warned that people trespassing on Coppabella or interfering with the station's stock without Hannah's written permission would be prosecuted 'without respect to persons'.

William Lehane seems to have set out at the start of 1874 to become a prominent man of the turf. He entered three horses, and had two accepted, for the main events at the Young races run in March — the £100 Publicans' Handicap and the £150 Burrangong Turf Club Handicap – but had no success in these. His horses also competed in some of the minor events and gained two second places – total winnings £6 10s. At the Yass races three weeks later, he had entries in six events and did somewhat better. His horses took two second places and three thirds, and then success came in the £10 Consolation Stakes for 'all horses beaten during the meeting, but not distanced; once round the course'. The winner was his seven-year-old You'll Do. 'This was simply a perfect race,' wrote the *Courier*.

Gertrude and Josephine Lehane.

The handicapping made it 'anybody's race'. The flag fell to an honest start, and then away the mob went keeping together as thick as thieves... Mr Lehane's victory was greeted with applause.

William was a steward at the May 1867 Murrumburrah races, but seems to have had little other previous experience on the racetrack. Two days before Christmas 1873, an advertisement appeared for a meeting to be held at Murrumburrah on 26 and 27 January 1874; this named William and John Murphy as stewards and nineteen-year-old Miles Murphy as honorary secretary. Those who read the fine print would have been surprised to see that gambling was to be strictly prohibited.

The advertisement was a hoax, the *Courier* acknowledged a week later. It added that Murrumburrah, 'through the action of some disreputable scoundrel or scoundrels', was fast acquiring 'an evil reputation' for practical joking:

> The latest phase that this form of larrikinism has assumed is forgery. Week before last, we received an order for an advertisement signed apparently by a well-known resident of Murrumburrah. Believing in its *bona fides*, we gave publication to the advertisement, only, however, to discover subsequently that the written authority ordering it was a forgery... The affair is being

carefully inquired into, and we are in hopes that justice will speedily overtake the criminal who perpetrated it.

The correct advertisement, published at the end of January, announced that the races would be held on 11 and 12 February with John Murphy as judge and Felix Murphy a steward. William and Miles Murphy were not on the list of officials, and there was no prohibition on gambling. The careful inquiry into the hoax seems to have had no outcome; Murrumburrah had long been, and long remained, a place where practical jokes were a frequent ingredient of small-town life.

Back in June 1864, an advertisement for 'Dillon's Races' at Murrumburrah appeared in the *Courier*, listing John Murphy as a steward. John Dillon disowned it in a letter to the paper and shortly afterwards another ad appeared listing no Murphys among the race officials. In June 1868, an ad announced that John Murphy was to sell the property of Murrumburrah blacksmith James Murray. The *Courier* reported a few days later,

> By the mail on Sunday last we received letters from Mr Murray, Mr Murphy and others stating that the advertisement was a stupid and malicious attempt at practical joking, the author of which we hope will be discovered and properly punished.

The victim three months later was a 'quiet, decent, old hawker' named Gilligan, who slept in his covered cart with the shafts propped up. 'One night some of the practical jokers knocked away the support of the shafts, which of course brought them plump to the ground, and Mr Gilligan nearly out of the cart head foremost.' They also clipped his horses' tails, depriving 'the poor brutes...of their means of keeping off flies.' The following month another fake advertisement for a sale of properties appeared, this time in the *Boorowa Express*. Then, in November 1868, 'a worshipper of Bacchus, having been a little too earnest in his devotions, was overtaken by a 'spiritual' prostration, and some persons thought that as he had 'lost his head' he should lose his hair also, and therefore applied the scissors... I think this *penchant* for practical joking will, sooner or later, have an unpleasant ending,' wrote the *Courier*'s Murrumburrah correspondent.

In April 1870, practical jokers set out to frighten a young man who spent his nights in the then half-built Catholic church at Murrumburrah. They 'despatched to the chapel a ghost, white sheeted and weird'. The victim, however, 'was not to be frightened so easily' and, when he got up and started to dress, 'the ghost 'skedaddled''. The perpetrators responded to the failure of their ploy by throwing stones at the young man. 'It must be owned,' the *Courier* said, 'that the whole affair was not of a very creditable character.'

Two years later, an advertisement appeared in the *Burrangong Argus* purporting to be for a concert and farce soon to be staged at Murrumburrah in aid of the town's Wesleyan church. It said a room provided by John Murphy was to be the venue and musical items would include 'Put me in my little bed' sung by Sarah Murphy. 'The parts assigned to the various persons mentioned are such as are supposed to give annoyance, and satisfy, perhaps, some petty spleen of the perpetrator,' wrote a correspondent who hoped the person responsible for the hoax would be caught and gaoled. The advertised date of the concert was four days before Sarah's marriage to William Lehane.

The victim of a hoax in April 1873 was a cordial maker named Blount from Spring Creek, near Young. Blount received a note purportedly from innkeeper John English requesting a large delivery in time for the coming Murrumburrah races. He prepared the order 'and started a man off with the goods in a spring cart':

> The day was wet, and the road boggy, and the load being heavy, about eighteen cwt., the man had all he could do to get to his destination in time. Arrive, however, he did, wet and weary, and we may judge of his surprise and chagrin when he was told that Mr English did not send the order, and knew nothing about it. If it is anything to be proud of, Murrumburrah can boast of holding some characters whose delight is in mischief, not fun, and in inflicting pain and annoyance upon their neighbours; and the predominant characteristics of whose dispositions are cowardice and cruelty. Mr Blount has, we believe, placed the matter in the hands of the police, and, should the individual who wrote the letter be detected, he may find that his smartness has brought him to the only place he would not disgrace, namely, a felon's dock.

Three months later, another fictitious advertisement appeared in the *Courier*, this time announcing plans for the auction of 'a respectable small settler's' property. On learning the ad was a fake, J.J. Brown handed the letter ordering it to the police. He was confident the perpetrator would be traced:

> We have examined the writing, and have no hesitation in arriving at the conclusion that it has emanated from the scoundrel who has on several previous occasions amused himself in a similar manner.

The hoaxes kept coming, however. The next was the advertisement for the 1874 Murrumburrah races that named William Lehane as a steward. In June 1876, 'a respectable young man' recently arrived in Murrumburrah found 'to his excessive annoyance' when preparing to dress for church 'that his most important garments were plentifully bestrewed with *mucuna pruriens*, vulgarly known as cow-itch'. This prevented his appearance at church. 'Of course nobody knew who did it,' commented the *Courier*. 'Nobody ever does!' Three months later, the paper's Murrumburrah correspondent seemed to think he was hot on the trail of the perpetrators. Following an event at which a local identity was presented with a cheap tin plate instead of the advertised handsome piece of plate, the correspondent concluded, 'from some remarks I heard dropped by one or two persons whom I shrewdly suspect to be 'experts' in practical joking', that this hoax had not gone quite as planned.

The 'experts' may have been identified, but they continued on their merry way. On a Sunday night in January 1877, about a dozen horses were removed from stables at the Criterion and Commercial hotels and elsewhere in the town and let loose in 'Mr Murray's paddock, where there is a good store of hay'. Murray had them all impounded, 'and it cost the owners a trifle to release them'. The *Courier* correspondent hoped those responsible would turn out to be 'no older than boys or hobbledehoys'. If they were caught, 'a dose of the cat-o'-nine-tails would be very salutary'.

In February 1881, the *Courier* reported that 'some scoundrel' had forged the signature of the local clerk of petty sessions on a fake marriage certificate. 'I hope this will be the last shameful, cruel, and heartless 'joke' perpetrated here, and that the inventors will be heavily punished,' a correspondent wrote. He went on,

Murrumburrah has been a sort of hell since ever I came here, and it even was long so before. Some two years ago the low larrikins shaved the tail of the horse belonging to the police magistrate, who had a distance of twenty miles to ride on his return home from circuit duty. Continually letters containing base, low, mean, libellous statements against ladies of respectable character are being sent to their husbands. A little time ago handbills were circulated (printed), containing scurrilous advertisements regarding two gentlemen who occupy good positions of trust. On two occasions, at and after midnight, have stones been dashed through the bedroom windows and smashed the glass. Repeatedly have gentlemen larrikins…rapped at my doors loudly and then walked on, laughing at the clever trick they were playing…

From 1881, Murrumburrah had its own newspaper, the *Signal*, which seems to have been more amused than scandalised by the activities of what it called the 'irrepressible Murrumburrah Ring'. In January 1885, it published a long story about a visit by a Salvation Army contingent from Goulburn under the block heading

War in Murrumburrah
The 'Ring' at Work Again
They Hoax the Salvation 'Harmy'
The Devil's Stronghold Fruitlessly Assailed
One Blackfellow Taken Prisoner by the Salvationists

The gist was that a letter had been sent to Goulburn suggesting that Murrumburrah would be fertile ground for army conversions; wealthy locals were ready to donate land and fund the building of 'barracks'; Murrumburrah already had upwards of fifty converts; and rooms had been booked at the 'Temperance Hotel' for army visitors. The Goulburn Salvationists rose to the bait and dispatched 'a chosen band of disciples, equipped with all the paraphernalia (from the *War Cry* to the kettle-drum) necessary for the conversion of this devil's stronghold':

Thus accoutred the attacking party, led on to battle by a warlike sergeant, and supported by an auxiliary of hallelujah lasses, commenced the assault on the Philistines. But, lo! They met not that co-operation within the walls of the city which they fondly hoped to find. No enthusiastic greeting awaited them; no anxious converts thronged to their standard; no block of land was ready to be conveyed to them; no banker was forthcoming to place £50 down for the benefit of the Army's fund; no 'Temperance Hotel' could be discovered wherein to rest their travel-worn limbs; and, finally, no writer of the delusive epistle was anywhere to be found. Crest-fallen they paraded the streets of the unholy city, in quest of the fabled hotel, the 'head centre' of the 'Ring' meanwhile dogging their steps, watching their every movement, and chuckling at their discomfiture with a broad Mephistophelian grin on his face, and a twinkle of devilry in his eye. Presently he approaches them, and with a face as long as a fiddle and a sanctimonious smirk on his countenance even broader than that worn by the Blind Creek El Mahdi; yea a smirk enough to win the favor of the oldest and most hardened 'hallelujah lass' in the 'Harmy's' ranks; he feelingly inquired wherefore they looked so dejected. The 'sergeant', as spokesman, thereupon explained their errand, stating the circumstances which brought them hither; and that just then they were in search of the Temperance Hotel. The 'Head Centre' then directed them to one of the local pubs, where as it unfortunately happened just at this particular time, there were an unusual number of 'drunks' on the verandah, engaged in mauling each other and making use of anything but Gospel phraseology...

The story goes on in similar vein. After having pewter pots hurled at them by the drunks, the Salvationists sought refuge in a tailor's shop. But the tailor turned out to be Catholic and impregnable to their 'hallelujah artillery'. They retreated towards the railway station at nearby Harden, and on the way 'collided with a Herculean darkey, whom they straightway enlisted as a 'brudder bones''. Then they set off 'in double quick time'.

That other durable Murrumburrah institution, the rivalry between the Murphys and John Dillon, had a shorter life than the practical joking. It was still in evidence, though, in 1873 – six years after Dillon circulated his petition calling for Miles Murphy's lease of the Murrumburrah run to be withdrawn (chapter 10). The *Courier* reported that the success of the town's race meeting held in April was 'due entirely to the energy of Mr J.A. Murphy, he being the only person in town who collected for the race fund, the other publicans holding aloof altogether'. Dillon shot off a letter to the editor saying he had, in fact, contributed £35. He agreed that he had 'kept aloof' from the meeting – 'having very good reasons, which I do not care to mention, for so doing'. He implied that John Murphy had written the report that appeared in the *Courier*.

I must do the correspondent the justice to state, that although he forgets to give merit where merit is due, he evidently has not forgotten the way to blow his own trumpet.

John Bourke, Murrumburrah auctioneer, butcher, poundkeeper and race meeting treasurer, leapt to Murphy's defence. His records showed, he claimed in a letter to the *Courier*, that Dillon's assertion that he had contributed £35 was 'utterly inconsistent with the truth'.

As in earlier times, the news from Murrumburrah as the 1870s progressed contained many mentions of the Murphys. At a bazaar held in April 1973, John's wife Mary Anne, Sarah Lehane and a daughter of John Dillon were among a large group of ladies who raffled and sold 'various handsome and useful articles'. About £250 was raised, more than enough to achieve the goal of clearing the debt on St Mary's Church. Originally the bazaar was to be held in a 'pavilion' erected at John Murphy's expense, but rain drove it indoors, to the Criterion Hotel's 'large room'. Wrote the *Courier* correspondent,

> I cannot conclude without eulogising the ladies, to whom all honour is due, not only for the artistic manner in which they arranged the different tables, but also for the energy they displayed in collecting money, and working those handsome articles, which only ladies can work, and of which I do not know the names.

Shortly afterwards, Murphy handed the Criterion over to a tenant publican, Thomas Allsopp. The Murrumburrah Cricket Club marked the event by arranging a dinner and ball at the hotel, with John and Mary Anne as guests of honour. The *Courier* described John 'as the mainstay of the club ever since its commencement', which may not have done justice to the role of his father, Miles, in the early days (chapter 12).

In November 1873, a fire on Kalangan destroyed two large sheds and their contents, which included a four-horsepower chaff-cutter. John estimated the loss at £200. The following month, Mary Anne gave birth to the couple's third child, Mary.

A sad event six months later was the suicide by strychnine poisoning of Catherine Dunn, a fourteen-year-old nurse girl employed by the Murphys. She was the daughter of a shepherd on Kalangan. The inquest heard that she had gone to the kitchen with a tumbler containing 'something like salts' and asked the cook for milk to drink it with. After swallowing the mixture, Catherine announced she had taken poison. She died soon after, following violent convulsions. The jury was told that Catherine had a passionate and excitable nature. Evidence was given that on the morning of the tragedy the station's overseer had accused her of stealing letters belonging to him and threatened to 'throw her on the fire' if she did not return them. If that provided the motivation for her action, the fact that John's supply of strychnine was not in its usual spot in his iron safe provided the opportunity. John told the inquest that, as the safe's latch was broken, he had temporarily placed the poison, clearly labelled, 'on the wall-plate under the eaves inside his office'. The jury concluded that 'the case was purely suicidal' and no blame should attach to any other person.

John's and Mary Anne's fourth child, Adeline, was born in March 1875. By the end of that year, the southern railway was rapidly approaching Yass and plans were being made

The children of John and Mary Anne Murphy. From left: Miles, Annie, Adeline and Mary.

for its extension to Binalong, Murrumburrah and beyond. In a worrying reminder of earlier events at Yass, word had reached Murrumburrah that its station was to be some distance – about one and a half miles – from the town centre. Murrumburrah's businessmen feared their enterprises would suffer; the subsequent development of the new town of Harden around the railway station showed they were right to be worried.

A public meeting called on 31 December to discuss the railway issue and other matters, including the need for a new courthouse and more police, attracted 'nearly all the principal men of business of the town'. A unanimously adopted resolution called for the station to be built 'in a more convenient spot'. Moving it, the manager of the local Oriental Bank branch, J.O. Atchison, said he had been 'given to understand from good authority that the station might be placed conveniently to the town at a cost of £2,500, which was a mere flea-bite in respect to the importance of the object in view'. Why had the out-of-town site been chosen? Atchison 'could not help thinking that it must be to suit some private end'. A *Courier* leader agreed, suggesting corruption might be involved.

The meeting decided a deputation should go to Sydney to press the town's case. John Murphy said he was already planning a visit and 'desired no payment' to be part of the delegation. Auctioneer R.P. Johnson was selected to go with him. A week later, the *Courier* correspondent observed that Murrumburrah 'has some smart, energetic men of business in it, though I think they do not pull very well together as a team intent on the advancement of the town; latterly, however, they have seemed to become more aware of the wisdom of united action.' Perhaps the correspondent was referring to the Murphy–Dillon disputes. Dillon joined the delegation a week after its departure, following news that Murphy and Johnson had received positive responses from the government on all issues except the railway.

Murphy was spokesman when the delegation reported back to a public meeting in Murrumburrah at the end of January 1876. He praised help given by the local MP, James Watson, who had 'very plainly pointed out' to the minister for works 'the easy and inexpensive method of bringing the railway terminus at least sixty or seventy chains [six or seven eighths of a mile] nearer the township'. The minister had promised to consult chief railway engineer Whitton on the matter, 'which gentleman will, we trust with all confidence, use his valuable assistance in meeting the view of the deputation on this most serious subject'.

John's optimism suggests he had not followed the saga of the Yass station site (chapters 16 and 18). It was dashed four months later when news came through that Whitton 'would not consent' to any change of plan. For the moment, though, the outlook appeared bright and the meeting concluded with much praise for Watson and the delegation. William Lehane was there, and 'in a very neat speech' endorsed another speaker's kind words about Watson. After the vote of thanks to the chairman the meeting adjourned to the Criterion Hotel, now run by John Murphy's twenty-one-year-old brother Miles. There, according to the *Courier*, 'the healths of Mr Watson and the several members of the deputation were drunk in an unlimited supply of Möet and Chandon.'

The railway finally reached Yass in mid-1876, with daily (except Saturday) services to and from Sydney beginning on 2 July. The timetable allowed just under nine hours for the 187-mile journey, with many stops along the way. No celebrations were held to mark this signal event, a precedent that was not followed by the people of Murrumburrah when their station opened in March 1877. John and Miles Murphy were on the committee chosen to plan the welcome for the first train. The great day, Monday 12 March, was declared a holiday and a 'huge crowd' and fifty or sixty vehicles greeted the arrival of the smoke-belching locomotive and eight carriages at one-twenty p.m. Dillon's Commercial Hotel proved unable to cater for all those with bookings for the special dinner held that afternoon; 'very many' had to be turned away. Speechmakers included Miles, who responded to James Watson's toast to the prosperity of the district. John was also present. In the evening a ball, bazaar and concert were held.

Much else had been happening in the meantime. Miles took charge of the Criterion at the start of 1876; the *Courier* predicted it would prosper under the new management as he and the whole Murphy family were 'generally popular'. Then in late May the hotel was advertised for sale, along with the other Murphy properties in Murrumburrah – the flour mill, store and various houses and allotments – and the Swan Inn, Binalong.

The timing of the planned auctions matched the provision in Miles Murphy senior's will (chapter 13) for his estate to be sold and the proceeds divided among the surviving offspring after young Miles turned twenty-one. The advertisement described the offerings at Murrumburrah as 'recognised and unmistakably admitted by shrewd and far-seeing business men to be the very pick of the town... advantage having been taken by the late Mr Miles Murphy at the first auction sale to secure the very eyes of the township'. R.P. Johnson auctioned these properties at the Criterion in early July, following a 'grand luncheon' hosted by John Murphy. Bidding was spirited and the prices obtained 'satisfactory'. Apparently, John and Miles bought the Criterion and the flour mill (which went for the 'high figure' of £3,100). The store, Sydney House, was acquired by Andrew Aiken, who had been running it for some time. Various local landowners and businessmen bought allotments in and around the town.

August 1876 brought success for John at an arbitration hearing over compensation for losses caused by the routeing of the railway through one of his paddocks. He claimed £500 and was offered £112. The arbitrators awarded him £425. In October, plans were announced for considerable additions to the Criterion Hotel, including a new wing. Whether this was wise in view of the distance of the Criterion from the railway station is doubtful. Less than two months after the arrival of the first train, the *Courier* noted that a 'small town' was 'beginning to show itself' beside the station buildings. A store had already opened, one hotel was being built and another was planned. Probably the drift of business from Murrumburrah to Harden contributed to the financial difficulties that overwhelmed the Murphys in the late 1870s.

First came another family tragedy, the death on 17 December 1876 at the age of twenty-five of Thomas Murphy. This occurred at a small settlement called Marsden's, west of Young. The circumstances do not appear to have been reported and, as usual with the Murphys, no

Thomas (left) and young Miles Murphy.

death certificate exists. A notice in the *Courier* advised that Thomas's funeral would leave St Mary's Church, Murrumburrah, at eight a.m. on Wednesday 20 December and arrive at Galong cemetery, just twelve miles away, at noon – a very slow procession. Thomas had been due to serve as clerk of the course at the Murrumburrah races on 21 and 22 December, a position he filled the previous year. John was to be judge and Miles among the stewards. Strangely, the *Courier*'s report of the race meeting contained no mention of Thomas or the other Murphys. No Murphy horses competed.

In 1877, young Miles was in charge of the flour mill and a tenant publican, Albert King, was looking after the Criterion. Miles carried on the family tradition of involvement in community affairs, joining the board of Murrumburrah's newly reopened – after a lapse of five years – public school in June 1877. The following March, he and John, who had served on an earlier school board in the late 1860s, were elected to a new Murrumburrah Progress Committee.

Miles faced a test of his maturity in May 1877, when the bookkeeper at the flour mill, John Hooper, drank himself to death. He told the inquest that Hooper had been drinking and unable to attend to his duties for about ten days; Hooper had also been in the habit of taking large doses of the patent medicine Chlorodyne (chapter 12). The mill's engine driver, John Byrom, said Hooper had not seemed suicidal the evening before he was found dead, and had drunk some soup and eaten 'a little fowl'. Byrom acknowledged that earlier in the evening he had taken Hooper a half-pint of gin: 'I then gave him a nobbler; at nine I gave him another, and left him the remainder; this morning at half past six I went into the bedroom and found him dead.' The jury accepted the opinion of the town's doctor, Thomas Archdall, that Hooper had died from serous apoplexy brought on by excessive drinking.

John Murphy took charge of the Criterion again during 1878. In mid-September, thieves stole three sides of bacon and a side of mutton, which the police soon located under the bed of the mother of two of the three men they arrested for the theft. At the trial at the circuit court in Yass, John told how he had led Senior Constable McGee to the stolen goods. 'I tracked the salt from my place towards prisoners' place,' he said. 'I tracked the salt to a fence, and I then sent for the police.' Two of the accused, who had pleaded guilty, received six-month sentences. The third was acquitted.

Miles appeared at the same court session, accusing a man he had drunk with at the Criterion of stealing his watch, chain and ring. Miles told the court that he and the accused, Philip Shelley, scuffled after the drinking session. Then he discovered his possessions were missing and marched Shelley to the police lock-up. The watch later turned up in a stable where Shelley had said he put it, and the ring and chain were found in Shelley's pocket. In answer to questions from Shelley, Miles told the court, 'I did shove you along the verandah; ...you threw me and I threw you; I insisted upon having my watch; ...you said, give me my hat and I will give you the watch...' Apparently unimpressed by Miles' account of events, the jury acquitted Shelley after just twenty minutes deliberation.

The following month, Thomas Allsopp, earlier tenant publican at the Criterion, bought the flour mill from the Murphys. Suggesting the transfer was not amicable, Allsopp took Miles to the Murrumburrah small debts court shortly afterwards alleging he had removed a corncracker from the mill between sale and delivery of the property. The magistrates decided the claim was not one that their court could hear because the sale had been for 'a considerable sum of money'.

The disposal of the mill at a time when the colonial economy was in recession was the clearest sign yet that the Murphys were facing financial difficulties. John's appearance in a January 1879 list of holders of conditional land purchases that had lapsed, through failure to provide necessary declarations or non-payment of interest, may have been another sign. The Kalangan pastoral run, acquired by Miles senior in 1856 and home of the family in the late 1860s and then of John and his family in the 1870s, was mortgaged to the Commercial Bank in 1874 – possibly an early indication of troubles to come. Kalangan's sale by auction in March 1879, to Albert Middleton of Boorowa, was a severe blow. Worse lay ahead.

20

Troubled times

In June or July 1874, the proud parents of ten-months-old John Augustine Lehane had him photographed by Robert Baxter of Young, a newly arrived 'artist photographer'. Baxter took a charming photo of the bright-eyed infant. William or Sarah wrote on the back, 'A most remarkable child. The pride of his mother, and terror of his father.'

William apparently was in an expansive mood around this time. After entering horses in most events at the Young and Yass races in March and April, he made a very generous donation – fifty guineas – in May to the building fund for St Mary's Catholic church, Young. As an encouragement to further fund-raising, he promised to give the same amount again when

John Augustine Lehane at ten months (left) and a little later.

subscriptions totalled £1,000. Apparently, the required money did come in quickly because Bishop Lanigan laid the foundation stone for the imposing granite edifice in December 1874 and it was opened less than two years later. However, it is unlikely that William's promised second donation eventuated.

During July 1874, he added 'a very valuable blood mare, of singular trotting capacity', bought in Sydney, to his stable of racers. This unfortunately died, following 'two days' illness', about a week after he bought it. Worse news came two months later; William was required by the insolvency court to show cause why his estate should not be sequestrated. He filed no objection to this course of action when the court met in Sydney on 8 October, and the sequestration order went ahead. A month later, he was declared in contempt of the court for failing to lodge a schedule of assets and liabilities within the allowed ten days.

The schedule as eventually presented in late December showed assets, of £9,701, substantially exceeding liabilities – £8,051 14s 1d, with £3,500 secured. These figures suggest that William could have quickly overcome his financial difficulties, but this was not to be. The insolvency court heard his account of his predicament on 14 December. The newspaper report is rather garbled, but an outline of events can be pieced together from it and from the report of an earlier related hearing.

Angus McKay, an agent for a company named Webb and Booth, initiated the insolvency proceedings. William had bought a large flock of ewes, more than 5,000, from this firm with a promissory note for £2,146 15s on which payment was due by 5 June. McKay demanded payment without success, as did another sheep dealer named Wilson who had supplied nearly 3,000 wethers on the strength of a promissory note for £818 7s. This one expired on 8 June. The purpose of William's purchases was to stock Younga Plains, a station he bought for £3,500 in February 1874. He had sold Narraburra the previous year, receiving between £12,000 and £13,000 for it in August 1873 (the month John Augustine Lehane was born there). With all that cash in hand, it's understandable that William felt he could afford to buy and run racehorses and give generously to the Young church appeal.

The money disappeared quickly, however. More than £6,000 went to paying off existing debts. Then in the closing months of 1873 William spent more than £3,000 on sheep, nearly £300 on a bullock team, a few saddle horses and a racehorse, then £100 on another racehorse. He bought more sheep, worth nearly another £2,000, in January 1874. Then he bought Younga Plains, drawing on £5,000 borrowed from Mort and Co. He mortgaged the property to Mort and Co. in July 1874, after being served with writs by the two promissory note holders, and that company took possession of the property the following month. It was a sorry tale of extravagant spending beyond capacity to pay.

At the end of 1874, William, Sarah and baby John were living at Young in a house rented from the manager of the town's Oriental Bank branch. Between January and April 1875, five meetings were held under the auspices of the insolvency court – one in Wagga Wagga, one in Young and three in Sydney – to give William's creditors the opportunity to prove their claims. Debts totalling nearly £350 were proved at the Young meeting; those seeking payment included two people working on Younga Plains and a carrier. During February, the official assignee sold for £436 three blocks of land totalling 264 acres that William had bought near Murrumburrah.

In early July, the insolvency court approved a scheme under which creditors would receive a first distribution from the estate – fifteen shillings in the pound. A second distribution, 1s 8d in the pound, was agreed three months later. A year passed; then in October 1876 William gave notice that he intended to apply for a 'certificate of conformity'. This would have confirmed that he had fulfilled requirements for disclosing his affairs, surrendering property and obeying court orders, and shielded him from any further claims by creditors. Obtaining the certificate proved no mere formality. When the court met in mid-November, William was directed to

> hold a special meeting for proof of debts within four weeks, at which meeting he was to attend, account for his insolvency, and give notice thereof to his creditors. Insolvent also to explain by affidavit, by the 13th February, his purchase of sheep on credit, and then placing them in his mortgage to Mort and Co.

Apparently this proved too difficult; on 27 February 1877, the court 'struck out of the list' his application because nobody turned up to support it. A certificate was never granted.

We have only a few glimpses of how William occupied himself during the long years of insolvency, and no information on how Sarah coped. There seems little doubt that he was a heavy drinker. William was among those who adjourned to the Criterion after the meeting on Murrumburrah's future in January 1876 to partake of the hotel's 'unlimited supply' of French champagne (chapter 19). Early one morning nine months earlier, the twenty-eight-year-old helped apprehend, at a Boorowa hotel, the thief of a horse that belonged to a publican, E.J. Dempsey from nearby Tangmangaroo. William told the man's trial in Yass,

> I was at Burrowa on the morning of the 1st April. About four a.m. that morning prisoner came into Leary's hotel for some liquor. I heard prisoner offering to race with a horse he had bought off a man with a fruit cart. I went outside, looked at the horse, and recognised it as the horse Standard, which about half an hour before Mr Dempsey told me he had missed from his stables at Tangmangaroo. I took possession of the horse. Prisoner asked me what business of mine it was to interfere; I said the horse was Dempsey's. Prisoner tried to retake possession of the horse; I would not allow him. I had Mr Dempsey called. Mr Dempsey came out and sent for the police. Prisoner walked away from the inn. When prisoner saw the police coming he ran away. He had said 'Here comes the police, it's time for me to skedaddle'.
> Prisoner: You may depend I did, and that quick.
> Witness continued: We prevented prisoner escaping.

The policeman who rushed to the scene told the court he found William holding the thief by the neck. Why William was at a hotel in Boorowa, and up and about at four a.m., was not explained. According to a report of insolvency court proceedings in October 1876, his place of residence was then still Young. Some time during the next couple of years, the family apparently moved to Murrumburrah; the Lachlan Electoral Roll for 1878–79 has William living there.

Like William, Hannah Lehane seems to have been in an expansive mood in mid-1874. Bishop Lanigan visited Yass towards the end of June to address the St Augustine's congregation on the proposed establishment of a Sisters of Mercy convent in the town. Hannah was there despite 'excessively inclement' weather, and promised to contribute an extremely generous £100. Hers was the biggest offered donation, nearly matching the combined £105 promised by Lanigan and the two Yass-based priests, Fathers O'Keeffe and O'Dwyer. At this stage, the total expected cost of erecting the building and bringing out a 'religious community of nuns' from Ireland was only £1,200. The full subscription list published in 1880 shows Hannah actually put in £105, plus £3 10s that she collected from others. Only the bishop and the wealthy retired storekeeper Thomas Laidlaw, who converted to Catholicism on his deathbed in 1876, contributed more.

In early November 1874, Hannah was back in Yass giving evidence at the court of petty sessions against William O'Dare and Samuel Jeffs, who had been charged with stealing and receiving five of her cattle. For the prosecution, police Sub Inspector Brennan said O'Dare told him he had bought the cattle 'from a man travelling' but was 'dashed if he knew' who this was. Brennan said Jeffs admitted he had bought the cattle from O'Dare but claimed he was unaware of a problem with them. Hannah told the magistrates the beasts, which were penned outside the court, were definitely hers; their brands proved it. She owned between 400 and 500 cattle, which had been mustered the previous February and again in May:

> Since the last muster it has been reported to me that some of my cattle were missing... I never parted with [the five cattle outside]; I know that my husband did not part with any cattle for six or seven years before his death, with the exception of one red poley cow, which he made a present of... I know my husband sold no cattle, because I managed his affairs for some years before his death...

O'Dare and Jeffs were sent to trial at the Yass Quarter Sessions the following January. There, a witness for the defence, Thomas Hardy, told the judge and jury that he and another man were with O'Dare when the accused bought the cattle, on the road between Binalong and Bowning:

> We stopped at Two-mile Creek to have some gin and water...each of us had two nips; a man came up to us driving five head of cattle; he asked for a light, and got one... This man wanted to deal with O'Dare for a horse... O'Dare afterwards gave £8 and the horse for the five head of cattle... O'Dare asked the man his name; he said it was Long, or Lloyd... I asked the man if the cattle he had sold were not Lehane's; the man replied that they were not, but that they had been bred by Mr Lehane, who was his cousin, and who had made them a present to him...

The jury accepted the crown prosecutor's advice to reject Hardy's evidence, and found both men guilty. At the sentencing hearing, Judge McFarland told O'Dare the case was a very sad one, 'aggravated by the fact that the prisoner had put Hardy into the box to tell a story which every one who heard it must have felt to be a wilful and deliberate lie'. He sentenced O'Dare to a year and nine months' gaol with hard labour and Jeffs to four years on the roads. This possibly was a miscarriage of justice. Jerry most likely did have relatives called Long; his sponsoring of the immigration of Kate Long, a twenty-year-old from Newmarket, County Cork, suggests this. She arrived on the same ship as his brother, Daniel, in November 1862. The St Augustine's parish register records that ten months later Kate gave birth to a daughter fathered by a Jeremiah Lehane – presumably Daniel's son of that name. Kate subsequently married a Yass blacksmith, William Clafferty.

Another drama for Hannah around this time was the death of Michael Waters, a sixty-year-old cook who worked at Coppabella. After drinking too heavily at the Five Mile Creek Inn (again a licensed hotel) on the Saturday between Christmas and New Year he fell into a creek while walking home. A brother of Mary Bodkin, the publican, found him there next morning and carried him back to the inn, where he complained of great pain in his side and breast. Mrs Bodkin told the inquest she rubbed him with oil, which relieved the pain. But then he got worse and 'I told him that I should send and inform his mistress, Mrs Lehane. He told me to do so, and also to tell her that…he was very bad, and that he wished her to see if she could do anything for him. I accordingly did so. Before receiving an answer from Mrs Lehane he was dead.'

September 1875 found Hannah in Yass again, placing an advertisement in the *Courier* announcing that sheep washing and shearing were to begin at Coppabella in early October. While in town she bought some five-shilling art union tickets in aid of the St Clement's Church of England organ fund. Her reward for this ecumenical gesture was three of the twenty-five 'framed oleographs and engravings' offered as prizes. Most likely the ticket seller was Joshua Shipway, publican at the Globe and a lay worker at St Clement's.

Shipway left the Globe soon afterwards, taking a job with the tramways in Sydney. Michael Reardon replaced him as publican in January 1876, paying £140 a year rent to Hannah. Like at least two of his predecessors, he soon fell into insolvency. The properties in Yass proved a continuing problem for Hannah over the next few years. A succession of publicans took on the Globe – Reardon's mother in February 1877, David Bernston in March 1878 and John Gardiner in February 1879. The old Braidwood Store building next to the Globe was advertised for 'moderate' rent in October 1876 and 'at a very low rental' in May 1878. In probably the biggest blow, J.J. Brown moved the *Courier* to new premises in Cooma Street at the start of 1878. All this change was probably linked to the gradual movement of Yass's business centre up the Cooma Street hill, away from the flood-prone intersection with Rossi Street.

On Coppabella, one of Hannah's main concerns seems to have been to secure as much land as possible as more and more of the run was made available for free selection. The *Courier* reported in January 1875 that her claims for pre-emptive leases over seven blocks totalling about 3,600 acres had been approved. Another pre-emptive lease, over 960 acres, was approved in March – in the name of young Jeremiah Lehane, then aged ten. Hannah's daughter Mary O'Hehir took up a forty-acre free selection in April 1875 and seven more the following month. Young Jeremiah took up forty acres in June. About a year later, in May 1876, two more pre-emptive leases were approved – 960 acres for Mary O'Hehir and 420 for seven-year-old Josephine Lehane!

Employees on Coppabella were among others who made 'friendly' land acquisitions. One was the overseer Michael Delahunty, who took up a 100-acre free selection at the end of 1875. Hannah hosted the marriage of Delahunty to Marianne Hobbs, her children's governess, at the Reedy Creek homestead in September 1877. Father Patrick O'Keeffe from Yass officiated.

Others who bought selections on the run were not so welcome. One sign of this may have been advertisements for boundary riders that Hannah placed in the *Courier* at the end of 1876 and in June 1877. In both cases the ad was headed 'Wanted immediately'. A January 1877 advertisement headed 'Notice and Caution' advised that the whole of Coppabella had been fenced and divided into paddocks. It warned, 'The public are hereby informed that persons injuring the fences or trespassing (by riding through the paddocks or otherwise) will be prosecuted as the law directs.' Three months later, the *Courier* reported that 'some malicious person' had set fire to and destroyed four miles of log fencing on Coppabella. 'The fence was set fire to in several places, and there is no doubt that it was the work of some spiteful individual.' Hannah offered a £50 reward for information leading to the conviction of the person responsible and advertised for people to build a replacement wire fence.

One man who took up land on and near Coppabella was Edward Browne, an immigrant from County Tipperary with connections to the Ryans of Galong. In December 1877, he appeared before the police court in Binalong charged with stealing a sheep belonging to Hannah. Following a complaint by Delahunty, a sheep with her brand was found in a mob that Browne was taking to market. Delahunty admitted in evidence that Browne's and Hannah's flocks had become mixed on many occasions over the past three years, and Browne had been cooperative in sorting them out. However, his relations with Browne had soured in recent times: 'I get nothing but abuse when I go near him.' Another Coppabella employee, Davis Nicholson, agreed that the sheep in question was Hannah's. He said he was on good terms with Browne, who until lately had been happy to let Hannah's employees retrieve any sheep that became mixed with his. Nicholson's description of a meeting between Delahunty and Browne gives an indication of the state of relations between the men: 'I heard Delahunty tell Browne...that two or three of Mrs Lehane's sheep were in his flock, and I heard Browne tell him he was a liar.' The magistrates dismissed the case, no doubt to Delahunty's great annoyance.

The rapidly completed Mount Carmel convent in Yass was opened with much ceremony in February 1878. Afterwards, 'upwards of seven hundred' people attended a grand luncheon in the schoolroom. Hannah 'provided' the head table, at which Bishop Lanigan presided. Other ladies looked after the other tables, all of which 'were laden with the choicest delicacies of the season'. Hannah may have been one of the region's biggest graziers and a major donor to the convent building fund, but her gender determined her role at an event such as this.

During the first part of May 1878, she looked after a road accident victim, Alice McEvoy, who had been midwife at the births of her children Josephine, John Thomas and Gertrude. Mrs McEvoy was knocked unconscious after jumping from an out-of-control Cobb and Co. coach between Gundagai and Albury. Taken to the Lehanes' at Reedy Creek, she was pronounced 'out of all danger' by Dr Perry of Yass, 'but the arm is so injured that it will take some time before she will be able to leave Reedy Creek'.

Mrs McEvoy had probably left by Thursday 30 May when a dramatic confrontation occurred between Hannah and Delahunty on one side and Edward Browne and his brother John on the other. 'Shocking Affray – Two Men Shot' shouted a special second edition of the *Yass Courier*. The *Burrowa News* treated the news much more sensationally under the heading 'Horrible Premeditated Attempted Murder': 'The most horrible premeditated attempt to murder by shooting that has ever been chronicled in the district occurred on the evening of Thursday 31st [*sic*] May, at Cumbamurra River,' claimed the *News*, 'the principal and intended victim of the revolting outrage being Mr Edward Brown [the spelling used in all the contemporary news reports], a selector, and the assailants Michael Delahunty, Felix Murphy and Mrs Lehane, in whose employ Delahunty and Murphy were.' Abandoning any pretence of objectivity, the paper went on,

> Mrs Lehane's ill-feeling and desire for revenge against persons selecting on her run is notorious. Mr Brown is an industrious honest man, and because he will not allow himself to be bounced or bribed out of his holdings, every hellish device that wicked, evil-minded men and women are capable of directing against him are practiced.

The *News* described Browne's prosecution for sheep stealing the previous December as 'one of the vilest…ever heard in a court of justice', adding that Hannah had a 'truculent craving for revenge'. The *Courier* tried to be impartial, but its first lengthy account of the shooting and preceding events also made Hannah look very much the villain of the piece.

The site of the shooting was a 320-acre selection on the Cumbamurra run, on Coppabella's northern border. According to the *Courier*, a James Ryan originally selected this block. He entered into a written agreement to transfer it to Browne, and the pair went to Boorowa to formalise the change of ownership at the local Crown lands agent's office. Ryan, unfortunately, died the night they arrived, so the transfer was not completed as planned next day. Browne was assured, though, that the agreement secured the land for him.

Despite this assurance, the block appeared in a list of forfeited selections published in the newspapers. Hannah seized the opportunity, hurrying to Boorowa to re-select it. A few days later she proceeded to the selection with Delahunty and thirty-three-year-old Felix Murphy, who had cattle on Coppabella, to try to take possession. They found Edward and John Browne at work there. An altercation ensued with both sides claiming ownership. Then Hannah and her companions left.

Two days later, Hannah returned with Delahunty and Felix. 'Words not of the most pleasant character' passed between them and the Brownes. Then Delahunty produced a loaded double-barrelled shotgun, which he fired, wounding Edward Browne in the left hand and John in the right arm. 'After receiving the shot,' the *Courier*'s report continued,

> Edward Brown called out (so goes our information which we consider trustworthy) to Mrs Lehane – 'Are you satisfied now; you have crippled us for life, if not mortally wounded us.' She replied – 'It serves you — — wretches right.'

Delahunty immediately rode to Binalong to make a statement to the police. He said he had picked up the gun for protection because the Brownes had hames (heavy pieces of wood from a horse's harness) in their hands and were flourishing them in a threatening manner. He cocked the gun and must have unintentionally pressed the trigger hard, making it go off. A messenger from the Brownes arrived at Binalong shortly afterwards and told a different story – that Delahunty had shot the two men without any provocation.

Hannah, Felix and Delahunty were charged the next day with shooting with intent to murder. Only Hannah was allowed bail, of £200. A week later the three appeared at the police court, Binalong, before a bench of three JPs who included Andrew Bogle Paterson, father of Banjo. The small courthouse was 'inconveniently crowded' during the three-and-a-half-hour hearing, the *Courier* reported. 'Numbers were gathered on the verandah and at the windows to hear as much as they could of the evidence.'

The first witness, Senior Constable Charles Walmsley of Binalong, provided more detail of Delahunty's statement to the police. As the three accused could not give evidence, this second-hand account of events was the only one presented from their perspective. Delahunty said, according to Walmsley, that on his, Hannah's and Felix's first visit to the disputed selection the Brownes abused Hannah and kicked her on the shin. Hannah told him to bring a gun for protection next time. On the second visit, the Brownes 'threatened to knock his brains out' with the half-hames they were flourishing. He walked towards them with the gun cocked, and 'in the excitement of the moment he must have pressed his finger too heavily on the trigger'.

Edward Browne appeared next. He said he returned to his shed after finishing ploughing on the day of the shooting and found Hannah and Felix there in a buggy. Delahunty was standing at a fire nearby. Hannah came over and demanded, 'Out of this shed, yourself and your horses, Brown.' When he refused to leave, Hannah called out: 'Mr Delahunty, go for a revolver.' Delahunty said he would '— soon make' Browne leave and struck him lightly on the face with the gun's muzzle two or three times. Browne went on,

> I told him to throw down his gun, it was not required…at this time I thought I saw something remarkable in his countenance, and went back in the shed along the side of it to the third post… I got the post between him and me. He made a step backwards like and then fired at me… Mrs Lehane, before Delahunty fired, called out three different times 'Fire on the wretch'… I called to Delahunty 'You have crippled me for life,' and Mrs Lehane called out 'It serves you right, you wretch'… I had before this a half-hames in my right hand. I did not attempt to strike him with the hames. My brother did not strike him or any of the parties…

Browne went on to describe Hannah's earlier visit to the block, accompanied by a little girl (presumably seven-year-old Gertrude Lehane) as well as by Delahunty and Felix Murphy. He said he had found Hannah's horses in the shed, eating his hay. When he tried to turn them out Felix came over with a gun in his hand and Hannah called out 'fire on the wretch'. Browne took no notice; after turning out the horses he went away and had his dinner. When he returned about an hour and a half later,

Delahunty...came up to me, put his fist up to my face, and said he would smash me. I had my hands down and told him he was at liberty to do so. Mrs Lehane came up close to me and said 'you coward, you are not game to strike an owl'. She had a tomahawk in her hand, she put it up in my face several times and said 'I'll brain you, you wretch.' I told her to go back, that I would have the matter settled in an easier way than that. I then went into the shed and kept walking up and down there until they left.

Under questioning by Hannah's counsel, J.H. Want, Browne elaborated on his account of her words before and after the shooting. 'She said 'shoot the — wretches'; she used such bad language that it could not be printed in the *Yass Courier*,' he said. Afterwards, 'she said 'it serves you — well right'.' He added that at the earlier confrontation he had not kicked Hannah on the shin as claimed by Delahunty: 'I believe I kicked a tin billy.'

The evidence of the next witness, John Browne, proved crucial when the case came to trial four months later. He said he had heard Hannah say to his brother, 'Brown, take these horses out until I put mine in', and had heard his brother refuse to do so. However, according to the *Courier*'s report, he told the court,

> I did not hear Mrs Lehane say anything to Delahunty before he went for the gun. When he came back with it, he said to my brother 'I'll soon shift you'... I could not take my eyes off the gun, for I expected my brother to fall every moment... I heard nothing said as I could not take my eyes off the gun...

The magistrates committed Delahunty and Hannah to stand trial when the circuit court next came to Yass, but discharged Felix. This meant he would be able to give his eyewitness account at the trial. Hannah was released on £200 bail with two sureties of £100, provided by John Murphy and George Eason. Delahunty's bail was £400. Hannah's squatter neighbour Richard Julian and Patrick Magennis, publican of the Bogolong Hotel and a relative of Julian's, offered the required £200 sureties.

Two days after the police court hearing, the Department of Lands in Sydney sent a notice to Edward Browne advising that the Cumbamurra block was his; its earlier forfeiture had been reversed. As the *Courier* noted, 'Had the Lands Department forwarded the...communication a few weeks earlier, the serious shooting affray at Cumbamurra would not have occurred.' In early July, Julian and Magennis applied successfully to the Yass police magistrate to be relieved of their bail undertakings. Julian said he suspected that Delahunty, who had moved to Sydney, intended to abscond from his bail and leave the colony. After spending more than a month in Yass gaol, Delahunty was bailed again in late August. This time, men named Nesbitt and Hewlett from Sydney provided the £200 sureties.

The circuit court sitting presided over by Judge Hargrave on 1 October 1878 was something of a family affair. The key witnesses in the two cases that came on before the trial of Hannah and Delahunty were John and young Miles Murphy, who gave evidence against men charged with stealing, respectively, sides of bacon and a watch and chain (chapter 19). Hannah and Delahunty faced two charges: shooting Edward and John Browne with intent to commit murder, and shooting them with intent to do grievous bodily harm. They had hired an eminent Catholic Queen's Counsel, Edward Butler, to lead their defence.

The trial started badly for Hannah, with Senior Constable Walmsley insisting that Delahunty had said in his statement on the night of the shooting that Hannah told him to go for the gun. Butler pointed out that the written record of interview did not include this, and Walmsley had not mentioned it in his evidence at the Binalong hearing. Edward Browne was called next, and largely repeated the evidence he gave at Binalong. Under cross-examination by Butler, he said Hannah spoke 'in her ordinary tone of voice' when she told Delahunty to fire at him: 'She might have been heard the length of this court-room; she was speaking, perhaps, a little louder than I am now.' He said his brother was at his side when he was shot. Felix was some ten or twelve yards away, just behind Delahunty.

John Browne's evidence also was generally similar to that given at the police court. However, he insisted that he had heard Hannah say 'shoot the wretch' after Delahunty got the gun even though the record of his statement to the police and the *Courier*'s report of his evidence at Binalong indicated the contrary. He claimed that when asked 'did Mrs Lehane say shoot the wretch?' he had said yes.

The tide began to turn for Hannah when Butler called Felix Murphy as the first witness for the defence. Felix said he drove Hannah to the selection in a buggy; Delahunty went there separately. There were no guns in the buggy:

> Mrs Lehane got out of the buggy and said: Brown, you are trespassing again. Delahunty took the horses out of the buggy, and was going to put them in the shed, when Edward Brown raised a hames in his hand and said: You or no other man will bring a horse in here. The next time I saw Delahunty he had a gun in his hand. Brown had the hames in his hand before Delahunty got the gun… John Brown then came with another hames. Mrs Lehane was standing at the fire, about twelve or thirteen yards from where the gun was fired off. Mrs Lehane said nothing to Delahunty. I was only three or four yards from Mrs Lehane. I don't think Mrs Lehane could have told Delahunty to go for the gun without hearing her say so. I was as close to her as Delahunty. When the gun went off I was nearer to Mrs Lehane than Brown. At the time the gun went off Mrs Lehane did not say shoot the wretch; she said nothing of the sort.

Cross-examined by the Crown prosecutor, C.J. Manning, Felix acknowledged that he could not swear Hannah did not tell Delahunty to take firearms to the block. 'I can't say whose gun it was Delahunty used,' he added. 'I can't say where he took it from; there was a tree between us.' Also he could not say whether Hannah saw the gun: 'I think her back was turned to Delahunty when he had the gun. I could not help keeping my eyes on Mrs Lehane.' Felix told the court that, after the shooting was over, Delahunty said to Hannah that he was sorry.

Hannah's solicitor, Edward Iceton, appeared next. He read a copy of a letter he had written to Hannah shortly before the shooting. The *Courier* did not report what it said, but it is clear from the judge's summing up that it supported her claim to the selection. Iceton then disputed John Browne's key testimony:

> I was present when John Brown gave evidence at the Police Court at Binalong. I did not hear him say one single word that would criminate Mrs Lehane. He said nothing about Mrs Lehane telling any one to go for a gun. I have a distinct recollection of Mr Scarvell [the Brownes' solicitor] repeating the question twice; Brown said no… What the witness has said here to-day is altogether contrary to what he said at the police office at Binalong.

James John Brown, who covered the proceedings at Binalong for the

Courier, was the next witness. The newspaperman gave a strange answer, if reported correctly, when asked about John Browne's claim that his report of the Binalong hearing was wrong in suggesting he had not heard Hannah say 'shoot the wretch'. 'I cannot say that the words were not used,' Brown said. He added immediately, 'If they had been they would have appeared in my report of the proceedings.'

J.J. Brown was the first of three character witnesses called. He said he had known Hannah since she came to the district: 'I have always known her to be a peaceful and respectable person, and never heard her name mentioned otherwise than with respect.' Bank manager Robert Pearson said he had 'known her always as a person of unquestionable character, and never heard that she was connected with any row.' Dr Isidore Blake said Hannah had been a visitor at his place, 'and I have never known a quieter or more ladylike person; for the last five or six years I have been intimately acquainted with the lady.'

In his final address, which took two hours, Butler made a point of the fact that Hannah and Delahunty had no opportunity to put their cases and Felix also would have had to stay silent if the Binalong magistrates had sent him to trial. He asked the jury whether they could 'think for one moment that Mrs Lehane was such a person as to be considered and branded as a bloodthirsty person'? He said the Crown had not produced a single word of evidence to prove that Delahunty had any intention of committing murder. The Brownes had clearly prepared for a fight with Delahunty and Felix, arming themselves with hames. It could not be believed that when Delahunty had the gun poking in Edward's face he placidly said, 'Put the gun down, it is not required'. 'The whole statement of Edward Brown was incredible from beginning to end,' Butler contended.

Judge Hargrave told the jury in what the *Courier* called his 'most careful' summing up that the prosecution had withdrawn the shooting with intent to murder charges. The twelve men sitting in judgment took nearly an hour to agree that Delahunty was guilty, and Hannah not guilty, of wounding with intent to do grievous bodily harm. 'His Honor said he quite agreed with the verdict,' the *Courier* reported, 'and he was bound also to say that in the whole course of his experience he never heard a case better defended than this case was by Mr Butler.' The judge sentenced Delahunty to two years' hard labour in Goulburn gaol.

Edward Browne went on to become a prominent landowner in the Binalong district. The doctor who attended him after the shooting told the court he did not expect his patient would ever be able to use his wounded hand again, and a photo from decades later shows it covered with a glove. It is said that shotgun pellets kept emerging from the wounds right up to Browne's death in 1910.

21

A new world

In early September 1878, while she was on bail awaiting trial, Hannah received a piece of very good news. She had won a silver medal for a sample of wool from Coppabella at the Paris Exposition Universelle. Only four other New South Wales wool producers achieved the same honour.

The *Yass Courier* greeted the news warmly. 'Our readers will be delighted to observe by English telegram in today's issue that Mrs Lehane, of Beremangra, has achieved the great distinction of having won a silver medal at the Paris Exhibition for wool,' it said. Maybe an item in the paper the previous September had prompted Hannah's entry. This announced that the New South Wales government wanted the colony to be represented at the exhibition and had called on the Agricultural Society to invite the cooperation of woolgrowers. The society issued a circular calling for entries of boxes of wool of various descriptions, to be delivered in Sydney by 1 January 1878. No charge would be made for entries, and showcases for the wool would be provided at government expense.

The Paris Exhibition of 1878 was one of the grandest of many staged around the world in the second half of the nineteenth century to celebrate achievements since the Industrial Revolution. The venue was a vast iron and glass hall similar to the famous Crystal Palace built in London's Hyde Park for the Great Exhibition of 1851. In 1879–80 Sydney staged a smaller version in the Garden Palace in the Domain, which was destroyed by fire in 1882. Melbourne followed a few months later. The Royal Exhibition Building, built for its international exhibition and the site of the ceremonial opening of Federal parliament in 1901, is a magnificent relic of the times.

Queen Victoria's heir, Edward, Prince of Wales, was among the distinguished guests at the Paris Exhibition. According to the *Courier*, he and the Imperial Duke of Austria spoke with astonishment about the display mounted by New South Wales, which included a variety of agricultural and mineral products as well as wool. 'They described the exhibits as indicating great wealth, and stated their opinion that the colony would become a great country,' the paper's London correspondent enthused. After the wool judging, a representative of the colonial government at the exhibition, Jules Joubert, wrote in triumph, 'The contest in [the wool] section has been the most severe, and I am proud to tell you we have beaten the whole world, not by favour, not by majority, but by the unanimous verdict of twenty of the best judges in the world.'

The successes in Paris prompted J.J. Brown to pen a philosophical leader for the *Courier*. Two strands of thinking were current, he wrote. One considered mankind was fast approaching the highest point of civilisation. War would be banished and peace and brotherhood prevail on 'this at present distracted planet'. The other thought civilisation a sham, 'our boasted advance over preceding ages a delusion'. Proponents of this view pointed to the new capacity to destroy human life 'in convenient batches' with weapons such as the Martini-Henry rifle and 80-ton guns. Brown was confident the optimists would prove correct:

> Everywhere we find the truth of the assertion that, not war, attended with devastation, famine, disease, and ruin, but peace, with plenty smiling on the earth, with the arts and sciences, with mental culture and physical and moral happiness, form the spirit of our civilisation... No better proof of the peaceful and therefore progressive tendencies of the age is to be found than in that presented by the great International Exhibitions that have been held within the last eight and twenty years. These may be said to form the trophies of peace. They are the indications of the spread of the feeling of brotherhood among the leading nations of the earth, and show that the barriers that have intervened to divide nationalities are fast being cast down in order that the European nations may be gathered together as members of the great family whose work is to christianise and civilise the remaining portions of the earth.

The *Courier* was an interested chronicler of the latest scientific advances. In September 1875, it reported the invention of the typewriter, 'a machine intended to supersede to some extent the pen for common writing'. The telephone was the next big invention, and trials began in the Yass region in 1878. Links were set up between towns on the telegraph line and groups gathered at each end to cooee and sing songs, and marvel at what they heard. When Yass, Boorowa and Young were connected on 1 July a rendition of 'We were marching through Georgia' by Miss Bell and Mr McNab in Young was 'clearly heard' in Yass. Listeners in Boorowa called 'grandly sung' down the line to Yass after a performance there by Mr Lassen. Next came early experiments with electric light. In January 1879, the *Courier* reprinted a long article from the *British Mercantile Gazette* reviewing progress, including work by Edison. Two years later, the people of Yass looked forward to a demonstration as a circus coming to town was to be 'Illuminated throughout by the dazzling Electric Light, the most remarkable invention of the age, literally turning Night to Day'. Unfortunately, the 'electric light apparatus' was damaged at Yass railway station 'and could not be brought into operation'. Instead, 'the tent was brilliantly illuminated by means of portable gas-lights'.

Sadly, Hannah, William Lehane and John Murphy, although only in their thirties and forties, did not live to see these inventions, and the many more that soon followed, become part of everyday life. Had they achieved their 'three score years and ten', Hannah would have seen the start of the twentieth century, John would have died just before the outbreak of World War I, and William would have lived through most of the war – that overwhelming demonstration that J.J. Brown's 'brotherhood among nations' was still some way off.

Hannah set out after her acquittal in October 1878 to further build the quality of the Coppabella wool clip, spending sixty guineas in mid-November on a 'valuable prize ram'. In January 1879, she was back in court in Yass over a new problem with her Rossi Street property. Soft-drink maker Patrick Sheekey had complained that household goods worth nearly £100 had been illegally locked up in a building he rented. Hannah told the court she had not given her agent authority to take this action, but added that she had never received 'one farthing of rent' from Sheekey. Judge McFarland was sympathetic, regretting 'that a verdict was bound to be given against Mrs Lehane, as she no doubt was innocent of the whole matter'. He fined her £5.

Hannah became ill soon afterwards. She died at a boarding house in Margaret Street, Sydney, on 1 June 1879 at the age of forty-six. The death certificate records that she had suffered from a uterine disease for three months, and names Dr Gilhooley as one of two doctors who attended her the day before she died. Jerry's daughter Ellen Lyons, then living at Balmain, certified the death, presumably having helped look after Hannah during her stay in Sydney. Ellen had suffered another tragic loss not long before, the death of her youngest child, five-year-old Elizabeth, on 16 December 1878. She and Annie Casey, owner of the Margaret Street boarding house and presumably a friend of Hannah's, are named on the death certificate as witnesses to Hannah's burial, which took place at Yass cemetery on 4 June. Father R.J. Carr of St Augustine's officiated. Most likely, Ellen and Annie accompanied the body on the train journey south, and then in the funeral procession up Rossi Street to the grave beside Jerry's.

In its report of Hannah's death, the *Courier* described her as a 'well-known and much-respected lady', and 'a person of great business ability' who 'for many years past managed a large station property with consummate skill and great success'. Among the challenges she faced on Coppabella were wool prices that fell sharply from the highs of the early 1870s, reaching a trough during the recession of 1878–79. Resulting financial pressures are probably the reason why the property was mortgaged to the Commercial Banking Company of Sydney some time between 1875 and 1878. Coppabella did not pass to young Jeremiah as Jerry had intended. Instead it was put up 'for peremptory sale' by auction 'by order of the mortgagees' on 14 July 1880.

The auctioneers, Harrison, Jones and Devlin of Sydney, noted in their advertisement that the property was being sold 'only on account of the death of the late proprietor, who had held it for many years'. They described it as 'compact and valuable', with an estimated area of 32,000 acres including 1,057 acres of purchased land and another 1,598 acres conditionally purchased. Improvements comprised an overseer's house, store and woolshed, men's huts, horse and stock yards and several large sheep paddocks, mainly fenced with wire. Some 12,000 superior mixed sheep, thirty-five head of cattle, ten working bullocks and twenty-three horses were to be included in the sale. 'Special attention should be directed to [Coppabella's] character as a wool-growing station, being unsurpassed for the healthy growth and superior quality of the wool,' the ad went on. 'The convenient situation of the run [on the main south road] enables every advantage to be taken of the markets, while it reduces the cost of working to a minimum, with the further advantage of enabling its owner to visit the metropolis within a few hours.'

The day before the sale, the *Courier* anticipated 'keen competition to secure the ownership of this fine property'. This seems not to have eventuated, probably because of the recent recession and decline in wool prices. The buyer was Thomas Broughton, proprietor of Muttama run, west of Jugiong, who paid what the paper described as 'the low figure' of £9,500. Broughton had been in the news a year earlier over various alleged hostile actions towards Muttama's free selectors, including depriving them of access to water and demolishing one man's hut. So Edward Browne and any other selectors who had found Hannah a difficult neighbour may not have welcomed Broughton's arrival as squire of Coppabella. His time there seems to have been brief; a *Courier* report named Austin Thomas Wiltshire as owner in May 1881.

With the death of Hannah, George Eason became sole executor of Jerry's will. The career of this prominent Boorowa district resident had taken interesting turns during the 1870s, when he was in his fifties and early sixties. He launched the weekly *Burrowa News* in June 1874, having bought the plant of the *Burrowa Advocate*, which ceased publication the previous year. The *News* apparently proved no money-spinner and he sold it to Malcolm Warner Burns, from northern Ireland, in 1877. Had Eason still been in charge in 1878, the paper's coverage of the Cumbamurra shooting incident (chapter 20) would surely have been much kinder to Hannah.

Eason was declared insolvent in August 1878, and two months later Gegullalong, the property he had run since 1858, was auctioned by order of the mortgagees. The schedule he filed with the court listed liabilities of about £2,989 and assets worth £4,172. These healthy-looking figures apparently proved fairly close to the mark, and he obtained his certificate of conformity in September 1879.

Eason died nine months later, on 6 June 1880 – at Beremangra, the Coppabella homestead. According to the *Courier*, since Hannah's death a year earlier he had 'principally resided' at Beremangra, 'looking after the interests of the [Lehane] children'. His death, from a heart condition, occurred on a Sunday evening, a little more than a month before Coppabella was to go to auction. 'While sitting in a chair reading, [he] suddenly expired, his head falling upon the book which he held in his hand,' the paper reported. Whether the children – Jeremiah (now fifteen years old), Josephine (eleven) and Gertrude (nine) – were home at the time is not recorded. Wherever they were, Eason's death was another traumatic event for them to cope with – as if the long illness and death of their mother, the dramas of 1878 and their father's death in 1874 were not enough.

In 1880, Jeremiah may still have been a boarder at St Patrick's College, a secondary school in Goulburn inaugurated by Bishop Lanigan at the start of the 1874 school year. Jerry gave £25 to this school's building fund, and Dr Forrest spoke at the opening: 'Let honour, intelligence, high cultivation of their natural gifts, with that Spartan chivalry which is, in the day of trial, the bulwark of freedom, be the aim and characteristics of young Australia,' he urged. The students' awards list for 1877, published in the *Courier*, shows Jeremiah taking out a prize for catechism.

Josephine was almost certainly already a boarder at Rosebank, a school run by the Sisters of the Good Samaritan in Sydney. A history published by the order records that she attended Rosebank 'from early childhood', and acquired 'a fine and wide standard of education. She excelled in literature, history and French (which she spoke like a native), in instrumental music, drama and singing.' Gertrude also may have been at Rosebank by 1880. Earlier, she and probably Josephine received their schooling at home from Marianne Hobbs, the governess who married the overseer Delahunty in 1877. Presumably Gertrude was the little girl who accompanied Hannah, Delahunty and Felix Murphy on their visit to the Cumbamurra selection two days before Edward and John Browne were shot in May 1878 (chapter 20).

At Murrumburrah, John Murphy decided at the start of 1879 that the time had come to make his will. Signed on 17 January, this left all his real and personal estate to his wife, Mary Anne. The fact that no separate provision was made for the four children in the event of her prior decease perhaps indicates that the thirty-five-year-old suspected his death was imminent. It occurred just three months later, on 19 April 1879 – a month after the sale of the family property, Kalangan.

The *Courier* reported that, because of continued ill health, John had gone to Sydney 'about a couple of months ago', and 'the attack' had 'terminated fatally' there. The *Burrangong Argus* was less cryptic, revealing that John died at Gladesville Asylum. The medical casebook records that he was admitted on 1 March with dementia. Staff were informed he had been in the habit of drinking excessively for some years and had 'been more intemperate than usual' over the past twelve months. He was weak and helpless, and speaking incoherently, on admission, and 'well-marked symptoms of cirrhosis of the liver' were observed subsequently. His condition gradually deteriorated. In its report of his death the *Argus* described him as

> A kind, generous, true man, whose hand was never closed against anybody who sought his assistance, and who succumbed with a broken heart, under difficulties, brought upon him because he was always too willing to share the difficulties of others. By his death, his townsmen have lost a good citizen, and his friends from out of their circle one who possessed instincts which, under any and all circumstances, stamped him as the true gentleman. His remains were brought up to Galong on Tuesday morning, and deposited in the cemetery at that place, many sincere mourners, from far and near, attending the funeral. Poor fellow! There are many who could have been easier spared.

John's story appears to be that of a good and able man who took on heavy responsibilities from an early age and eventually buckled under the pressure. An inclination to spend carelessly probably contributed to his downfall and so, no doubt, did his drinking. It seems he did not inherit his father's instincts for entrepreneurial success. John took charge of the Murphy store on the wild Lambing Flat goldfields at the age of eighteen – an indication of Miles' confidence in his ability. His choice by the local Catholics as their spokesman to welcome the visiting Archbishop Polding in 1863 is a sign of the respect the twenty-year-old quickly earned. Back in Murrumburrah, the deaths of Miles and Anne in 1869 left him, at the age of twenty-six, with heavy responsibilities as head of the family. His involvement in community and church activities never flagged.

The Murphy family vault at Galong cemetery.

Probably his brother Miles junior arranged the erection of the Murphy family vault at Galong cemetery, which stands as a monument to Miles and Anne, their sons Robert, Patrick, Joseph, James and Thomas, as well as to John and Mary Anne (who died at Murrumburrah in 1926). John's body was brought to Galong by train from Sydney on 22 April, and 'a large concourse of mourners in buggies and on horseback' took part in the afternoon procession from the railway platform to the cemetery. The *Courier* named many of those present. As well as Mary Anne, John's three surviving siblings Felix, Miles and Sarah, and William Lehane, they included two priests, prominent district landholders, and Murrumburrah businessmen including John Dillon. 'Doubtless there would have been many more had the procession moved from this town, or had longer notice been given,' wrote the Murrumburrah correspondent, 'for Mr Murphy was so generally well known in and around Murrumburrah, and had so many friends and well-wishers among all classes, owing to the kindness and liberality of his disposition, that everyone about here cannot but feel a deep sadness at his death.'

When probate was granted on John's will in May 1879, the value of goods sworn was less than £1,000. Apparently there were also substantial debts against his name because the following October the estate – administered by Mary Anne, who was now running the Criterion Hotel – was declared insolvent. Representatives of a deceased lawyer from Wagga Wagga, Henry Donovan, launched the insolvency proceedings. At a creditors' meeting in December Andrew Aiken, owner of the store established by the Murphys at Murrumburrah, proved a debt of nearly £100, J.J. Brown of the *Courier* showed he was owed about £20 and four other men proved debts totalling more than £60. Another £16 debt was proved at a further meeting the following February.

Despite an order for compulsory sequestration of the estate issued in October 1879, Mary Anne apparently remained in charge of the Criterion. Two months after John's death, she advertised that a 'new store' was being opened at the hotel 'with a splendid assortment of goods, bought at extremely low prices, which must be cleared out in a few weeks'. Perhaps this was an unsuccessful attempt to forestall already threatened insolvency proceedings. Following the creditors' meetings, in April 1880, a visiting reporter from Sydney's *Town and Country Journal* referred to 'Mrs Murphy's Criterion Hotel', noting that it was 'an excellent hostelry'.

Six months later, the estate of Miles Murphy senior became the target of a new insolvency action, this time launched by the storekeeper Aiken. Again, sequestration was ordered; presumably assets that had passed to Felix, Sarah and Miles were now drawn into the net as well as those in John's estate. Perhaps these were vexatious proceedings; no debts were proved at creditors' meetings held in Young and Sydney in late 1880 and early 1881. The crisis apparently passed quickly. Later in 1881, Mary Anne donated to Murrumburrah's St Mary's Church a stained glass window inscribed 'In memory of John Aloysius Murphy'. It is still there, as the centre panel in a group of three behind the altar. The others commemorate John Dillon and the blacksmith James Murray, both of whom died in 1884.

Unlike Hannah Lehane and John Murphy, William Lehane was mentioned only occasionally in the press. So his last years have been impossible to track in any detail. In September 1880, he attended an election meeting at Binalong, which suggests that he, Sarah and seven-year-old John Augustine were still living in the Binalong–Murrumburrah district. William was one of a number of men who 'spoke highly in favour' of the Catholic lawyer Thomas Slattery, who proposed standing for the new Legislative Assembly electorate of Burrowa. The *Courier* endorsed Slattery's policy of making life easier for free selector farmers by abolishing interest charges on their payments, and was pleased to see him elected.

Some time during the early 1880s, William obtained a job with the Lands Department as an inspector (or assistant inspector according to one reference) of conditional purchases. Inspectors had the often-unpopular task of checking that free selectors fulfilled their legal requirements to live on and improve their land. The job appears to have been based at Wagga Wagga, and a photograph in an old Lehane album probably confirms that this town became, at least temporarily, home to the family. It shows the four daughters of Morgan O'Connor, then aged between about ten and eighteen. Perhaps the doctor from Yass – an old acquaintance of Jerry and the Murphys who transferred his practice to Wagga Wagga in 1873 (chapter 18) – befriended William and Sarah when they moved to the town.

The first inspectors of conditional purchases began their rounds of farmers' blocks in 1874. In 1875, they numbered only five, and so must have had very large territories to cover. They were paid £350 a year, plus an allowance for travelling expenses. The inspection force grew rapidly – to nine in 1876, fourteen in 1877 and twenty-four in 1878 – and so did antagonism in the bush to them and to the process they were part of. Selectors accused by inspectors of failing to fulfil their obligations were summoned to special courts of inquiry to explain why their blocks should not be forfeited. A proposal to do away with the inspectors was debated in the colonial parliament in June 1877 but rejected by a large majority. One speaker claimed many of them accepted free accommodation from squatters while drawing their twenty-five shillings a day allowances; in too many cases they had become 'the despicable tools of the squatters'. Another accused inspectors of regularly being drunk on the job.

The inspectors' positions survived major changes to the land laws made after an inquiry in 1883 identified big problems with the free selection system. The commissioners found 'unintelligible chaos, in which the rights and interests of all mainly concerned have been the sport of accident, political interest and departmental disorder'. The system had 'barred the advance of honest enterprise in all directions and has at the same time opened a door for the entrance of every phase of abuse and fraud, to be shared in by persons of all classes and conditions'.

Changed arrangements included the establishment of local Land Boards, which took on the task of determining whether landholders were complying with their conditions of tenure. The Wagga Wagga board held one of its regular meetings at the end of September 1885, and William most likely reported to it. A month later the *Wagga Wagga Advertiser* carried the following news:

> For some weeks Mr William Lehane, Assistant Inspector of Conditional Purchases in this district, has been lying at the Australian Hotel here in a critical state. His friends will learn with regret that that gentleman died on Tuesday morning [3 November], at the comparatively early age of 38 years.

William did not leave a will. The letter of administration of his intestate estate, dated April 1886, records that the 'estate and effects' had been granted to Sarah. The sworn value of the goods in his name was 'under £75'. The letter gives Sarah's place of residence as Gunning, a village about halfway between Yass and Goulburn. Presumably, the family had moved there; the fact that William's death occurred at one of the town's hotels suggests Wagga Wagga was no longer home when he died. The Registry of Births, Deaths and Marriages holds a notification of William's burial at Wagga Wagga Cemetery on 4 November 1885, but there is no death certificate and hence no official record of the cause of death. Most likely alcohol contributed. A paragraph in the *Murrumburrah Signal* described William as 'a gentleman widely known and much respected in this and the surrounding districts' and added, 'the cause of death is said to have been enlargement of the liver'.

22

Into the twentieth century

The sorry endings to the stories of William and John Murphy would be a dismal note to conclude on. So this chapter briefly traces the lives of other second- and some third-generation Lehanes and Murphys. Successes and good times reminiscent of the days of Jerry and Miles mingle with the inevitable failures and sadness.

William's wife (and John's sister) Sarah appears to have inherited the endearing qualities of her mother, Anne Murphy (chapter 13). The successful life of John Augustine Lehane suggests she was a good nurturer and wise guide to her child, who was only twelve when William died. At some stage, probably after young John left home, Sarah moved to Mount Wilson in the Blue Mountains. In April 1901 the forty-eight-year-old came down to Sydney for an operation at Lewisham Hospital, and died two days after the surgery.

Many besides her twenty-seven-year-old son and two surviving brothers, Felix and Miles, mourned her. Wrote the *Murrumburrah Signal*, 'She was of a lovable nature and a true woman, and her demise is deeply regretted by her numerous relatives and friends in these parts.' According to the *Yass Courier*, she was

Sarah Lehane.

as fine a girl as ever breathed. She was loved and respected by all who knew her. The name of Sarah Murphy will ever remain green in the memory of her old schoolmates in and around Yass, Binalong and Murrumburrah.

John Augustine Lehane, known as Jack, had a clerk's job in Melbourne when he married Elizabeth Mitchell at St Monica's Catholic church, Essendon, on 28 June 1899, a little less than two years before his mother's death. Elizabeth was the youngest of five children of Irish emigrants James Mitchell from Manorhamilton, County Leitrim, and Mary Spellissy from Ennis, County Clare. James and Mary had married in the gold town of Castlemaine in October 1862; he was then a groom and she a servant. He later worked for the Victorian railways.

Jack and Elizabeth moved to Coorparoo, Brisbane, in late 1899 or early 1900. There, according to the birth certificate for their first child, Felix, born on 18 July 1900, Jack was employed as a woolbroker – the start of a long and successful career in the wool trade. By 20 May 1905, when the second child, Claire, was born, the family had moved to Randwick, Sydney, and Jack had become manager of Pine Valley wool scourers of Botany. Then in 1910 they moved to Melbourne, where Jack was a wool-buyer

Jack (John Augustine) and Elizabeth Lehane.

Jack and Elizabeth took this photo of their children, Felix and Claire, with them on their 1914 round-the-world trip.

with Ostermeyer, Dewez & Van Rompaey and later Kreglinger & Fernau.

The family settled in Kew and the children attended nearby Catholic schools; Felix went to Xavier College and Claire to Genazzano F.C.J. College. Both had happy memories of their childhood. One of Claire's fond recollections from old age was being wrapped in a pink blanket one night in 1910 and carried to a window to be shown Halley's comet. She remembered the family's enjoyment of Jack's recitations of Byron's tirade against Lord Elgin of Elgin Marbles fame ('Athena, thy plunderer was a Scot...') and C.J. Dennis's reworking of Shakespeare's *Romeo and Juliet* in *The Sentimental Bloke* ('Wot's in a name?' she ses. 'Struth, I dunno.'). A great occasion at the age of about thirteen was a visit to the stage version of Steele Rudd's *On Our Selection*.

Jack's work required round-the-world voyages for discussions with the principals of his firm in France and Belgium and with the companies it supplied. He apparently went alone on the first trip, in 1911. Elizabeth accompanied him on the second, just before the outbreak of World War I in 1914. They took Claire on their first post-war visit, in 1924. She met a young British army officer, Gordon Maclean, on the ship, the parents met his family in England, and two years later he came to Melbourne to marry her. After army postings in Hong Kong and Cairo the young couple settled in England. Felix accompanied his parents on their next voyage, in 1928–29. He was also now a wool buyer with Kreglinger &

Fernau, based in Sydney, where in 1933 he married Jessie Vicars, daughter of a prominent manufacturer of woollen cloth.

Both children of Jack and Elizabeth married non-Catholics and severed their links with the faith of their forebears; the parents also left the Church. One of Jack's stories passed down in the family suggests he was a sceptic from an early age:

> A member of the family was thought to be dying and the family and priest were gathered around her bed. Jack, aged about seven, had slipped in too. Seeing him there, the priest handed him a small bottle and told him to run down to the church and collect some holy water. It was raining outside, so Jack, being practical, collected some water from a puddle outside the front door, paused for the appropriate number of minutes, and returned, breathing heavily. The holy water was duly administered, the patient recovered, and the priest turned to Jack saying: 'There you are, my boy. You've witnessed the power of holy water.'

Elizabeth wrote a lively diary of the 1914 trip to Europe and America. One thing that stands out is a strong consciousness, fourteen years after Federation, of being Australian. Early in the voyage she commented on the dress sense of the ship's passengers: 'We feel the Australians hold their own very well so far.' When Lord Loch, son of a former governor of Victoria, came aboard at Aden with his retinue he asked whether there were any Australians on board. 'I hope he will be satisfied with the specimens,' Elizabeth wrote. 'They [the Lochs] are a most ordinary looking party.' When another ship passed theirs in the Suez Canal 'we tried to find out if there were any Australians on board, but we had no reply. We supposed there were not.'

She noted reminders of home, in one place hearing gramophone records of Melba and in another just missing a performance by Percy Grainger. She also liked making comparisons. In the south of France 'the trees and general colouring' were 'very much the same as on our coast', but there were 'better wattle and gum trees than I have ever seen in Australia'. After visiting several 'dirty, dark, old, mouldy' churches in Italy and France she observed, 'These old cities look very dirty after ours, and one feels they are good to see, but the new and wholesome cities to live in – every time.' A French 'Train de Luxe' was fine, but no better than 'our

Limited'. She thought operas were staged 'quite as well' in Melbourne as in Paris. London's Kew Gardens were grand as a park, but as botanical gardens could not compare with Melbourne's. The beach at Brighton was a disappointment: 'It is composed of huge pebbles or stones, rounded by the wash of the waves but horrid to walk on, and the water as muddy as the Yarra, far more so.'

Costs tended to be lower in Europe. At one grand house the couple visited in France a man was paid ten shillings a week to look after about one and a half acres of garden and a very capable domestic 'who does everything' received £1 2s. 'They think it too much. When I told them what we paid, they exclaimed.' In Bordeaux, Elizabeth paid nineteen shillings for a pair of boots that would have cost £2 7s in Melbourne. Another comparison left her home town far behind. In Paris, she 'took some measurements of the footpaths to settle an argument about the widths of Melbourne streets and these.' It was no contest: 'Walked back along the Champs Elysées, feasted my eyes upon it and thought of people calling St Kilda Road the finest in the world. Bosh!'

Elizabeth loved the French capital: 'Paris is music, wickedness, gaily lawless. The whole place is brilliantly lighted. Music of the best arrests the ear at every café... It is a Dream City.' And she was very well looked after there by the head of Jack's firm, Alfred Van Rompaey, and his family: 'I am seeing and doing Paris in a style any titled lady might envy, everyone so kind to me I sometimes wonder if I am really myself.' The Van Rompaeys took Jack and Elizabeth to a new home they were creating from an old monastery, which they intended to call 'Australie'. 'They say it is where I am to stay next time I come here,' Elizabeth wrote. 'I was even shown my room. I shall never forget the kindness I have met with from those good people.'

The diary provides some interesting insights into Jack's character. Early in the voyage, 'Jack won another game of chess from the Purser'; the next day, he 'beat the Captain at chess.' At the ancient city of Carcassonne in southern France, 'Jack saw something here that interested him very much, the tomb of Simon de Montfort.' In London, 'We first went to the Kenilworth Hotel, a very nice place but according to Jack run by wowsers, which did not suit him.' They soon transferred to the Waldorf. At Hampton Court, 'We went into the maze and were much amused at the distress of so many people unable to get out. Jack worked it out scientifically so we got out without assistance, but it is most intricate and I'm sure I should be there yet if left to myself.'

Among the most poignant passages is a reference to the son of a businessman Jack dealt with in Bordeaux. He was 'a nice lad and speaks English very well. He spent 2 years in England and now has to put in 3 years in the Army; I'm afraid he won't know much of his English at the end of that time at the rate he is going.' The war was only months away.

Jack and Elizabeth crossed the US and Canada by train, and boarded a ship for Australia at Vancouver. The last diary entry, for 19 June 1914, was written two days after they left Honolulu bound for Fiji. 'Good weather and enjoying trip immensely,' Elizabeth wrote. This was just nine days before the assassination of Archduke Francis Ferdinand of Austria, the event that proved the trigger for the conflagration, which began in earnest in August.

The Lehanes' host in Vancouver in June 1914 was Jack's cousin Frank Lyons, son of Jerry's daughter Ellen and John Perry Lyons. 'He took us for a motor drive all about Vancouver,' Elizabeth wrote. The next morning he saw them off, accompanied by one of his small sons. Frank, who was then forty-three, three years older than Jack, had been a criminal lawyer in the city since 1911. He moved to North America in 1908 after working as a lawyer in Sydney. Before establishing himself in Vancouver he did legal work in the US connected with the infant aviation industry.

Jack evidently regarded Frank as quite a character, and the drive around Vancouver may have provided the basis for another of his stories. When his wife was showing signs of distress at his wild driving Frank allegedly called out, 'I'll curse and you pray and we'll get there somehow!' Like Jack, Frank seems to have let the family religion slide. According to another story, Frank's devout Catholic fiancée insisted that he go to Confession before their marriage. Since she was adamant, he agreed and she accompanied him to the church. He went into the confessional; she knelt in a nearby pew. Then she heard a loud Irish voice saying, 'Get out, get out, I'll not give you absolution!' When Frank came out, she hurried him down the aisle asking what had he said? 'Well,' he replied, 'I thought I'd start with an easy one so I told him I made fun of the priests, particularly the Irish ones.'

It would be good to be able to tell cheerful stories about other members of the Lyons family, but the little information at hand is sad. The deaths of Frank's father John Perry Lyons and two of his sisters, Ellen and Elizabeth, in the 1870s have been mentioned (chapters 14, 18 and 21). His mother, Ellen, just lived to see the end of World War I, dying at the age of seventy-four at St Vincent's Hospital, Sydney, on 19 November 1918, eight days after the armistice. None of her five children were there to comfort her in her last days; only Frank was still alive and the war would have prevented any thoughts of his returning.

Her second son, a commercial traveller also named John Perry, died in January 1916. Ten months earlier, at the age of forty-three, he had enlisted as an army private, ready to fight for King and Country. After seventy-three days training at Liverpool camp he was discharged as medically unfit following the flare-up of an apparently pre-existing heart condition. John died at the Garrison Hospital, Sydney, leaving a wife and two children. An army plaque marks his grave at Rookwood Cemetery. His mother was buried in the same plot.

Another of Jack Lehane's cousins was the noted Brisbane physician Sir Ellis Murphy. Born in 1895, Ellis was closer in age to Jack's son Felix, and the two holidayed together as youths on a farm near Murrumburrah owned by the family of Archie Stewart, brother-in-law of Anne Murphy, wife of the first Miles. Felix was best man at Ellis's wedding and later visited Ellis and his family on wool-buying trips to Brisbane. Ellis was senior physician at the Mater Misericordia Hospital before World War II, saw service in the Middle East and Ceylon between 1940 and 1943, and was senior physician at Brisbane Hospital for ten years after the war. He did much else, including chairing the Queensland division of the Red Cross and the Work Assessment Committee of the Australian Heart Foundation, and serving on a CSIRO advisory committee and the board of trustees of the Queensland Art Gallery. He was also a keen sailor; the Wynnum Manly Yacht Club's annual Sir Ellis Murphy Night Race Series commemorates him.

Ellis was the eldest child of Miles Murphy, eighth and longest-lived of the nine offspring of the first Miles. After the death of his brother John in 1879, Miles apparently tried his luck at goldmining on the new Temora field, which extended on to the Narraburra run, birthplace of Jack

Lehane. Later he worked as a 'wool traveller' with Pitt, Son and Badgery. Miles was thirty-nine years old when he married Josephine Grenenger, daughter of a German-born tanner living in Braidwood, and nearly sixty when the last of their eight children was born.

In a sign that broader family ties remained strong, Miles and Josephine attended the wedding of Felix Lehane in 1933. Miles died at the age of eighty-nine ten years later, and was buried with Catholic rites at Rookwood Cemetery. Miles' older brother Felix Murphy also lived to a considerable age, dying at Liverpool Asylum for the Infirm and Destitute, Sydney, in 1926. The death certificate records that the eighty-four-year-old was unmarried, had been a labourer and had a Catholic burial at Liverpool Cemetery.

More cousins, and contemporaries, of Jack Lehane were the four children of John and Mary Anne Murphy. The first-born (in 1870), Annie, became a teaching nun – Sister Mary Aloysius – at the Sisters of Mercy Convent in Yass, and died there of tuberculosis in 1917. Her brother Miles, born in 1871, died of the same disease ten years earlier in Sydney, where he had gone to seek medical help. He was only thirty-six, having lived just one year longer than his father. This Miles, who did not marry, was an auctioneer and stock and station agent in Murrumburrah, and secretary of the local turf club and pastoral and agricultural association. The *Murrumburrah Signal* described him as 'quiet, unassuming and possessed of all those qualities which win the esteem of men and women', and noted that he had been buried alongside his aunt, Sarah Lehane, at Rookwood Cemetery. The younger daughters of John and Mary Anne, Mary (born 1873) and Adeline (born 1875), outlived their mother, who died in Murrumburrah at the age of eighty-two in 1926. Mary married a lawyer working in Murrumburrah, Joseph Foley, and raised a family there.

The children of Jerry and Hannah Lehane were also Jack's contemporaries. The older daughter, Josephine, became Sister Mary Gregory of the Sisters of the Good Samaritan and had a successful teaching career. According to a history of the order, she was 'endowed with talents far beyond the usual. Her personality was vibrant, strong and most attractive. As well as charm of manner and appearance, she was endowed with keen perception and an incisive mind.' She had excelled at school, and 'to her high proficiency was added the power to impart knowledge which helped her both as a secondary school teacher and as a music teacher to lead her pupils to outstanding success. The coloratura performance of one of her pupils in operatic arias absolutely delighted an audience in 1931, at which the writer was present.'

The second daughter, Gertrude, also set out to become a nun, but left the Good Samaritan novitiate in 1890, the year Josephine took her profession of vows. Five years later, she married Philip Tasman Susman at the Glebe Road District Registrar's Office, Sydney. He was one of thirteen children of a Jewish emigrant from Germany who had become a prominent merchant in Hobart. Philip and Gertrude had two sons, both of whom went to Sydney's Church of England Grammar School and became doctors. Eric (known as Gus), born in 1896, began his medical studies in 1916 after returning from Gallipoli, where he had been wounded. During World War II he served as surgeon lieutenant commander on HMAS *Westralia* and his brother Maurice (known as Mick), born in 1898, was specialist surgeon at casualty clearing stations in Greece, Syria and northern Australia. The Eric Susman Prize, awarded annually by the Royal Australasian College of Physicians for contributions to knowledge in internal medicine, serves as a memorial to the older Dr Susman, who is remembered for his flamboyant style, wit and excellence as a teacher. Maurice, a pioneer in various areas of surgery, took to the skies as an amateur pilot from the 1920s. Recollections of this doctor include his frequent protests, in letters to medical journals and newspapers, about sloppy use of the English language.

Although Gertrude's life took a very different course to Josephine's, the two evidently remained close; the newspaper notice of the nun's death in August 1944 refers to her as the 'dear sister of Mrs G. Susman'. Twenty-six years earlier, Gertrude was present when the tragedy-scarred life of their half-sister Ellen Lyons drew to a close. Ellen's death certificate names her as the informant.

The story of Jeremiah, brother of Josephine and Gertrude, remains largely a mystery. He did not inherit Coppabella as his father intended, but became proprietor of the family properties in Rossi Street, Yass, when Hannah died. As well as the Globe Hotel – which in the early 1880s became a boarding house run by a Mrs Powell – these were the old *Courier* and Braidwood Store buildings and another office and residence. Jeremiah arranged for them all to be auctioned in October 1892, at the depth of the 1890s depression. A baker, John Fonville, bought the Globe for £400, a figure that the *Courier* aptly called a bargain. The other buildings went for a total of £770. Jerry paid £6,500 for this real estate in 1861 and made many improvements and additions. What he would have thought of it being sold thirty years later for less than a fifth of that sum scarcely bears contemplating.

The next news of Jeremiah is from early 1924, when he was fifty-nine years old. Concerned for the welfare of her unmarried and probably alcoholic brother, Josephine arranged with the superior general of her convent, St Scholastica's, Glebe, for him to be paid a £4 per month pension. This was the interest on a bank deposit of £1,000. 'Trusting this will relieve you of all responsibility and anxiety,' wrote the superior general, Mother Marcella, in a letter telling Josephine that the convent's council had approved the arrangement. 'I am very grateful to you for all the trouble you are taking about this business and I trust in the Sacred Heart to repay you and our Institute a thousandfold,' Josephine replied. Her letter provides a little additional information: 'My brother is at Burradoo [in the highlands south of Sydney] still. He is feeling better and as the people have gone to the seaside for a holiday, he is staying quietly there minding the place for them and will be there for a week or so more.'

Jeremiah received this pension for the rest of his long life. In February 1951, the solicitors who transmitted the payments wrote to the superior general after a visit by the old man to their office. They noted that he had not shown any effects of drink lately, and apparently was reasonably well cared for at his Millers Point boarding house. He had told them his health was fair and he felt quite able to carry on. 'He is particularly religious,' they added.

Jeremiah lived nearly another two years, dying in his room in late 1952. The death certificate says he had 'no occupation' and never married. Sadly, it also indicates that he was alone when he died, recording that death occurred 'on or about' 25 November. His nephew Dr Maurice Susman was the informant; apparently Gertrude's family had kept in touch with the old man. A Requiem Mass was held for him at St Brigid's, Millers Point, which is the oldest surviving Catholic church in Australia (opened 1835) and just a stroll around Walsh Bay from where Jerry landed 113 years earlier. He was buried at Northern Suburbs Cemetery.

Jeremiah died seventy-nine years after his father and seventy-three years after his mother. Having been born in 1864, he was, nevertheless, old enough when their lives ended in the 1870s to retain clear memories of them and their times. What stories he could have told.

Postscript
James John Brown and the *Yass Courier*

The newspaper is...the alpha and omega of bush literature. Destroy, or even hamper, it and at once the largest section of those colonists whose mind should be expanded are left without the means of intellectual recreation.

So wrote James John Brown, proprietor and editor of the *Yass Courier*, in an August 1867 leader calling for the scrapping of the postal charge on newspapers. 'The chief literature in which the people, more especially those located away from the towns, can indulge is the newspaper,' he went on. 'They cannot enjoy the luxury of the mechanics institute or the book club. In their isolated position all that they can learn of the outer world must be derived from their weekly or bi-weekly newspaper.'

It took many years, but the campaign waged by Brown and other newspaper proprietors against the charge eventually succeeded. Brown celebrated its abolition from 1 January 1874 by reducing the cost of an annual subscription to the *Courier*, paid in advance, from a maximum of £1 14s to £1 – just over twopence an issue.

Newspapers of the mid-nineteenth century appear puny things compared with today's colourful multi-page productions, but they packed a lot in. Small advertisements filled page one of a typical four-page *Yass Courier*. Pages two and three contained opinionated leading articles, brief overseas and local items received by telegraph, reports from correspondents in surrounding districts, 'local and general' news paragraphs written by *Courier* staff or culled from other papers, letters to the editor and more advertisements. Page four might contain a poem and a book extract – for example, the *Courier* serialised Jane Austen's *Pride and Prejudice* between September 1876 and March 1877 – or longer articles often extracted from British papers. Space was always found for government announcements on matters such as land sales, impounding notices, produce prices and other useful information.

Journalistic conventions were very different from today's. For example, while most news items were brief, some reports, usually of speeches and court proceedings, could be very long and detailed. Many items were opinionated, but opinions were not attributed to interviewees as they are now; newspaper interviews were a later development. Unlike the news paragraphs, correspondents' reports and, particularly, letters to the editor were often lengthy – and, to today's eyes, in need of heavy editing. There were, of course, no photos; usually small drawings in advertisements were the only illustrations.

The country newspapers were locally owned and produced, and their proprietors were important figures in their communities. Apart from word of mouth, the newspapers were, for most people, the only source of information about what was happening locally and in the wider world. For many they also provided the only access to creative writing. J.J. Brown's leaders on postal charges may have been prompted partly by self-interest, but they did not exaggerate the importance of the colonial newspapers. Now, preserved on microfilm, the papers are a vital resource for people wanting to learn about life in early Australia.

James John Brown began his newspaper career as an apprentice printer on Scotland's *Inverness Courier*. This, he told his Yass readers in March 1878, was 'the most scholarly weekly newspaper of the three kingdoms'. Its editor, Robert Carruthers, a doctor of laws, was a biographer of the poet Pope. 'The title of this paper [the *Yass Courier*] was adopted in recollection of the kindness and careful training received by the writer from Dr Carruthers,' Brown wrote.

Shortly after winning promotion to the Scottish paper's shorthand reporting staff, Brown, aged about twenty-one, set off for the newly discovered Victorian goldfields. He dug without success, then returned to journalism – first on the Melbourne *Argus* and soon afterwards the *Goulburn Herald*. With ambitions to strike out on his own, he may have noted with interest a September 1855 advertisement in the *Herald*. This offered an entire printing plant for sale, comprising an 'excellent Demy Press, new and complete, with sufficient Type (second-hand) to start a newspaper, together with fancy type, leads, cases, composing sticks, brass rule &c. &c.' The ad went on to suggest anyone starting a newspaper at Albury, Braidwood or Yass had 'a first-rate chance of doing well.'

Brown recalled later that he chose Yass as the site for his paper on the advice of the storekeeper Thomas Laidlaw, a fellow Scot. During the extended periods when business was slow in the town and advertising hard to attract he wondered whether he had made the right decision. He noted in October 1873 that a third newspaper had started in Albury, and had 'a good display of advertisements – as the Albury journals always have... Seventeen years ago attractive inducements were held out to ourselves to take up the ground at Albury instead of Yass, and we need scarcely say that we have very frequently since regretted not having done so.'

Brown and a partner, Charles William Morgan, brought out the first issue of, to give it its full title, *The Yass Courier and General Advertiser for the Southern Districts of New South Wales* on 6 June 1857. Morgan soon moved on, first to the *Adelong Mining Journal and Tumut Express*, which began publication in October 1858, and then to the *Miner*, which he launched at Lambing Flat in February 1861 and transferred to Forbes at the end of that year. When that venture soon failed he set himself up as a solicitor in Young. With Brown as sole proprietor, the *Yass Courier* continued to appear weekly until May 1860, and then twice weekly except for a short period of weekly publication in 1864 (chapter 7).

The first two issues of the *Courier* have been lost, but the *Sydney Morning Herald* noted the arrival of the first, observing that 'in every respect it does credit to the district.' The *Herald* reported its policy statement:

> The *Courier* will advocate what is known as the liberal and progressive in politics. The extremes of Conservatism and Liberalism will be avoided. Every measure tending to advance the social and moral interests of the colony will receive its support. Religious discussions will at all times be avoided, as inconsistent with the duties of a general newspaper or chronicle of passing events, and also as tending to excite bitterness of feeling where harmony and unanimity should be cherished.

In line with its liberal and progressive agenda, the *Courier* observed in November 1857 that federation was 'a desideratum of unspeakable consequence'. It backed free selection and was confident the Robertson Lands Bill of 1860 would protect small farmers from 'the greedy grasp of the rich monopolist'. A leader in July 1866 opposed tariff protection while arguing for the development of manufacturing industries. A target of the paper's anger in 1870 was the legal system's more lenient treatment of people who embezzled thousands of pounds than of those convicted for stealing cattle worth only a few pounds. In 1871 the *Courier* argued forcefully against the traffic in Polynesians to the Queensland sugar fields, which it compared to the slave trade to America.

In 1872, Brown announced he had changed his mind about capital punishment; he now opposed it. He favoured equal voting rights for all men, declaring in 1876 that there should be no class distinctions in government (there was no suggestion that women also might vote). Shortly afterwards, rumours of a colonial visit by the Prince of Wales produced this colourful response:

> Already, doubtless, have great pastoral and commercial magnates imaged to themselves hoped-for future scenes wherein they play no inconspicuous parts with the aforesaid Imperial Hope as the bright cynosure in the foreground. Visions of knighthood, and of C.M.G.-hood, have doubtless not spared the aching sight of many a colonial mayor and wealthy softgoodsman in connection with this rumoured trip of the Prince of Wales to the antipodes of the province whence the name of his title is derived. We are utterly unable to conceive of any good purpose which these so-called royal progresses are intended to subserve.

In 1877, the *Courier* declared that 'the hope for the future lies in that liberalism which seeks to do just things for the sake of justice and simple righteousness – in the liberalism of men like Gladstone who can overmaster once cherished convictions because in principle they were untenable, who dare to overturn institutions, however time-honoured, which are based upon the doctrine of inequality – inequity 'writ large'.' In 1879, the paper argued strongly in favour of trade unions 'as a counterpoise to capitalistic and banded professional pressure'. A year later it called for home rule for Ireland. Brown attributed the intense nationalism of the Irish to the harshness of British rule, comparing the situation of the Irish to that of the Jews, who had suffered 'oppressions which a so-called Christianity thought it holy and right to wage ceaselessly through centuries of ignorance and bigotry against the race of Israel'.

An 1881 leader argued that the Imperial honours system – 'the conferring of knight commanderships and knight grand crosses of illustrious orders' – had resulted in legislators putting British interests ahead of colonial needs. 'It is doubtless in the nature of things for politicians of the adventurer class as they grow old to grow conservative – it is a course that pays!' Brown wrote. 'Statesmen of the heroic type, however, grow more liberal as their years advance.' He named Peel and Gladstone as examples, and contrasted them with colonial 'Liberals of the old times' such as Henry Parkes and John Robertson who 'are now eaten up with Jingoism'.

Brown may have had himself in mind as one whose liberal instincts strengthened with age. To today's reader, the glaring exception to the *Courier*'s liberal stance in its early years is its attitude to the Chinese in Australia. A leader in 1860 described them as an inferior race displaying thieving habits, treachery and 'abominable propensities of an unspeakable character'. 'Their further introduction must be prevented, and the present stock got rid of as rapidly as law, without undue harshness, can accomplish,' it argued. By 1864 the paper had become a little friendlier, noting that Chinese were growing vegetables successfully 'in spots most discouraging to Europeans'. In 1866 it conceded that 'the Chinese are capable of teaching our farmers, and, indeed, some other branches of society, two lessons, if not more'. The first was adaptability – turning successfully to a new occupation (vegetable growing) when the gold ran out. Second was their skill in meeting the challenges of poor soil and inadequate rainfall. The following year Brown noted that many Chinese had displayed great ingenuity and industry, and were law-abiding. He still opposed further Chinese immigration, but thought those already in the colony should be allowed to stay.

The *Courier* was a frequent critic of community apathy. For example, in May 1863 it lamented the recent demise of a Yass dramatic society, a committee promoting the establishment of a market in the town, and the Yass Pastoral, Agricultural and Horticultural Society (after its first show). 'When will a new era dawn upon us, witnessing the cooperation which is necessary for the advancement of the general interest?' the paper wondered. Brown made efforts of his own to diversify the region's economic base, including promoting cotton growing in the early 1860s and sugarcane planting in the early 1870s. His early confidence in prospects for both crops soon dissipated.

The need for sectarian harmony was a constant preoccupation. Brown was pleased to observe at a fund-raising gathering in 1862 that 'on one platform, in brotherly love, and moved by one common spirit of sympathy, were the ministers of the three denominations of Christians who have distinctive places of worship in the town'. His language could become very strong when such harmony was lacking. For example, the Anglican Bishop of Sydney was well known to have a 'dogmatic, despotic, autocratic temperament', he wrote in 1868. Six years later, he described those running the Sydney *Protestant Standard* as 'malignant bigots' propagating 'shameless virulence'. Father Patrick O'Keeffe of St Augustine's, Yass, was the target of Brown's sharp pen in 1879. He was a 'vulgar ranter' whose anti-Protestant sermons were largely to blame for the establishment of an Orange Lodge in Yass. A year later, Brown noted that the Yass convent was 'a splendid monument' to O'Keeffe's 'energy, zeal, and enterprise'; sometimes he changed his mind about people.

Harsh words were common in the colonial press, and in September 1878 Brown was the target of a tirade from Malcolm Warner Burns, proprietor of the *Burrowa News*. In a leader headed 'A trifle personal', Burns described Brown as 'a contemptible itchy fellow' with a 'detestable' character, and 'a blackguard of the lowest priggish kind, unpossessed of one manly thought'. 'If we have to recur to the matter,' he added, 'there will be a brief reference to the abominations surrounding draggle-tail drunkenness, and Sussex-street debauchery.'

This appeared between the magistrates' hearing and the trial in the Cumbamurra shooting episode involving Hannah Lehane, an event that Brown and Burns chose to report in very different ways (chapter 20). One might have thought Burns' outburst would relate to a major issue such as that. Instead the trigger was a letter to the *Courier* about the management of the Burrowa Town Band. This referred to a *Burrowa News* leader that suggested the financially strapped band be broken up 'because of the large number of 'dry hash' people in Burrowa who are eager for the music, but after the manner of Canning's Friend of humanity to the Knife-grinder, 'Give thee sixpence! I'll see thee damned first!" The anonymous letter to the *Courier* supported continuation of the band and said the people of Burrowa were generous, not miserly.

It went on,

The remarks of the editor of the *Burrowa News*...are what all might expect from such a worthy. Has he, too, the reader may ask, forfeited the confidence of the people of the Burrowa district? Certain it is he loses few opportunities of bespattering them with phrases so peculiarly his own. There is something said of the bird that fouls its own nest that might be applicable.

Brown responded to the 'A trifle personal' leader by suing Burns for libel. Reporting this development in the next *Burrowa News*, Burns reprinted the offending article and resumed the attack. Brown was now a 'bully and braggadocio' and a 'low hectoring' person. 'When Mr Brown can be 'deprived of his good name, fame, and reputation' [the alleged result of the libel], there will be some chance to colour the rainbow and blacken a sweep', Burns added. Brown did not return fire in his paper, but would have been pleased when the Yass magistrates committed Burns to trial for libel. No trial occurred, however. For reasons that were not reported, the attorney-general 'declined to file a bill' in the case.

Brown faced competition on his home turf from July 1879 when the *Yass Tribune* appeared. Publisher was Andrew Brander, who had moved his plant from Gunning to the larger town and incorporated his *Gunning Times* into the new paper. The *Courier* described the *Tribune* as 'a small penny paper', but generously wished it 'a long and prosperous future'. Brown took his first gentle swipe at it in August:

Wonderful! A contemporary announces that 'some' eating apples have just 'come' into Yass a distance of six miles. Our devil – the impudent knave – asks whether the apples are locomotive – whether they rolled, walked, or ran into town; if not either of these, he 'guesses' that the apples must have flown. As a last hazard he admits it is just possible that they may have 'eaten' their way through the mud into town. Now, Youngsters, wake up, and solve our devil's doubts.

Letters critical of the *Tribune* started appearing soon after. The first described the new paper as 'your temporary local contemporary'. Then two complained of misreporting – about the price of eggs in Yass and the proceedings of a Pastoral and Agricultural Association meeting. Things became more serious in early January 1880 when Brown accused the *Tribune* of 'wholesale appropriation' of copy from the *Courier*. 'The whole transaction is the most impudent, mean, and contemptible that could possibly have been perpetrated in a small town by a so-called brother journalist,' he wrote. Unfortunately, the issues of the *Tribune* published in its early years have been lost, so we will never know what it had to say about Brown and the *Courier*.

A sign that the *Courier* was feeling the competition was Brown's decision in 1881 to match the *Tribune*'s three times a week publication schedule. The cost of a subscription remained £1 a year. Brown's article announcing the change coincided with the start of the *Courier*'s twenty-fifth year of publication. 'Many are the changes that have occurred in this town and district during the past twenty-four years!' he wrote. 'These changes, so far as has been possible, are chronicled in the twenty-four volumes now ranged at our side. Did time and space permit an interesting local history could be written from the particulars recorded in our pages since June, 1857.'

Brown thanked subscribers and advertisers for their support, and noted that 'some hundreds of those whose names are on our books have been subscribers from the commencement'. He went on,

> The thoroughly independent course we have steered in the past will be followed in the future. While carefully avoiding giving unnecessary offence to any, still, when duty demands, we shall not hesitate to 'call a spade a spade'. It is pleasing to us to know that the *Courier* has always held a high position in the ranks of the colonial press. We shall continue to do what in us lies to maintain that honourable position. After so long and arduous a career, the time cannot be far distant when we shall have to lay down our pen – to be taken up, we trust, by those who have been carefully trained so to conduct the *Courier* as to increase its reputation for ability and to rigidly maintain its character for thorough independence.

Brown may have been feeling tired, but he still had interesting things to say in his leaders. In April 1881 he was concerned that young Australians appeared much more interested in sport than learning. 'A race of splendid animals is springing up in the colonies, while the thoughtful, soulful man is sinking further back into the limbo of the past,' he wrote. 'In two generations we shall have the gladiators among us again, but the gladiator's brains will have descended from his head to his muscles – mind will have become a traditional attribute decidedly rare and unfashionable.' The following July he attacked the New South Wales governor, Lord Loftus, for attending the Randwick races rather than a special commemoration day at Sydney University. He thought the governor, 'a paid servant of the colony', had a duty to encourage by his presence 'those events which go to make the colony's history'. Brown noted that 'rather than sever the tie which binds us to the mother land we tax our revenue to support a Governor, a Viceroy – we give our allegiance to aristocratic dead-beats and diplomatic fiascos...' He concluded, 'It is such gubernatorial misdeeds as those we now note that give reason to the cry and logic to the argument that it is desirable to consolidate the Australasian colonies into a Republic.'

Brown died five months later, on 19 November 1881, at the age of fifty-one. 'He died literally in harness, worn out by work – hard, conscientious, constant work, faithfully executed in the interests of this town and district,' the *Courier* recorded in an obituary probably written by Allan Wood, who took over as editor. Wood was a son of James Wood, author of the series 'Early Recollections of Yass' by 'A late digger' (chapter 8).

The obituary described Brown as 'the trusty friend, the kind and considerate employer, the straightforward, truth-loving, honest man'. It went on,

> For over a quarter of a century, in conflict with many difficulties, through good report and evil report, James John Brown fought loyally, consistently, and persistently, ever on the Liberal side, for popular rights, and against every form of cliqueism and faction... He made the 'Courier' a power. Many of those local institutions which are now the pride of the district owe their origin and success to lively suggestions made in these columns by his fertile brain. The son of an old Waterloo hero, he possessed much of the pugnacity of the soldier, and all the courage!

The object of Brown's life, the obituary added, was to make the *Courier* a first-class provincial journal. 'That he succeeded in attaining his object is the expressed opinion of competent critics, yet this success did not yield satisfaction to himself,' the article went on. 'Heavy domestic troubles prevented him from doing much that he desired to do with the view of further increasing the usefulness and popularity of this paper.'

What this cryptic comment refers to is unclear. The paper recorded two tragic events in his life, the deaths of an infant daughter in 1867 and of his thirty-nine-year-old wife, Frances, in 1876. In December 1874, Brown put the *Courier* and a second paper he had launched a year earlier, the *Burrangong Chronicle*, up for sale by auction. The announcement inserted by the auctioneers, Richardson & Wrench, said urgent business affairs required Brown's early departure for England, compelling him to sell the papers. The crisis must have blown over; Brown did not leave Yass or the *Courier*. He sold the *Chronicle* soon after his wife's death in 1876.

The obituary heaped praise on Brown's ability as a newspaperman, suggesting that 'in a wider sphere he would have ranked as a Greely [presumably Horace Greeley, founder of the *New York Tribune*] or a Bennett [probably James Bennett, founder of the *New York Herald*]'. 'He was a shrewd observer, a close reasoner, and a pregnant writer. In the mechanical part of newspaper work he was an adept. To this may be added that he was a first-class shorthand reporter.'

The *Goulburn Herald* noted in its long obituary that nearly all businesses in Yass 'put up their shutters' when news spread of Brown's death:

> The respect in which Mr Brown was held may be designated universal... The deceased gentleman was far above the ordinary class of country newspaper editors, possessing superior ability as a writer... [He] was a good father, a kind master, a faithful friend, an able journalist; and when the great benefits which have been conferred on the town and district through the means of his pen are taken into consideration, all little differences which have arisen between him and a few of the residents sink into oblivion... The funeral yesterday afternoon was one of the largest that ever took place in Yass, and further showed the sense of the loss sustained, and the respect in which the deceased gentleman was held.

On Brown's death, ownership of the *Courier* passed to a Sydney businessman, George Robert Whiting. He was one of three executors named in Brown's will. *Courier* readers may have remembered Whiting from a long letter he wrote to the paper in March 1880 on alternative sewage disposal methods. Whiting was highly critical of a suggestion from Chief Justice Sir James Martin that instead of sewering Sydney the city authorities should encourage people to install 'earth closets'. These were popular in England in the second half of the nineteenth century. The idea was that fresh soil put into the closet's bucket after use would prevent smells and disease; then vegetable gardens could be fertilised with the used soil. Whiting feared Martin's plan would prove 'the means of laying the seeds of the greatest epidemic the Australians have ever experienced'.

The *Courier* assured its readers, in a leader most likely written by Allan Wood, that the paper would maintain its liberal and independent outlook. The publication schedule reverted to twice a week in January 1882 and Whiting moved on a month later, selling the business to Wood, who remained in charge for thirty-two years. He sold the paper in June 1914, just before the outbreak of World War I, and died a year later at the age of sixty-seven. The *Courier* recorded that James John Brown had taken Wood on as an apprentice at the age of eleven. So, apparently, Wood joined the paper in 1859, just two years after its launch, and worked for it for a remarkable fifty-five years.

The *Courier* carried on until March 1929 under a succession of publishers. Last was John Titus Cunneen, who inserted the line 'The Pioneer Newspaper – Estab 1856' under the masthead (he was out by a year; Brown would never have made such a basic error). Cunneen sold the paper to Albert Mudge, proprietor of the rival *Tribune*, who with his son published the merged product as the *Yass Tribune-Courier* until 1955. Then, with a switch from broadsheet to tabloid format, it became simply the *Yass Tribune*. The *Courier* was a notable paper in its early decades, but the upstart that irritated Brown in his last years proved more durable.

Appendix

Who's who: Lehanes, Murphys and some close relations

FORREST Very Rev. Dr John, son of a sister of Mary Lehane, arrived from Ireland 1860

LEHANE Catherine, daughter of Daniel and Ellen, arrived from Ireland 1865

LEHANE Claire, daughter of John Augustine and Elizabeth, born 1905

LEHANE Daniel, brother of Jerry, arrived from Ireland 1862

LEHANE Elizabeth (née Mitchell), wife of John Augustine

LEHANE Ellen, daughter of Jerry and Mary, born 1844 (see LYONS Ellen)

LEHANE Ellen (née McAuliffe), wife of Daniel, arrived from Ireland 1865

LEHANE Felix, son of John Augustine and Elizabeth, born 1900

LEHANE Gertrude, daughter of Jerry and Hannah, born 1870 (see SUSMAN Gertrude)

LEHANE Hannah (née Bourke), second wife of Jerry

LEHANE Honora, relationship to Jerry unclear, arrived from Ireland 1856, married John Vicq

LEHANE James, son of Jerry's brother Pierce, arrived from Ireland 1856

LEHANE Jeremiah (Jerry), arrived from Ireland 1839

LEHANE Jeremiah, son of Daniel and Ellen, arrived from Ireland 1857

LEHANE Jeremiah, son of Jerry and Hannah, born 1864

LEHANE Jessie (née Vicars), wife of Felix

LEHANE John Augustine, son of William and Sarah, born 1873

LEHANE John Thomas, son of Jerry and Hannah, born 1869

LEHANE Josephine, daughter of Jerry and Hannah, born 1868

LEHANE Mary (née O'Connor), first wife of Jerry

LEHANE Sarah (née Murphy), wife of William (see MURPHY Sarah)

LEHANE William, son of Jerry and Mary, born 1847

LYONS Elizabeth Augusta, daughter of John Perry and Ellen, born 1873

LYONS Ellen (née Lehane), wife of John Perry (see LEHANE Ellen)

LYONS Ellen, daughter of John Perry and Ellen, born 1869

LYONS Frank, son of John Perry and Ellen, born 1870

LYONS John Perry, married Ellen Lehane

LYONS John Perry, son of John Perry and Ellen, born 1872

LYONS Mary Agnes, daughter of John Perry and Ellen, born 1867

McCARTHY Peter, son of Jerry Lehane's sister Margaret, arrived from Ireland 1866

MURPHY Adeline, daughter of John and Mary Anne, born 1875

MURPHY Anne (née Ellis), wife of first Miles

MURPHY Annie, daughter of John and Mary Anne, born 1870

MURPHY Ellis, son of Miles and Josephine, born 1895

MURPHY Felix, son of Miles and Anne, born 1844

MURPHY James, son of Miles and Anne, born 1858

MURPHY John, son of Miles and Anne, born 1843

MURPHY Joseph, son of Miles and Anne, born 1847

MURPHY Josephine (née Grenenger), wife of second Miles

MURPHY Mary, daughter of John and Mary Anne, born 1873

MURPHY Mary Anne (née McNamara), wife of John

MURPHY Miles, arrived from Ireland 1841

MURPHY Miles, son of Miles and Anne, born 1854

MURPHY Miles, son of John and Mary Anne, born 1871

MURPHY Patrick, son of Miles and Anne, born 1849

MURPHY Robert, son of Miles and Anne, born 1846

MURPHY Sarah, daughter of Miles and Anne, born 1852 (see LEHANE Sarah)

MURPHY Thomas, son of Miles and Anne, born 1851

STEWART Archie, brother-in-law of Anne Murphy, arrived from Ireland 1862

STEWART Sarah (née Ellis), sister of Anne Murphy, emigrated with husband Archie

SUSMAN Gertrude (née Lehane), wife of Philip (see LEHANE Gertrude)

SUSMAN Eric, son of Philip and Gertrude, born 1896

SUSMAN Maurice, son of Philip and Gertrude, born 1898

SUSMAN Philip, married Gertrude Lehane

WALSH David, son of Jerry Lehane's sister Honora, arrived from Ireland 1856

Sources

For most chapters the principal source is the *Yass Courier*. In some cases the date on which an item appeared is given in the text; elsewhere the approximate date can be inferred from the context. Other sources are listed below.

Page

7, 10 O'Farrell, Patrick 2000. *The Irish in Australia*. Third edition. University of New South Wales Press, pp. 57, 80.

7 Campbell, Malcolm 1997. *The kingdom of the Ryans: the Irish in south west New South Wales, 1816–1890*. University of New South Wales Press.

9 Articles from the *Kerry Evening Post* and *Cork Standard* reprinted in the *Sydney Gazette*, 12/11/1839.

9 Vamplew, Wray (ed) 1987. *Australians: Historical Statistics*. Fairfax, Syme & Weldon Associates, Sydney, pp. 27, 28.

10 O'Mahony, C. and Thompson, V. 1994. *Poverty to promise: the Monteagle emigrants, 1838–58*. Crossing Press, Sydney, pp. 1–2.

10 Fitzpatrick, David 1994. *Oceans of consolation: personal accounts of Irish migration to Australia*. Cork University Press, p. 534.

10–11 Morton, H.V. 1932. *In search of Ireland*. Methuen, London, p. 105–106. (quote from description by Mr and Mrs S.C. Hall of emigrants' departure).

11, 15 Lewis, Samuel 1837. *A topographical dictionary of Ireland, comprising the several counties; cities; boroughs; corporate, market, and post towns; parishes; and principal villages; with historical and statistical descriptions*. Reissued 1970 by Kennikat Press, USA.

11–12 McCarthy, Joe 1966. Life World Library: *Ireland*. Time-Life International (Nederland).

15 Duhallow Heritage Project 1994. *Newmarket Court (1725–1994)*. Kanturk, Ireland.

16, 17, 46, 73 Entitlement Certificate of persons on bounty ships, 1832–42. State Records NSW: CGS 5314, [Reels 1304, 1330]. Assisted immigrants to New South Wales, 1838–96. SRNSW: CGS 5316, [Reel 2135].

16–17 Madgwick, R.B. 1937. *Immigration into Eastern Australia 1788–1851*. Longmans, Green. London.

17 *The Australian* (Sydney), 26/11/1839, 30/11/1839.

18 *Sydney Herald*, 25/11/1839.

19, 27 Maclehose, James 1839. *Picture of Sydney and Strangers' Guide in New South Wales for 1839*. Reissued 1977 by John Ferguson, Sydney, pp. 68, 78, 99.

19-20 Marshall, A.J. 1970. *Darwin and Huxley in Australia*. Hodder and Stoughton, Sydney. pp. 36–37.

20–24, 27–30 Wilson, Gwendoline 1968. *Murray of Yarralumla*. Oxford University Press, M Mowle, S.M. c.1899. Journal in Retrospect. National Library of Australia MS 1042.

22 Clarke, Patricia 1991. *A colonial woman: the life and times of Mary Braidwood Mowle, 1827–1857*. Allen & Unwin, Sydney, p. 58.

22–25, 27–30 Murray, Terence Aubrey, and Murray, James 1838–1845. Letters to S.M. Mowle. Murray Family Papers, National Library of Australia MS 565/Series 1.

26 *Freeman's Journal* (Sydney) 11/8/1883.

30 *Goulburn Herald*, 28/4/1849, 2/3/1850, 26/10/1850.

31 *Goulburn Herald*, 21/9/1850, 26/3/1852, 3/4/1852.

33 Death of Mr W. O'Connor, *Burrowa News*, 21/6/1912.

33 *Goulburn Herald*, 29/5/1852, 25/9/1852, 15/1/1853, 19/2/1853.

33 McNaught, Jean 1997. Butts and certificates of the first publicans' licences 1830–1860.

34 *Goulburn Herald*, 21/10/1854.

37, 269 Barnard, Alan 1958. *The Australian Wool Market 1840–1900*. Melbourne University Press.

46 Young and District Family History Group. *Pioneers of the Lachlan, Murrumbidgee and County King pre-1860*.

46 Musgrave, Sarah 1973. *The wayback*. Third edition, Bland District Historical Society, West Wyalong, NSW, p. 4.

46–47 Maher, Rev. Brian 1988. *Memories of Yass Mission*. St Augustine's Parish Sesquicentenary Committee, Yass.

47 O'Connor, Morgan 1861. *Rise and Progress of the Yass Mission* (facsimile: Library of Australian History, North Sydney 1984).

47–48 *Sydney Morning Herald*, 23/12/1844.

48 Finlayson, Frank C. undated. *History of Binalong*. Compiled for the Back to Binalong Committee (typescript).

48–49 *Goulburn Herald*, 28/4/1849, 26/1/1850, 13/4/1850.

50–52 *Goulburn Herald*, 22/3/1851, 25/6/1853, 29/7/1854, 11/11/1854, 30/12/1854.

53 Southwell, H.A.T. 1937. History of the Settlement and Growth of the Murrumburrah District (published in the *Murrumburrah Signal*, 11/11/1937–13/1/1938).

53 Littlejohn, R.A. 1979. *Early Murrumburrah: historical notes*. Harden–Murrumburrah Historical Society, p. 25.

53–54 *Goulburn Herald*, 19/8/1854.

58 *Miner* (Lambing Flat), 6/2/1861, 13/4/1861.

59–60 *Miner*, 22/6/1861, 13/7/1861.

62, 73 Persons on bounty ships to Sydney, Newcastle and Moreton Bay ('Board's Immigrant Lists'), 1848–91. SRNSW: CGS 5317, [Reels 2473, 2478 and 2483].

63 *Miner*, 6/4/1861, 24/4/1861, 27/4/1861, 15/5/1861.

64 Bookham School Centenary Committee 1982. *Bookham Public School centenary, 1882–1982, including local school & family histories*.

76 Gilmore, Lorna H. c1988. *The O'Malley heritage: a history of the family of Patrick O'Malley and Julia Downey*. L.H. Gilmore, Coolamon, N.S.W.

76–77 Shiel, D.J. 1983. *Ben Hall, bushranger*. University of Queensland Press.

76, 290 Maroney, Ross 1987. *Old Young*, vol. 2. Local History Publications, Orange.

77 Camm, J.C.R. and McQuilton J. (eds) 1987. *Australians: a Historical Atlas*. Fairfax, Syme and Weldon Associates, Sydney, p. 213.

77 Clark, C.M.H. 1978. *A History of Australia*, vol. 4. Melbourne University Press, p. 204.

85 *Sydney Morning Herald*, 6/1/1865 (reprint of article from *Yass Courier* 4/1/1865).

86–87 Barrett, Max 1995. *Galong Cemetery*. Church Archivists' Press, Virginia, Qld, p. 12.

88 *Goulburn Herald and Chronicle*, 17/5/1865.

90 *Miner*, 11/9/1861, 24/11/1862.

90 *Burrangong Courier*, 10/5/1862, 16/7/1862, 6/8/1862, 11/10/1862.

105–6 *Goulburn Herald*, 7/7/1855.

106 Prendergast, Ann 2000. The Benedictine Schools and Students of Colonial Sydney. *Australian Catholic Historical Society Journal*, vol. 21.

106–108 *Freeman's Journal* (Sydney), 26/12/1857, 17/10/1860, 26/12/1860, 30/1/1861, 25/12/1861, 20/12/1862, 23/12/1863.
107 *Australian Dictionary of Biography*, vol. 4, 1851–1890, 1972. Melbourne University Press. Entry for Dr John Forrest.
107 Cable, K.J. 1964. The University of Sydney – 1850–1880. *The Australian University*, 2/3.
107–08 *Freeman's Journal*, 9/5/1874.
108 *Sydney Morning Herald*, 6/8/1883.
108 *Daily Telegraph* (Sydney), 6/8/1883.
109 *Freeman's Journal*, 12/4/1865.
109 St John's College, University of Sydney 1987. Directory of Johnsmen.
110 *Goulburn Herald*, 20/10/1853.
113–115 *Wagga Wagga Express*, 28/4/1866.
129 *Maryborough Chronicle*, 10/1/1874.
143 *Goulburn Herald*, 7/10/1868.
152–53 Maher, Fr Brian 1997. *Planting the Celtic Cross*, Canberra. p. 151.
166 *Freeman's Journal*, quoted in *Yass Courier*, 5/5/1866.
169 *Freeman's Journal*, 17/4/1869.
203 Deniliquin *Pastoral Times*, quoted in *Yass Courier*, 17/2/1871.
232 *Sydney Morning Herald*, quoted in *Yass Courier*, 27/6/1873.
234 *Burrangong Chronicle*, 3/1/1874.
235 *Maryborough Chronicle*, 10/1/1874.
239 *Burrangong Argus*, 13/4/1872.
241–42 *Murrumburrah Signal*, 10/1/1885.
246–247 *Burrangong Argus*, 8/7/1876.
247 Harden–Murrumburrah Historical Society, in conjunction with Harden Shire Council, 1988. *A brief history of the Harden–Murrumburrah district*, p. 9.
251 *Sydney Morning Herald*, 15/12/1874.
258 *Burrowa News*, 8/6/1878.

269 *Sands Alphabetical Directory (City and Suburban)* 1877. Sydney. Entry for Annie Casey.
270 *Burrowa News*, 20/9/1878.
271 *Freeman's Journal*, 7/2/1874, 22/8/1874.
271, 284–85 McEwen, Sister Mary Dominica 1989. *A living stream resource book: Sisters of the Good Samaritan, 1857–1924*, Glebe Point, NSW, pp. 50–51.
272 *Burrangong Argus*, 23/4/1879.
272 Gladesville Medical Case Book 1878–79, SRNSW: CGS 5031, [4/8165].
274 *Town and Country Journal*, quoted in *Yass Courier*, 13/4/1880.
274 *Sydney Morning Herald*, 18/12/1880, 10/3/1881.
274 *Town and Country Journal*, 7/11/1885.
275 *Australian Encyclopaedia*, 1958. Angus and Robertson. Vol. 2, p. 234.
276 *Wagga Wagga Advertiser*, 15/9/1885, 5/11/1885.
276 *Murrumburrah Signal*, 7/11/1885.
277 *Murrumburrah Signal*, 20/4/1901.
283 *Who's Who in Australia 1974*. Entry for Sir Ellis Murphy.
284 *The Sun* (Sydney), 11/7/1933 (report of Lehane–Vicars wedding).
284 *Murrumburrah Signal*, 27/9/1907, 13/9/1917.
285 *Medical Journal of Australia* 1959. Obituary, Dr Eric Susman. 2, 338–40.
285 *Medical Journal of Australia* 1989. Obituary, Dr Maurice Susman, Vol 151, 483.
286 *Sydney Morning Herald*, 27/11/1952.
289 *Goulburn Herald*, 22/9/1855.
290 *Sydney Morning Herald*, 9/6/1857.
293–94 *Burrowa News*, 6/9/1878, 13/9/1878, 20/9/1878.
297 *Goulburn Herald*, 22/11/1881.
298 *Yass Tribune*, 29/9/1955.

Picture credits

Page
12, 13, 14 Kenneth Maclean.
20 Portraits, T.A. Murray, Plate No. NL7817. By permission of the National Library of Australia.
21 Sketch attributed to Obadiah Williams of Queanbeyan. R4056, Plate No. NL372/2. By permission of the National Library of Australia.
26 Kenneth Maclean.
38 *Illustrated Sydney News*, 16 December 1865, p. 4. By permission of the National Library of Australia.
47 Oil by J.E. Grube. Plate No. NL24086. By permission of St Augustine's Church, Yass, and the National Library of Australia.
48 Whitehurst collection, Plate No. 329. By permission of the National Library of Australia.
54 *Town and Country Journal*, 1 July 1876, p. 28. By permission of the National Library of Australia.
74 *Illustrated Sydney News*, 15 April 1865, p. 5. By permission of the National Library of Australia.
83 *Illustrated Sydney News*, 16 June 1865, p. 1. By permission of the National Library of Australia.
99 *Illustrated Sydney News*, 15 July 1865, p. 9. By permission of the National Library of Australia.
125 *Town and Country Journal*, 10 April 1880, p. 697. By permission of the National Library of Australia.
131 *Illustrated Sydney News*, 16 August 1867, p. 216. By permission of the National Library of Australia.
144 *Illustrated Sydney News*, 16 September 1867, p. 233. By permission of the National Library of Australia.
154 *Illustrated Sydney News*, 7 August 1868, p. 25. By permission of the National Library of Australia.
156 Pencil sketch by Stanley Leighton. R.4164, Plate No. NL24228. By permission of the National Library of Australia.
175 Whitehurst collection, Plate No. 436. By permission of the National Library of Australia.
182 Whitehurst collection, Plate No. 1169. By permission of the National Library of Australia.
187 Whitehurst collection, Plate No. 806. By permission of the National Library of Australia.
188 Whitehurst collection, Plate No. 282. By permission of the National Library of Australia.
195 *Illustrated Sydney News*, 6 September 1870, p. 37. By permission of the National Library of Australia.
208 Whitehurst collection, Plate No. 359. By permission of the National Library of Australia.
213 Whitehurst collection, Plate No. 419. By permission of the National Library of Australia.
230 Whitehurst collection, Plate No. 849. By permission of the National Library of Australia.

Index

A

Aborigines 22, 112, 143, 159, 161, 162
Aiken, Andrew 247, 273
Albert, Prince Consort 40
Aldworth family 13, 15
Aldworth, Richard Oliver 18
Alexandra of Denmark, Princess 92
Alfred, Duke of Edinburgh 143, 147, 150
Allan, William 215
Allman, Emily 208
Allman, George 35, 42, 56, 99, 113, 129, 133, 136, 147, 179, 182, 196, 203–04, 208, 209, 218, 219, 220
Allsopp, Thomas 243, 249, 272
Archdall, Dr Thomas 248
Arramagong 46, 76–77, 81
Atchison, J.O. 245
Atkinson, Capt 58, 60

B

Back Creek 61
Barber, George 228
Barber, Samuel 73, 129
Barnes, J. & G. 151
Barnes, John 80
Bartholomew, Mr 207
Baxter, Robert 250
Beckham, Edgar 35, 49, 50, 52, 53, 56, 57, 205
Beechinor, Rev. J. 18
Belmore, Earl of 150, 154, 155, 161, 176
Bendenine 34, 39
Benjamin, Sarah 92, 93, 94
Beremangra 266, 270
Bermingham, Fr Patrick 41
Bernston, David 256
Besnard, John 9

Besnard, Nicholas 36, 39, 40, 50, 56, 125
Besnard, Nicholas jr 217
Binalong 39, 43, 48, 49, 51, 55, 56, 57, 65, 70, 72, 76, 82, 85, 87, 95, 97, 100, 124, 126, 133, 137, 141, 151, 158, 167, 168, 170, 171, 199, 201, 205, 244, 246, 257, 259, 262, 263, 264, 274, 278
Binalong bridge 51, 52, 171, 191
Bishop, Thomas 134, 136
Black Jack 111, 112, 114, 115, 131, 133, 142, 158, 159, 162
Blake, Dr Isidore 148, 196, 200, 201–03, 233, 264
Blount, Mr 239
Blue Cap 141–42
Bodkin, George 114, 115, 116, 118, 121
Bodkin, Mary 141, 184, 255
Bogalara 73, 129
Bogolong 34, 38, 64, 88, 110, 118, 156, 177
Bookham 34, 64, 74, 101, 149
Bookham Inn 74, 156
Boorowa 26, 33, 45, 56, 64, 76, 81, 98, 102, 146, 173, 197, 209, 215, 217, 249, 253, 258, 268, 270
Bourke, Edward 111, 112, 114, 115, 122, 123
Bourke, Governor Richard 16
Bourke, John 243
Bourke, Michael 73
Bourke, Michael & Mary 73
Bourke, Mr (lock-up keeper) 189
Bourke, Robert 121, 122, 141
Bowning 8, 33, 94, 110
Bowning Inn 31, 33
Bowning station 31, 34

Brady, Const. Edward 122
Braidwood Farm 24
Braidwood Store 65, 176, 206, 256, 285
Brander, Andrew 294
Brennan, Fr Michael 30, 47
Brennan, Sr Sgt, later Sub-inspector 68, 131, 145, 203, 254
Broughton, Henry 215
Broughton, Thomas 270
Broughton, W.H. 228
Browne, Edward 257, 258, 259, 260, 261, 262, 263, 264, 265, 270
Browne, John 258, 259, 262, 263
Brown George 131
Brown, Henry 191
Brown, H.H. 17
Brown, J.J. 6, 8, 39, 45, 120, 123, 175, 178, 181, 193, 195, 204, 206, 207, 210, 211, 213, 222, 227, 229, 234, 240, 256, 263, 264, 267, 268, 274, 288, 289, 290, 291, 293, 294, 295, 296, 297
Burke, Edmund 41
Burns, Malcolm Warner 270, 293, 294
Burrangong 82, 90, 97, 170, 199, 205, 215, 236
Burrowa 45, 75, 253, 274, 293
Burton's Circus 205
bushfires 37, 110
bushranging 45, 46, 65, 73, 75, 76, 77, 78, 79, 81, 82, 83, 84, 85, 86, 88, 89, 121, 122, 141, 142
Butler, Edward 262, 264
Byrnes, Ann 34, 35, 65
Byrnes, Charles 65
Byrom, John 248

C

Callaghan, Judge 35, 59, 69, 70, 72, 94, 95
Campbell, David 81
Campbell, Dr Allan 157, 178, 181, 208, 209, 222, 232
Canowindra 77
Carr, Fr R.J. 269

Carruthers, Robert 289
Casey, Annie 269
Cassidy, Michael 203
Castlelyons 11, 12
Castlemaine 229, 278
Catholic mission, Queanbeyan 29
cattle stealing 70, 110, 115, 116, 117, 130, 133, 158, 185, 220, 254, 291
Chapman, Const. 116
Cheeke, Justice 130
Chinese, feeling against 45, 57, 59, 60, 62, 292
Chisolm, Frederick 84
Chlorodyne 156, 157, 248
Clafferty, William 255
Clarke, Rev. W.B. 186
Cobb and Co. 128, 257
Coffey, Fr Nicholas Joseph 27
Collector 30, 33, 85
Colls, Thomas 130, 206, 222
Commercial Bank 188, 191, 229, 249, 269
Commercial Hotel, Murrumburrah 102, 138, 139, 151, 163, 173, 174, 240, 246
Commercial Hotel, Yass 130, 155, 161, 189, 207, 222,
Conlon, Michael 201
Cooleman Plain 22
Cooma Cottage 89, 228
Cooper, Joseph 105
Cootamundra 163, 173
Coppabella 8, 33, 34, 36, 37, 62, 64, 65, 69, 73, 78, 95, 100, 104, 105, 110, 111, 116, 118, 121, 122, 131, 133, 141, 142, 158, 159, 175, 178, 183, 191, 219, 233, 235, 255, 256, 257, 259, 266, 268, 269, 270, 285
Coramundra 162, 163
Corby, Michael 117
Cottrell, James 206, 222, 231, 233
Cottrell, Robert 141
Cowper, Charles 58, 59, 100
cricket 162, 163, 164, 166, 173, 174, 199, 216, 220, 243
Criterion Hotel, Murrumburrah 53,

57, 80, 98, 101, 125, 126, 139, 151, 166, 173, 174, 199, 240, 243, 246, 247, 248, 249, 253, 273, 274
Cumbamurra 223, 258, 261, 270, 271, 293
Cunneen, John Titus 298
Cunningar 53

D

Dalley, William Bede 113, 114, 115, 117, 130
Darwin, Charles 19
Davis, David 84
Dawson, James 199
Dease, Christopher 179, 194, 201, 202
Delahunty, Michael 256, 257, 258, 259, 261, 262, 263, 264, 271
Demondrille 53, 151
Dempsey, E.J. 253
Denny, Thomas 198
Devereux, John 59
Diggers' Arms, Lambing Flat 63
Dillon, Fr George 192
Dillon, John 98, 102, 138, 139, 151, 152, 162, 163, 164, 173, 174, 238, 242, 245, 246, 273, 274
Dinnir, Samuel 68
Dolby, 'madman' 62
Donegal Relief Fund 55
Donovan, Henry 273
Donovan, Rev. A. 18
Douro 34, 112, 183
Doyle, G. 128
Doyle, John 83
drought 21, 22, 37, 74, 89, 110, 120, 168, 186, 193
Drummond, Mrs 157
Drummond, Thomas 156
Duce, Jerry 141, 142
Duigan, Fr Richard 147, 148, 151, 152, 169, 178, 180, 181, 182, 183, 184, 192, 200, 202, 203, 204, 220
Dunn, Catherine 243
Dunne, Fr Patrick 200, 201, 203, 204
Dunn, John 84, 85, 87, 88
Dwyer, James 131, 133

E

Eager, Charles 9
Eason, George 76, 215, 218, 227, 261, 270
economic depression/recession 28, 30, 120, 249, 269, 270, 286
Edward, Prince of Wales 92, 266
electric light 268
Emerald Isle Hotel, Sydney 73
emigration 9, 10, 16
Emily, jolly-boat 191
Empire Hotel, Lambing Flat 62, 63, 64, 65
English, John 53, 70, 98, 138, 151, 162, 173, 239
Enniscorthy, County Wexford 46
Eugowra 77

F

Farnell, J.S. 232
Faucett, Peter 35, 100, 113, 115, 125, 142
Fenians 146, 147, 149
Finch, C.C. 157
Finnegan, Fr Henry 185, 199
Fitzpatrick, Michael 139, 181, 183, 193, 194, 232
Five Mile Creek 184, 191
Five Mile Creek Inn 65, 114, 116, 118, 121, 141, 255
Flannery, Edmund 123
floods
 1852 33, 186, 188, 189, 190
 1864 83, 89
 1870 171, 178, 186, 188, 191, 193
flour mill, Murrumburrah 96, 101, 125, 126, 134, 135, 138, 151, 162, 170, 171, 215, 217, 247, 248, 249
Foley, Joseph 284
Foley Troupe 174
Fonville, John 286
Forbes 61, 67, 76, 81, 86, 170, 290
Forrest, Benjamin 26
Forrest, Sarah (née O'Connor) 26
Forrest, Very Rev. Dr John 26, 64, 73, 107, 109, 128, 147, 183, 216, 217, 271

Fortune of War Hotel, Yass 175
free selection 181, 256, 275, 290
Freestone, Anthony 134, 136

G

Gaffney, Walter 143
Gallagher, Fr John 234
Galong 7, 35, 39, 83, 248, 257, 273
Gardiner, Frank 45, 65, 77, 78, 79, 89
Gardiner, John 256
Garry, Dora 124
Garry, James 124
Gegullalong 219, 270
Gibbes, Colonel John 21
Gibson, Rev. John 149, 179
Gilbert, Johnny 79, 80, 81, 82, 84, 86, 88, 96
Gilhooley, Dr James 26, 183, 216, 269
Gilhooley, Mary Ann (née Forrest) 26, 216
Gilligan, Mr 238
Gipps, Governor George 20
Gleeson, Thomas 50
Globe Hotel, Yass 65, 66, 67, 68, 69, 91, 92, 94, 97, 101, 121, 130, 141, 152, 155, 175, 178, 187, 189, 194, 196, 197, 200, 206, 207, 210, 212, 214, 220, 222, 230, 231, 236, 255, 285
Godfrey, Henry 67
gold, discoveries of 31, 45, 56, 61, 127, 129, 151, 212, 222, 223, 289
Gorth, Nathaniel 36, 116, 118
Goulburn 33, 117, 139, 176, 200, 206, 208, 209, 220, 224, 241, 271
'government ditch', Yass 213, 233
Grainger, Percy 280
Grenfell 46, 127, 164
Grew, William 68
Grove, W.E. 17
Grundy, Francis 229
Gundagai 33, 36, 38, 84, 102, 110, 112, 121, 158, 177
Gunning 276, 294

H

Hall, Ben 45, 46, 76, 77, 78, 79, 80, 81, 82, 84, 86, 88, 96, 141
Hanly, Rev. Dean James 70, 72, 100, 123, 140, 158
Harbottle, Mr 100
Harden 242, 244, 247
Hardwicke 222, 223
Hardy, Thomas 254
Hargrave, Judge 262, 264
Harris, John 53, 126
Harry the Cook 93
Hart, James MLA 109
Hart, Peter 111, 112, 113, 115
Hassett, Miss 197
Hassett, Richard 36, 175, 178, 194, 195, 196, 197, 212
Hawton, Mr 70, 71
Hayes, Mr 84
Hibberd, Mary 94
Higman, John 99
Hilly, Owen 94, 97, 141, 175
Hoare, John 116, 117
Hobbs, Marianne 256, 271
Hooper, John 248
Hooper, Mr 146
horse-racing 48, 52, 82, 85, 96, 150, 174, 236, 248
Hovell's Creek 33
Hovell, William 228
Howard, William 78, 137, 171, 198
Hume, Andrew Hamilton 215
Hume, Frederick 205, 226
Hume, Hamilton 34, 35, 58, 89, 100, 190, 194, 209, 228
Hume, John 228
Hume, John K. 209
Hume, Mrs 209
Hurst, Mr 122

I

Iceton, Edward Arthur 220, 236, 263
Illalong 34, 56, 149
Imperial Duke of Austria 267
Intercolonial Exhibition, Sydney 195, 198

Ireland, history 11, 12, 41
Isaacs, Robert 113, 115, 125

J

Jackson, Thomas 75
Jeffs, Samuel 254, 255
Jockey Club, Yass 97, 210, 220
Johnson, R.P. 245, 246
Johnstone, Thomas 116
Johnston, John 151
Jones, John 123
Joubert, Jules 267
Jugiong 36, 64, 74, 84, 88, 110, 113, 116, 119, 159, 162, 184, 191
Julian, Richard 88, 141, 261

K

Kalangan 53, 57, 65, 70, 75, 78, 82, 85, 104, 167, 170, 215, 243, 249, 272
Kangaroo Reefs 223, 233
Kangiara 46
Kavanagh, Fr Michael 29
Kelly, John 87
Kiandra 56
King, Albert 248
King Andy 161
King, William 50

L

Laidlaw, Thomas 179, 180, 229, 254, 290
Lake George 20, 24, 28, 30, 33, 85, 228
Lambing Flat 7, 45, 57, 58, 59, 60, 62, 63, 65, 67, 70, 71, 73, 75, 76, 78, 80, 83, 89, 90, 94, 97, 127, 171, 272, 290
Lamb, Mr 34
lamb with two heads 69
Lancashire Distress Fund 74, 90
Langan, Patrick 123
Lang, Rev. John Dunmore 38
Lanigan, Bishop William 139, 140, 152, 199, 200, 203, 210, 251, 253, 257, 271
Lassen, Mr 268
Lee, John 133

Lee, William 24, 28
Lehane, Catherine 74, 156
Lehane, Claire 278, 279
Lehane, Daniel 11, 62, 63, 73, 156, 255
Lehane, Elizabeth (née Mitchell) 278, 279, 280, 281, 282
Lehane, Ellen (daughter of Pierce) 26
Lehane, Ellen (mother of Jerry) 11
Lehane, Ellen (née McAuliffe, wife of Daniel) 74
Lehane, Felix 278, 279, 283, 284
Lehane, Hannah Maria (née Bourke) 73, 95, 105, 111, 156, 158, 169, 175, 197, 204, 212, 217, 218, 219, 232, 235, 253, 256, 257, 258, 259, 260, 261, 262, 263, 264, 266, 268, 269, 270, 274, 284, 293
Lehane, Honora (sister of Jerry) 64
Lehane, James 36, 62, 64, 175
Lehane, Jeremiah (Jerry) 11, 15, 24, 26, 27, 28, 30, 31, 33, 34, 35, 36, 39, 43, 47, 48, 62, 63, 64, 65, 66, 69, 73, 75, 76, 78, 82, 91, 94, 95, 99, 100, 104, 106, 109, 110, 111, 113, 115, 116, 117, 118, 121, 125, 128, 129, 130, 131, 132, 133, 141, 142, 154, 156, 158, 159, 162, 167, 168, 175, 178, 183, 185, 191, 194, 197, 200, 201, 203, 204, 205, 206, 207, 210, 212, 213, 214, 215, 216, 218, 219, 223, 225, 226, 229, 231, 232, 233, 234, 255, 269, 271, 284
Lehane, Jeremiah (son of Daniel) 73, 111, 112, 113, 115, 159, 255
Lehane, Jeremiah (son of Jerry) 105, 156, 204, 218, 219, 256, 269, 271, 285, 286, 287
Lehane, Jessie (née Vicars) 280
Lehane, John Augustine (Jack) 78, 233, 250, 251, 252, 274, 277, 278, 279, 281, 282, 283, 284
Lehane, John Thomas 105, 175, 183, 257
Lehane, Josephine 105, 156, 204, 219, 256, 257, 271, 284, 285, 286

Lehane, Margaret (sister of Jerry) 11
Lehane, Martha 62
Lehane, Mary (née O'Connor) 25, 26, 27, 29, 30, 33, 36, 40, 62, 64, 73, 88, 105, 227
Lehane, Pierce (brother of Jerry) 11, 27, 36
Lehane, Sarah (née Murphy) 48, 169, 170, 216, 217, 233, 239, 243, 250, 252, 273, 274, 275, 276, 277, 284
Lehane, William (son of Jerry) 30, 47, 48, 64, 73, 78, 106, 107, 108, 109, 114, 140, 143, 149, 171, 199, 216, 218, 219, 233, 234, 236, 237, 238, 239, 240, 246, 250, 251, 252, 253, 268, 273, 274, 275, 276, 277
Lehane, William (father of Jerry) 11
Lehane, William (son of Daniel) 74
Lehane, William (son of Pierce) 27
Lennan, Patrick 123
Lillingston, Rev. Frederick 146, 147, 148, 149, 154, 179, 181, 187, 188, 190, 193, 203, 211
Loch, Lord 280
Loftus, Lord 296
Long, Kate 255
Louis of Orleans, Prince de Conde 166
Lovat, Fr Charles 47
Lynch, Mr 100
Lyons, Dr William 117
Lyons, Eliza 128
Lyons, Elizabeth Augusta 233, 269
Lyons, Ellen (daughter of John and Ellen) 233, 283
Lyons, Ellen (née Lehane) 29, 30, 63, 64, 128, 159, 183, 219, 233, 235, 269, 282, 285
Lyons, Frank Joseph 233, 282
Lyons, John Perry 63, 128, 129, 183, 219, 233, 235, 282, 283
Lyons, John Perry jr 233, 283
Lyons, Mary Agnes 129, 233
Lyons, Michael 128

M

Macansh, William 205, 215
MacKillop, Mother Mary 15
Maclean, Gordon 279
Macleay, William 56
Maclehose, James 19, 27
Macnamara, Patrick 197, 207, 212, 213, 214
Macquarie, Governor 99
Magennis, Patrick 261
Magennis, Rev. Patrick 39, 55
Maher, Matthew 109
Manning, C.J. 263
Mannus 29
Marcella, Mother 286
Marks, Jacob 95
Marshall, John 16, 17, 18
Martin, James 56, 100, 124, 130, 155, 298
Martin, William 196
Maryborough 129, 183, 219, 235
Massy, Charles 29, 33, 215, 226
Matthews, Mary 162
Mayoh, Ellen (née Lehane, daughter of Daniel) 74
Mayoh family 74
Mayoh, Nora (née Lehane, daughter of Daniel) 74
McAlroy, Fr Michael 40, 42, 63, 139, 185
McEncroe, Archdeacon 109, 119, 147
McEncroe, Edward 119
McEvoy, Alice 257
McFarland, Judge 255, 268
McGee, Sr Const. 248
McKay, Angus 251
McMahon, Thomas 162
McNamara, Mary Anne 169
McNamara, Michael 169
Mechanics Institute, Yass 160, 181, 209, 219, 222, 227, 232, 233
Mehaffee, Catherine 133
Melbourne Cup 216
Middleton, Albert 249
migrant ships
   Joseph Cunard 46

Mary 16, 17, 18, 19
Miller, George 94, 95, 231
Milora 140, 167, 170, 177
Minehan, Daniel 34
mineral discoveries 177, 223
Mitchell, James 278
Morgan, Charles William 290
Morgan, 'Mad' Dan 86
Morris, William 36
Mort, Thomas Sutcliffe 31
Mowatt, Francis 20
Mowle, Mary (née Wilson) 24, 30
Mowle, Stewart 21, 22, 23, 24, 25, 27, 29, 30, 33
Mudge, Albert 298
Mulgrew, Mr 124
Murphy, Adeline 244, 284
Murphy, Anne (née Ellis) 46, 96, 102, 123, 140, 167, 168, 170, 272, 277, 283
Murphy, Annie 198, 284
Murphy, Felix (son of Miles) 46, 47, 78, 82, 106, 137, 169, 170, 173, 198, 199, 216, 217, 238, 258, 259, 260, 261, 262, 263, 264, 271, 273, 274, 277, 279, 284
Murphy, Felix (father of Miles) 46
Murphy, James 140, 167, 170, 273
Murphy, John Aloysius 46, 78, 85, 90, 97, 107, 127, 134, 138, 139, 151, 169, 170, 173, 185, 187, 198, 199, 205, 215, 217, 227, 237, 239, 242, 243, 246, 261, 268, 271, 273, 274
Murphy, Joseph 48, 106, 140, 216, 273
Murphy, Josephine (née Grenenger) 284
Murphy, Margaret 46
Murphy, Mary 151
Murphy, Mary Anne (née McNamara) 169, 217, 243, 271, 273, 274, 284
Murphy, Michael 156
Murphy, Miles (son of John) 205, 284
Murphy, Miles jr 123, 170, 217, 237, 246, 248, 249, 262, 272, 273, 274, 277, 283, 284
Murphy, Miles sr 43, 45, 46, 47, 48, 50, 51, 53, 55, 57, 58, 59, 65, 69, 71, 72, 74, 75, 76, 77, 78, 80, 82, 87, 95, 96, 97, 98, 99, 101, 104, 123, 125, 126, 134, 135, 136, 137, 138, 139, 140, 146, 151, 154, 162, 163, 166, 167, 168, 169, 171, 173, 191, 199, 216, 218, 234, 242, 243, 246, 249, 272, 274, 277, 283
Murphy, Patrick (son of Miles) 140, 273
Murphy, Patrick (father of Winifred) 151
Murphy, Robert 48, 140, 273
Murphy, Sir Ellis 283
Murphy, Thomas 123, 169, 170, 199, 217, 247, 273
Murphy, Winifred 151
Murphy's store, Binalong 48, 50, 51, 70, 71, 96, 137, 169, 171, 199
Murphy's store, Lambing Flat 46, 58, 60, 70, 71, 78, 90, 170, 272
Murphy's store, Murrumburrah 90, 96, 98, 170, 171, 198, 246, 273
Murray, Dr James 23
Murray, James 98, 238, 274
Murray, Leila 29
Murray, Mary (née Gibbes) 21, 27
Murray, Mr D. and troupe 68
Murray, Terence Aubrey 19, 20, 21, 22, 23, 24, 25, 27, 28, 29, 30, 31, 42, 176, 215, 231
Murray, Tommy 22
Murrimboola Creek 53, 168
Murrumburrah pastoral run 53, 57, 104, 138, 139, 242
Murrumburrah village 53, 55, 59, 70, 76, 78, 80, 85, 86, 90, 96, 98, 100, 102, 125, 126, 127, 137, 138, 140, 150, 151, 152, 162, 163, 164, 166, 167, 169, 170, 171, 173, 174, 183, 198, 199, 201, 216, 218, 237, 239, 241, 242, 244, 245, 246, 248, 253, 271, 274, 278
Muttama 177, 270

N

Nanima 223
Narraburra 78, 104, 105, 109, 142, 168, 216, 218, 219, 233, 234, 251, 283
Nelligen 39
Nelson, Const. Samuel 85
Newmarket, County Cork 11, 13, 25, 26, 36, 255
Nicholson, Davis 257

O

O'Brien, Cornelius 7, 34, 35, 39, 42, 49, 56, 125, 155, 175
O'Brien, Fr William 148
O'Brien, Henry 27, 34, 67, 74, 100, 112, 119, 182
O'Brien, Mrs (Henry's widow) 182, 183, 200, 207, 208
O'Connell, Daniel 12, 75, 97
O'Connor, Cornelius 25
O'Connor, Daniel 27
O'Connor, Jerome 27
O'Connor, Very Rev. Dr John 217
O'Connor, Margaret,(née Roach) 25
O'Connor, Dr Morgan 64, 140, 147, 148, 154, 167, 181, 183, 200, 201, 202, 204, 210, 211, 217, 226, 228, 275
O'Connor, William 25, 33, 64
O'Dare, William 254
O'Dwyer, Fr 254
O'Farrell, Henry James 145, 150
O'Hehir, John 73
O'Hehir, Mary 73, 217, 256
O'Hehir, Susan 169
O'Keefe, Jeremiah 26, 64
O'Keefe, Johanna (née O'Connor) 25, 64
O'Keeffe, Fr Patrick 254, 256, 293
O'Meally, John 46, 76, 77, 78, 80, 81
O'Meally, Patrick 46, 76, 81
O'Neill, Fr 98
O'Neill, Sub Inspector 110, 112, 113, 115, 116
Oriental Bank 82, 245, 252

P

Papal infallibility 210
Paris Exhibition 266
Parkes, Henry 148, 232, 292
Parry, Sgt Edmund 84
Pastoral and Agricultural Association, Burrangong 205
Pastoral and Agricultural Association, Yass 74, 177, 187, 215, 220, 225, 227, 292
Paterson, Andrew Bogle 56, 259
Paterson, Banjo 34, 56, 259
Paterson, John 34, 35, 56, 125, 149
Patison, Alexander 66, 68, 69, 91
Patison, Mary 66, 68
Pearce, Mr 69
Pearson, Robert (bank manager) 264
Pearson, Robert (cook) 133
Perry, Dr 258
Phillip, Capt Arthur 120
Polding, Archbishop 27, 47, 97, 106, 109, 272
Pottinger, Sir Frederick 77, 78
Powell, Mrs 285
practical jokes, Murrumburrah 238–42
Pryor, Frederick 119
Purefoy, Judge 123, 124, 129

Q

Quail, Charles 59, 65, 70, 94
Queen Victoria 40, 92, 126, 143, 150, 160, 266
Quinn, Bishop James 130

R

Reardon, Michael 255
Reardon, Mrs 256
Reedy Creek 33, 62, 76, 78, 116, 133, 141, 156, 158, 183, 191, 212, 216, 217, 234, 235, 256, 258
Remmington, Arthur 222
Ridley, Rev. W. 160
Ringwood, Patrick 143
Riordan, Fr 202, 204
Ritchie, James 188, 189, 194, 222

Robertson, John 56, 290, 292
Robinson, Sir Hercules 226
Rose, A.C. 116
Rosebank school 271
Ross, Robert Scott 125
Russell, John 131, 133
Russell, Mr F. 82
Ryall, Mr 111
Ryan, James 258
Ryan, John Francis 131, 133
Ryan, John Nagle 35, 56, 58
Ryan, Ned 35, 39, 49
Ryan, Timothy 137

S

Salvation Army 241, 242
Scarvell, Mr 263
Schafer, Christian Frederick 130
Scott, John 96
Shaw, John 181
Sheahan, John 110, 111, 113, 125, 159, 185, 220
Sheahan, Philip 111, 113
Sheekey, Patrick 205, 268
Shelley, Philip 249
Shipway, Joshua 93, 214, 222, 223, 230, 255
Sinclair, James 31
Sing Quong, James 199
Slattery, Thomas 274
Smith, George 156, 157
southern railway 53, 128, 176, 206, 224, 229, 244, 245, 246
southern road 31, 37, 38, 84, 141, 213, 218
Spellissy, Mary 278
Spring Creek 131, 133, 239
Squatter's Arms Hotel, Yass 94
Star Inn, Reedy Creek 33, 36
St Augustine's Church, Yass 40, 47, 152, 185, 192, 210, 253, 255, 269, 293
St Augustine's School, Yass 123, 140, 182, 200, 203, 232, 233
St Clement's Church of England, Yass 146, 255
Steffanoni, Louis 228

Stewart, Archie 167, 283
Stewart, Sarah (née Ellis) 167
St John's College, University of Sydney 26, 55, 64, 73, 107, 109, 114, 147
St Mary's Cathedral, Sydney 25, 27, 73, 99, 119, 220
St Mary's Church, Murrumburrah 98, 139, 152, 199, 243, 248, 274
St Mary's Church, Young 250
St Mary's College, Geelong 128
St Mary's College, Lyndhurst 106, 140, 166, 216
St Mary's temporary Cathedral, Sydney 128
St Omer 23
St Patrick's College, Goulburn 271
St Patrick's College, Melbourne 128
St Patrick's Day dinner, Yass 39, 56, 217, 220
St Paul's College, University of Sydney 107
strychnine 36, 243
Sullivan, Henry 149
Susman, Dr Maurice 285, 286
Susman, Eric 285
Susman, Gertrude (née Lehane) 105, 197, 204, 219, 257, 260, 271, 285
Susman, Philip Tasman 285
Sutherland, J. 193, 232
Swan Inn, Binalong 48, 50, 51, 54, 56, 95, 124, 137, 167, 205, 246

T

Tangmangaroo 253
Taylor, James 36
Taylor, Mary 36
telegraph 39, 103, 150, 219, 220, 235, 268, 288
telephone 268
Theatre Royal 93
Throckmorton, C.L. 177
Throsby, Patrick 76
Tipperary Gully 59
Turland, William 77
Turner, Thomas 205
typewriter 267

V

Van Rompaey, Alfred 281
Vaughan, Archbishop 107
Vicq, Amelia 64
Vicq, Arthur 64
Vicq, Honora (née Lehane) 62, 63, 64, 88, 149, 183
Vicq, John 62, 63, 65, 88, 94, 101, 118, 125, 149, 156, 177, 183, 223
Vicq, Mary 64
Vicq, William 64

W

Wagga Wagga 102, 112, 113, 119, 130, 140, 142, 227, 252, 273, 275, 276
Walker, Henry 235
Walmsley, Sr Const. Charles 259, 262
Walsh, David 64
Walsh, Mr (solicitor) 113
Wantabadgery 119
Want, J.H. 261
Waring, Peter 111, 113, 114, 115
Waters, Michael 255
Watson, James 232, 245, 246
Watt, Charles 157
Webster, Barry 131
Webster, George 131, 133
Weddin Mountains 46, 77, 127
Welman, James 126
Wentworth, William Charles 46
White, George 223
White, James 45
Whiting, George Robert 297
Whitton, John 229, 230, 245
Williams, 'The Towney' 35
Wilson, Dr Thomas 24
Wilson, John 127, 134, 135, 136
Wilson, Mrs 134, 136
Wiltshire, Austin Thomas 270
Winderradeen 30
Windeyer, Charles 17
Windeyer, John W. 119
Windeyer, Louis Adam 220
Windeyer, Walter O. 119
Woden 23
Wood, Allan 296, 298
Wood, James 103, 296
Woolgarlo 177
Wotton, William 205

Y

Yarralumla 19, 20, 21, 22, 23, 25, 27, 28, 29, 30, 63
Yass 7, 27, 34, 37, 39, 44, 45, 47, 48, 56, 59, 60, 65, 66, 67, 69, 74, 75, 89, 90, 92, 94, 97, 99, 100, 103, 104, 110, 120, 123, 125, 130, 137, 145, 146, 148, 150, 152, 154, 161, 166, 168, 169, 176, 177, 178, 181, 183, 185, 186, 189, 190, 191, 193, 195, 196, 198, 199, 201, 203, 204, 205, 206, 209, 210, 211, 212, 213, 214, 217, 220, 222, 226, 229, 230, 232, 236, 245, 250, 256, 268, 290, 292, 294, 297
Yass bridges 186, 187, 193, 199, 206, 207, 208, 210
Yass convent 253, 257, 284, 293
Yass Permanent Railway Progress Committee 206
Yass Show 74, 178, 187, 198, 205, 214, 218, 225, 226
Young 45, 74, 82, 83, 90, 170, 202, 205, 215, 236, 250, 251, 252, 253, 268, 290
Younga Plains 251, 252
Young, Sir John 130
Yuill, Mr 80

Z

Zouch, Arthur 69

www.ingramcontent.com/pod-product-compliance
Lightning Source LLC
Chambersburg PA
CBHW071805080526
44589CB00012B/689